W9-CHT-544

I Can Dream Again
The Jimmy Jack Story

Table of Contents

FOREWORD

by Rev. David Wilkerson

Founder of Teen Challenge
Author of *The Cross and the Switchblade*
Founder of Times Square Church

When I founded Teen Challenge over 50 years ago, I had no idea that God would multiply this movement to over 1,000 centers around the world. From the beginning, my vision has been to introduce young people to Jesus Christ and then get them back on the streets, witnessing for the Lord. Today God is raising up a mighty army of Spirit-filled soul winners and evangelists out of former drugs addicts and gang members.

Jimmy Jack is one of those miracles. I first met Jimmy in New York City at one of my street meetings in 1985. This young, zealous, Brooklyn Teen Challenge graduate thanked me for starting Teen Challenge and shared with me that almost all of his family went through Teen Challenge. When he told me his mother had been a prescription drug addict, the only thing I could think to say was, "Boy, you had a messed up family." Rescuing young men like Jimmy, as well as ladies and entire families through the love of Jesus Christ, is the mission of Teen Challenge.

Jimmy reminded me of my response years later when he told me 38 members of his family had encountered Jesus through the Teen Challenge ministry. I responded, "You have a miracle family."

Recently, when I ministered at his church, Freedom Chapel, in Amityville, New York, I was blessed so see so many that had been touch by the hand of God. I have had the opportunity to personally challenge Jimmy to seek the Lord in deep prayer, to keep his heart pure, and his ministry biblically sound. I have heard him preach, and the fruit of his ministry is a testimony of his faithfulness and obedience to the call of God on his life.

I am honored to know Brother Jimmy Jack. I rejoice in the great work of grace Christ has done in his heart and the influence he and his family have had. One day in glory, what a corner of praise there is going to be from all those saved by grace through this ministry.

ACKNOWLEDGMENTS

"I have been blessed to be a spiritual father to many 'sons' over the years in my ministry with Teen Challenge, but in Jimmy Jack I gained not only a spiritual son, but an entire family. Like the family sagas in the Old Testament, this book tells the story of the triumphs and, at times, the struggles of the Jack family through the lens of Jimmy's journey from drug addiction to salvation and a life now devoted to the ministry of Jesus Christ. I hope you will be as blessed as I was in reading this thrilling testimony."

Don Wilkerson
Founder, Teen Challenge International

"The most unlikely person to be in the ministry is probably the person who is the pastor and the director of the great Christian drug program—Teen Challenge in Long Island. He was at different times hopeless, a mess-up, a rebel, and more. Since his conversion, though, God has used his words to touch people's hearts, and I thank Him for His grace on Jimmy Jack's life."

Jim Cymbala
Senior Pastor, Brooklyn Tabernacle

"When I first met Jimmy Jack and heard his story, two words came to mind - "Only God." I thought, "Only God" could change a heart like this! "Only God" could rescue at the devil's doorstep. "Only God" could give purpose and use Jimmy Jack to do what he is doing. For the past ten years, I have personally witnessed God working in and through Jimmy Jack to lead Long Island Teen Challenge. His life is a miracle, his work is a miracle, and in the following pages you will be drawn to the One he serves."

Bill Kirk
Assistant Superintendent
New York District of the Assemblies of God

"We love Jimmy Jack here in Shreveport, Louisiana, at Shreveport Community Church. Having him is always an incredibly refreshing experience. Jimmy not only has a grasp of the Word and an ability to communicate in the language of our culture, but he also has the cutting edge that can be felt by everyone present. The joy of the Lord shines on his countenance. He receives my highest recommendation for ministry."

Denny Duron
International Evangelist
Pastor of Shreveport Community Church, Shreveport, Louisiana

DEDICATION

I dedicate this book to the special people who influenced my life, bore my pain, carried my burden, and never gave up on me!

To my godly mother, Adele Jack, who instilled within me compassion for humanity. Despite her painful life journey, she instinctively fought for the oppressed people of society with loving zeal and a heart full of passion that only could have come from heaven. Mom exemplified the heart of Christ for a hurting world from walking in Washington, D.C. with Dr. Martin Luther King, Jr., to feeding the wounded of society in the local soup kitchen. Besides her love for society, Mom was always there for me in my time of need. She left this earth on October 5, 1999, knowing her mission was completed. I love you, Mom, and miss you very much.

To my father, Alexander Hugh Jack, who fought through World War II, a German prisoner of war camp, and his own inner war? Being mentally, physically, and emotionally wounded through the war, he pressed on to be one of the pioneers of Little League baseball and public high school basketball and wrestling tournaments on Long Island, New York. He advanced to college-level coaching and became one of the first athletic directors of the largest school district on Long Island. Dad demonstrated the courage, creativity, and perseverance that I would later realize was imparted in my life. These qualities helped me achieve the goals God had for me.

To my faithful wife, Miriam. During the most crazed periods of my life, Miriam endured humiliation, rejection, abuse, and mental anguish due to my ungodly actions. Yet, she saw something in me that few could even imagine—a young man who really wanted to share his love with the world, but was too bound and confused by drugs to do so. My precious wife stuck it out with me. As she helped guide me in the ways of righteousness, God blessed Miriam with biblical attributes: Ruth's dedication, Hannah's ability to travail, Esther's boldness, and Mary's, the mother of Jesus, wisdom and discernment. Miriam, you are one of the greatest mentors. God has blessed you to help develop my life. I love you, sweetheart. You're the best!

The Lord has blessed us with three beautiful, miraculous, loving, loyal multi-talented, and God-fearing children, more than we could ever dream of: David, who has a precious gift of love, compassion and humor for all people; Dionnza, a gifted vocalist, songwriter and worshiper; and Dominique, a born leader with a heart for ministry. They have all have sacrificed so much to stand with Miriam and me as we pioneered Long Island Teen Challenge, Freedom Chapel, Rock the Block and Teen Challenge World Outreach.

To Bobby and Dianne Lloyd. Even in Bobby's gangster years, he always protected my family. My sister, Dianne, married Bobby in 1979, not realizing he was addicted to heroin. A former heroin addict herself, she had given her heart to Jesus while in a secular drug program. Dianne was faithful to the Lord and did everything in her power to help Bobby, knowing there must be a Christ-centered drug program for him. She searched and found Brooklyn Teen Challenge. Courageously, Bobby entered Teen Challenge in 1984. Both Bobby and Dianne faithfully prayed for me, and finally convinced me to attend a church service where Bobby was singing with the Teen Challenge choir. At the service, I witnessed the supernatural power of the Holy Spirit and was forever changed. While I was at the threshold of death, God used my sister to rescue me and get me to Brooklyn Teen Challenge on November 4, 1984, where I joined Bobby in the program. That's where my journey began!

To Joe and Elaine Cedzich, pastors of Sheepgate Assembly of God in Baldwin, New York. I thank the Lord for your being the first pastor who ever prayed for me, Miriam, Billy, and the rest of my family, eventually leading us to Teen Challenge. In the providence of God, the name of your church has been prophetic. It has brought many into the Kingdom and sent them out into the harvest field.

To David and Don Wilkerson. These men of God have been my personal mentors, pouring years of counsel, guidance, and wisdom into my heart. They have strengthened my hand to the plow in the frontline ministry to which God called me. Their example in street ministry ignited a passion within me that has been the heartbeat of my calling. David Wilkerson had a fervent passion for the youth of his generation and started Teen Challenge in 1958. His brother, Don, then teamed up with him. Today, Teen Challenge is the largest and most successful drug program in the world and dedicated to helping people become mentally sound, emotionally balanced, physically well, and spiritually alive through the power of God's love.

I would like to thank Times Square Church staff, Senior Pastor Carter Conlon, Barbara MacKery, Gail Paulson, and John Curley for their support of my life, family, and ministry.

To my first mentors at Brooklyn Teen Challenge, who poured the Word of God into my life when I was an infant in Christ: Mike and Kay Zello, Norman Miller, Kevin Hennessy, Sandy Segrest, Bob and Chris Bushman, Yolanda Planas Cartagena, Ben and Lila Torres, Dave and Patty Batty, Ralph DeMattico, Kevin Mikkelson, Mr. Ingram, Ralph Rodriguez, Mrs. Davis, and, especially Pete and Damaris Rios.

To John and Esther Castellani, who opened their hearts and lives to Miriam and me as I served as northeast representative for Teen Challenge International, USA.

To my Bible college president, Maurice and Marcia Lednicky; coaches

Kirk and Lynn Hanson; and to my professors, Dr. Opal Reddin, Dr. Charles Harris and Gary Bruegman who imparted to me not only a sound theology, but also the demonstration of love that is the essence of all theology.

A special thanks to Denny and DeAnza Duron and the church family and pastoral staff of Shreveport Community Church in Shreveport, Louisiana, for their love and inspiration in my life. Denny was the first person to encourage me to write this book.

To Pastor Jerry Stewart and his wife, Joan. Pastor Jerry was one of the first pastors to embrace our vision for Long Island and served as the first chairman of the board of our ministry. Both have been a vital part of our ministry and personal lives through thick and thin. Also, many thanks to the Long Island Teen Challenge Board of Directors who have been so encouraging through the years.

To Pastor Bill Kirk and his wife, Laura, who have been a Barnabas, "brother of encouragement," in the vision God has given me.

To Ron and Liz Wellbrock, Doug and Cindy Twohill, Jean Imisberg and Gus Schad, who have been a vital part of our ministries. You have given sacrificially and been a strength and support in so many ways.

To my brothers and sisters who I love very much. I thank them for being by my side and showing me unconditional love throughout the years. Through the storms of life and a painful journey we have all experienced, I am so thankful for the grace of God that has taken us through and is sufficient for the work that will continue in our lives.

I would like to acknowledge the partnership of Global Teen Challenge and Bernie Gillott. Through countless hours, weeks, and months of writing, editing, and rewriting this manuscript, he has truly helped me craft the words and phrases that capture the sights, sounds, and emotions of my miracle.

To Joanna Dagley, Sarah Simmons, Ann Floyd, Tami Spallino, Dawn Trivolis, and Carol Patterson who helped me write my book. Your patience, care, and compassion have inspired me.

And to many more have influenced my life to make not only my dreams come true, but all those whom you have inspired to dream again.

Some of the names in *The Jimmy Jack Story* were changed to protect the privacy of individuals who were such a part of the miracle. The only name that matters is Jesus Christ.

Chapter 1
The Broken Dream

Miriam and I at a local bar, empty and broken.

TRAGEDY IN MANHATTAN

My yellowish-orange, 15-passenger school van was so beat up it had several windows missing. I hadn't registered or insured it, because any money I hustled was used for my party life. Somehow it got me where I wanted to go—but never really where I needed to be.

Billy and I went to the Lower East Side of New York City in that van to cop four bags of heroin. That was all we could afford. Billy was my best friend; but even more, he was like my twin brother. We parked near Norfolk and Houston streets. I snorted one of the bags, and then we cooked the other three bags so Billy could shoot the dope in his vein.

We got water from a leaky fire hydrant on the corner and poured it into a carbon-charred spoon to liquefy the powdered heroin. I held a lighter under the spoon while Billy cooked it up. Straining it through a cigarette filter to keep the impurities out, we drew the potent fluid into the syringe.

Most of Billy's veins were already destroyed and had collapsed from constantly sticking needles in his hands, feet, and arms, so it was hard to find a good vein. I helped Billy tie off his upper arm with a belt, and he frantically searched for a good vein. I held his bicep to get a vein. He finally penetrated a usable vein and then shot the three bags of heroin into his arm.

Within seconds, the very thing I always feared came upon us. Billy looked at me in panic and utter shock as he said, "Jimm—...!" He fell out of the van before he finished getting my name out. I realized he had overdosed. The bags we bought must have been uncut, pure heroin. That's how people die.

Billy was on the street turning blue in front of my eyes. He wasn't breathing. I jumped out of the van in panic and began mouth-to-mouth resuscitation. With my hands on his chest over his heart, I was pumping his heart up and down, crying and screaming, "Come on, Billy!" His hear stopped beating and he stopped breathing. I lifted up his limp, lifeless body. I smacked him, hugged him, and tried to make him walk. We both fell to the ground.

Billy was closer to me than a brother. Now it looked like I had killed him. "Billy, wake up! You can't die! You can't die!" I screamed. "Don't do this to me, Billy! Wake up!"

We knew addiction was a monster but never thought we would feel the sting of its poison. Now facing the reality that I had held the arm of my best friend to inject the deadly poison into his vein while he overdosed, I had to ask, "Who is the monster now?"

Here we were, lying in the gutter of New York City—two young men in our twenties living life on the threshold of death. Now it had finally arrived. Our potential was destroyed, our dreams broken, and seemingly all hope gone.

Some have said that when you die your life passes before your eyes. Focused as I was on reviving Billy, my own mind flashed back to the memories of the crazy things we did together growing up.

RUNNING WILD IN THE STREETS

When we were young, we anxiously waited for Mister Softy, the ice cream man, to drive down our block. We climbed on the back of the truck, stood on top of the bumper, and rode all over town, visiting our friends who were waiting for ice cream. Then, we would jump off, give each other a high five, and dash off to the next adventure. During snow-storms we hung on the bumpers of cars, squatting down with our boots on top of the icy, snow-packed roads and sliding through the streets. We called this "skitching." We grew up looking for a challenge and a thrill, but Billy was always one step ahead of me in terms of danger.

When we were bored, Billy and I climbed the gutters of St. Agnes Cathedral School which was adjacent to my house. We called it "scaling." After we scaled the walls, we climbed on top of my roof.

Then, Billy scampered across the roof, jumped on top of the adjacent 5-story brick building, and ran on top of the capstones. He ran across the ledge with no fear that the tiniest little slip could send him plummeting to his death. I frantically screamed, "Billy, get down! Get off!" He laughed and ignored me because he had no fear of heights. That's just how Billy lived: always on the edge.

When I first became friends with Billy, my father and I were driving down my block. We saw Billy climbing up the gutters and drain pipes of the school next to my house. My dad said, "See that kid, Jimmy? He's no d--n good, and I want you to stay away from him."

"Oh, Dad, I already met him. He's my friend,"

I said, "Well, you need to stay away from him," was his firm response.

When he said that, Dad was trying to protect me from Billy. Maybe he should have been protecting Billy from me. After I found out how my dad felt about Billy, I had to lie and sneak around to continue hanging out with him. My father had great wisdom and saw things that I was blind to as an impulsive self-willed kid. At the time, my dad was on the edge of a mental breakdown. This was one of the last instructions he gave me before he went into the psychiatric ward.

My dad knew I had great potential, especially in athletics. But, he also knew the odds were against me, and I was on a road that would destroy every dream he had for me. My father, a World War II tail gunner who spent two years in a German prisoner of war camp, had seen young men tortured, suffer, and die.

As I look back, I often wonder if he believed this same suffering would become part of my life. I believe Dad sensed the stench of destruction and death in our future. He tried to warn and separate us, but to no avail. I would have saved so much pain and suffering if I had listened to him and learned from the pain of Dad's personal war. World War II not only impacted Europe, the world, and the USA; it also wounded our family.

Chapter 2
"Automatic Jack,"
A P.O.W. Who Made It Back

My dad (top row, far right), the crew,
and their B-17 Bomber.

FIGHTING TO LIVE

Through the sound of exploding anti-aircraft fire, the haze of soot, and the acrid stench of spent and burning shells, they battled.

Alexander Hugh Jack fought like a hero. He clutched the dual handles of his 50-millimeter machine gun in the cramped gunner's nest, wedged in the tail of a B-17 on a mission deep behind enemy lines. They beat out a deafening cadence of fire against wave after wave of enemy Messerschmitt Me 262's who unleashed their torrid of fire to intercept the payload of twelve 500-pound bombs destined for Germany. My father was a tail gunner on a B-17 with the 325th Bomb Squadron, 92nd Bomb Group, United States Army Air Corps. He fought for his country. He fought for his family. In the end, he fought for his life.

Battle though he did, my father was shot down over Brussels, Belgium, on his 13th mission and was captured by the Nazis on March 2, 1944. His life had started with such promise. How could it end here?

FIRST THINGS FIRST

Born in Ocean City, New Jersey, on August 25, 1921, my father was a son of old age and an embarrassment to his parents. As a child, my dad was passed off as his much older sister Jessie's child. Without supervision, he became independent and ran around with no accountability. You could say he had the call of the wild in his life. As a teenager, my dad and his friends would romp bareback on horses through the undeveloped land of what is now Oceanside, Long Island, New York.

On one occasion, he and his buddies broke into a mortuary. Some hid in caskets, while others brought in some unsuspecting acquaintances and scared the devil out of them. Another time, they made moonshine in someone's bathtub and got so drunk one of them fell in the tub. My dad never lost his love for moonshine. Either by DNA or environment, his own children eventually emulated this character trait.

Then, there was my mom. Adele Marie Buchan was born into a middle-class Scottish white family at home on July 30, 1922. She was the oldest of five children. My grandfather literally caught her as she shot out of the womb. In 1924, her little sister Marjorie died soon after birth. Little Anne was born in 1930, and, in 1933, a set of twins, a boy named Jimmy and a girl named Jessie, joined the family. Mom got her strength and fortitude from her mother, who exemplified strength even when one of the twins, Jessie, succumbed to pneumonia and died at 11 months old.

Grandma was an excellent role model in times of hardship, tragedy, and even the death of her children. She made the best of what she had and whatever she faced. This prepared mom for the death of her own child some 30 years later. Her dad, Herbert Buchan, was a veteran of World Wars I and II. She was an avid reader. He encouraged her to search books for knowledge, wisdom, and encouragement at a time in history when this was a rarity for women. He allowed her to express her feelings, hopes, and dreams that people of every race, color, and creed could live in peace, love, and harmony.

He never understood the interracial composition of his daughter's family, but encouraged her efforts to promote freedom and equal rights. In a time when girls were considered second-class citizens, my grandfather taught my mother everything a father would teach a son. Frequently, he hugged her and called her his "pearl." Her parents inspired her with hope, determination, and perseverance. This was more than inspiration; it was also a burden for her. She was living in a time of America's history when following that inspiration would have her swimming against the current throughout her life.

A LOVING ATTRACTION TO A LONG JOURNEY

My dad and mom met on Easter Sunday 1935. He was 14 and she was 13. The magnetic attraction between them continued during junior high and high school. My father was high-strung, opinionated, and headstrong. Mom was an over-achiever, low-keyed, but headstrong, too.

Mom played the violin and Dad played the drums in the school orchestra. Both were varsity athletes. Swimming was one of their leisure activities. She taught him to jitterbug, and together they won many contests in local theaters. As compatible as they were in certain areas, they had a few differences. The cliché says, "Opposites attract." However, in their case, my parents complemented each other. Their love and their conflict never ended. "Until death did they part!"

Mom loved basketball and Dad loved baseball and football. He is in the Hall of Fame at Oceanside High School. In 2005, he was officially inducted into the Circle of Pride at Oceanside High School.

My mother went to Blue Ridge College in upstate, New York and excelled in basketball. By the spring of her second year, they were engaged and then married on November 21, 1942, shortly after World War II broke out. Against my mother's wishes, Dad enlisted in the Army Air Corps, leaving her alone and pregnant at age 21. When their first child was born, he received an emergency furlough to see her and the baby. In a few days, he was back on the front lines.

MISSING IN ACTION

My dad went off to war as a patriotic soldier, dedicated to fighting for the United States. My mom worked during the war, and they wrote letters back and forth. Suddenly, after a year, my mother stopped getting letters. One day, while weeding her "victory garden," she was called to the front of the house. There stood a uniformed Army officer holding the yellow piece of paper wives dreaded seeing. Panic seized her heart as she looked at the words.

The telegram came from the War Department, Adjutant General's Office in Washington.

Dear Mrs. Adele Marie Jack, The Secretary of War desires me to express his deep regret that your husband, Staff Sergeant Alexander J. Jack, 32,684,807, Air Corps, has been reported missing in action over Germany since 2 March 1944. Your husband's plane, on his 13th mission, has been shot down over Germany and he is presently MIA (missing in action). When we identify his whereabouts, you will be further notified. J.A. Ulio, Major General.

With only ten missions left before Dad could come home, his B-17 Flying Fortress was shot down. My mother did not know if he was even alive. She faced the frightening reality of being a war widow. However, Mom's faith and prayers prevailed. We later learned that Dad had parachuted from the burning plane, injuring both legs as he landed in the hands of the enemy. The army uniform issued on mission days included a shoulder holster and 45-caliber automatic pistols. These were no match for the German infantry men who overran their position. After being captured, my father was in a German prisoner of war camp for 14 months.

The P.O.W. camp was a place of torture. In Stalag V, as sergeant, my dad was singled out for extraordinary abuse and punishment in an effort to get information. After 14 painful months of incarceration, he was liberated by English troops under Major Lightfoot at Fallingbostel, Germany, in May 1945. It was weeks before my mother would find out that he had been liberated from the P.O.W. camp, but no one could have predicted how long it would take to get the P.O.W. camp out of him. While she rejoiced in his return, my mother had no idea the struggles that lay ahead.

After the war was over, my father was honorably discharged with military medals: Air Medals, European-African-Middle Eastern Campaign Medal, World War II Victory Medal, Good Conduct Medal, Honorable Service Button, Aerial Gunner Badge, Bronze Service Star, Bronze Oak Leaf Cluster, Distinguished Service Medal, and the Purple Heart.

Like so many other faithful veterans, Dad left the military full of mental anguish and anxiety. He never talked about the war nor confided details to us. Once when I questioned Dad about the war, the only thing he shared was a humorous memory. In the mornings, all prisoners were required to line up according to the number on their concentration camp uniform. To pass the time during this lengthy roll call, Dad and his friends often switched places causing the number sequence to be out of order. The German officers would become confused as they were required to manually line up all the prisoners as Dad and his friends all laughed. It was only through my father's friends and other soldiers who had been there that we learned that the P.O.W.'s ate rats and dogs in order to survive. They saw their comrades tortured or abused and experienced intense pain and misery.

The traumatic experiences and atrocities he bore as an American P.O.W. followed him home from that replacement depot. Dad never successfully blocked out the memories. The images of the shooting and killing from his tail gunner position plagued him for the rest of his life. More than this, the guilt of the women and children killed or maimed by the deadly payload of bombs delivered from the belly of his B-17 tormented him most. As the tail gunner, he witnessed the devastation of the bombs that dropped from his plane more vividly than his fellow airmen. This, combined with his P.O.W. experiences, became more terrifying as the years passed by. The only things that anesthetized his pain were alcohol and prescription drugs. They called it good old-fashioned booze—always available, always dependable, but it was oh so deadly when mixed with those pills.

A NEW LIFE AND A FRESH START

After his honorable discharge on September 22, 1945, Dad applied to Cortland State College (now State University of New York College at Cortland) for the Physical Education Certification program. He was accepted with all fees and tuition paid by the G.I. Bill. Mom and Dad took their three-year-old daughter, Sandy, and moved to Cortland. Mom was pregnant with Russell and nauseous, a state she would experience for the next 12 years.

Campus life was challenging. Money was scarce and housing was cramped. My mother tutored my dad through college, sometimes reading his books and writing his papers. In fact, she was officially awarded half a degree the day he graduated. In spite of his postwar stress, the pressures of campus life, and the children, my father played shortstop on the baseball team and kicked extra points for the football team.

Because of his leg injuries from the war, he could not kick in cleats. He was known for the games he won kicking fields goals with his Army-issued combat boots. The Cortland students called him "Automatic Jack." This nickname followed him until the day he died. After graduation they left for a new life on Long Island with their two children.

Mom and Dad started working at a day camp owned by a close friend. By September, Dad had his first position: physical education teacher, football coach, and assistant trainer at Hofstra University. After several months, a position opened in the Levittown School District, which grew to become one of the largest districts on Long Island. Dad was hired as the first male teacher on staff in the district.

My father excelled as head coach for the Levittown School District, climbing to the position of athletic director for the entire school district including three high schools, two junior highs, and numerous elementary schools. My dad hired all the coaches for each school.

My father established the first Baseball Little League of Levittown and founded the Long Island Nassau County basketball championships, wrestling championships, and many other athletic programs and events. His goal was to help young people use athletics to excel. With all these accomplishments, there were still inner wounds that lay dormant and would eventually erupt because of the immense pain he experienced. The memories of the war he silently endured led to mental breakdowns and stays in psychiatric wards.

As the school system grew, so did the Jack family. By 1958, Dad had 17 schools to supervise, and my mom had nine children at home. There were happy times— Christmases or birthdays— but as the years went on, the happy times were fewer and further between. Life became more and more unbearable, unhappy, and unmanageable for both of them. Alcoholism and the emotional damage of the war began to take its toll. Dad's heart was wounded, and like so many good fathers, he was tormented by

RIBUNE, Levittown, N.Y., Thursday, June 2, 1966   NINE

Surprise Testimonial for A. Hugh Jack

More than 125 professional colleagues, friends and relatives joined together last Thursday night at the Holiday Manor to honor A. Hugh Jack, Supervisor of Physical Education and Athletics in School District 5. In photo above, Anthony J. Di Benedetto presents citation to

My dad receiving an award for his achievements for the expansion and development of high school athletics on Long Island.

the fear that his own children would be hurt. He did not want us to experience the pain he had endured.

HIS OWN PRIVATE PRISON

In 1960, my father surprised my mom by purchasing an old colonial house in Rockville Centre, New York, one town away from where they grew up. With nine kids ages 2 to 17, my mother hoped the change would do him good and the family would be more comfortable in a larger home. My father was a carpenter by hobby, and they worked together as a team—renovating, painting, and wallpapering. She said they were the best years of their lives.

Because of the trauma my father brought home from the war and the rejection he suffered from his own parents, he was never able to say, "I love you." He could be violent, but he protected and provided for us just as any father would. He had emotional barriers. Learning to guard his emotions protected him in the prison camp and helped him to survive; but, this tactic now held him prisoner of his own silence.

My oldest sister eloped and left home within a year. Then, my oldest brother, Russell, got his girlfriend pregnant, abruptly got married, and left home.

In 1968, when my 17-year-old sister, Marianne, got pregnant, doctors detected that she had leukemia. She died months later following a brief, painful illness. It devastated the entire family. The only good news was that her daughter, Eva Marie, miraculously survived the intense chemotherapy. Six weeks after Marianne's death, my father took another emotional blow. My 16-year-old sister, Dianne, confided, "Daddy, I'm pregnant."

In my father's world, pregnancy meant a young woman had to leave home, get married, and endure her shame alone. Dianne had just been accepted to Cortland State College and now that dream was over. The realization that another child he loved was about to leave him and suffer the consequences of bad decisions, coupled with the fear that her future was destroyed, drove him deeper into the bottle.

His family was falling apart and he was helpless to change it. He tried to sedate the pain, which only triggered his violent temper. Dad erupted into rages over small things—too much salt in the food or one of the children outside with no shoes. Small encounters turned into violent rages. The neighbors often ran over to calm my father.

The police were called to the house after my dad broke furniture or threw bowls of food against the walls. It seemed like the house shook. My mother's attempts to disarm my father only flamed the volcanic anger within him. My father finally began to manifest the pain of that World War II P.O.W. camp and the pent-up pain held in for so many years. His anger was unpredictable, especially when he was drinking. This led him to psychiatrists whose only remedy was antidepressants.

We all remember when Dad gave up the fight to survive. Marianne had died, my sisters were becoming pregnant, and everyone was leaving home. Dad put on his pajamas and robe and rarely took them off. He went into depression, was given an early retirement from the school district, became a 100 percent disabled veteran, and secluded himself in the living room chair.

The accumulated weight of family pressure and the memories of the war that he silently endured led to his first mental breakdown resulting in stays in psychiatric wards. After the mental breakdowns, he was admitted into three psychiatric hospitals and given electric shock treatments. My mother began to have breakdowns as well.

THE WAR WITHIN WINS

With no accountability, my siblings and I lived as our emotions and bodily appetites dictated. Despite conflicts, sibling rivalry, and the times we fought with each other, there was a fierce loyalty in our household. If anyone touched any of us, we had each other's back.

Dad could be violent. We would fight, and all kinds of things would go on in the house, but he always provided for us. When he had control of his faculties, he proved how much he cared in the only ways he knew how.

My father had talents in carpentry, athletic coaching, and leadership dynamics. He was only able to share these with me until I was 8 or 9 years old. Because of his mental illness, I missed out on a lot growing up, but the principles and philosophies of life and athletics he did share with me were valuable resources when I finally came to my senses.

My mind snapped back to the crisis at hand. We were in lower Manhattan with no help, and I thought my friend was dead. I was sobbing hysterically and began to cry out to God, "Please don't let Billy die."

All of our hopes and dreams were dying in my arms.

Chapter 3
A White Boy in a Black World

My second family (the Smith's) and I (far left)
during the "Billy Laan Teen Challenge Basketball Tournament."

I looked at Billy's lifeless body one more time when, out of nowhere, two paramedics appeared. I still don't know where they came from, but the older asked me coldly, "What's going on here?"

Their question was short, and my answer was even shorter as I screamed, "Heroin overdose!"

Another junkie walking by on the street, realizing that we must have gotten some potent stuff, excitedly asked, "Wow, where did you cop the stuff?"

There was no urgency in the efforts of the paramedics, barely older than Billy and I, as they backed their van up and opened the rear doors. Years of rescuing the casualties of drug infestation made them callous to my cries. They reacted as though he was dead and there was no need to rush.

I lifted Billy's limp, lifeless body up into the van with all the strength I had. I yelled, "Now, you work on him. You get to work on him!" There was no way I was going to just let Billy die without trying to help him. Here we were two vibrant, charismatic, gifted, athletic, young men from middle-class America with explosive potential, now hopeless, dying drug addicts.

CAREFREE DAYS - WHO CARES?

We lived in a white neighborhood in Levittown for a short time after I was born, because of Dad's job with the Levittown School District, then we moved to Rockville Centre. The demographics of our new town were 90 percent white and 10 percent black. The religion was predominantly Roman Catholicism as the diocese was in Rockville Centre. As such, one of the major schools was St. Agnes.

Our 4-bedroom, 2-story colonial-style home on Osborne Place in Rockville Centre had an attic that my father and older brother, Russell, renovated into two extra bedrooms. Dad converted the porch into a big den, which eventually became a bedroom, giving us a total of seven bedrooms. They also built a nice patio out by the above-ground pool in the backyard. With nine children to house and feed, we could not afford a carpenter or painter to maintain our home, so all us boys learned carpentry.

Those were wonderful, carefree days, filled with laughter, because we were not old enough to know our home was dysfunctional. We had picnics when the weather was nice. We jumped off the roof into the pool. One day so many kids jammed into the pool that it literally exploded, and we had to go "pool hopping" by sneaking into the neighborhood pools or the local golf course that had a private in-ground pool to cool off our energetic zeal.

The living room had a big fireplace. The long table in the large dining room looked like the Last Supper when all eleven of us sat down for a meal. Since I was the youngest, I sat next to Mom at one end of the table and two of my older brothers, Johnny and Hughie, sat at the other end next to Dad. He liked them beside him so he could whack them when they misbehaved. They seldom disappointed him.

When Dad whacked one of them, my knees would shake and the milk in my cup would begin to ripple. My father would yell, "Jimmy, stop shaking! You're gonna vibrate the milk out of the cup."

One of my brothers would stick up for me and say, "Leave him alone." He would get another crack upside the head. I would shake more, and the cycle would repeat itself until someone was sent up to their room or thrown out of the house.

The house on Osborne Place was decent, but it needed a paint job. Because it was located behind St. Agnes Elementary and High School, kids from both schools threw debris out the classroom windows and littered in our backyard. The schools were only 20 feet from the house and the school kids often looked into our home, including our bedroom windows.

We were always under the microscope of the community. As a young boy, I wished our house looked nicer. The white community rejected and mocked us, because we opened our home to help black and Spanish families in their time of need. As I look back, I realize that God's destiny for my life was to be raised with multicultural, interracial families.

The same environment that resulted in so much emotional pain, rejection, insecurity, and severe drug abuse would later cause me to plunge into the arms of Jesus to receive healing. The healed wounds of this painful life were the training ground that would enable me to embrace a hurting world.

NEW FRIENDS, NEW CULTURE

Billy was one of my first white friends. He hung around our home so often he became like one of the family. Since we had moved from an all-white community to Rockville Centre, we had not seen many people of color. When we moved there, my older brothers, Hughie and Johnny, discovered a pond several miles from our new house. One day, a new neighborhood friend, Tommy, and his father took them fishing. "Smith Pond," as it was called, was next to the black neighborhood. My brothers noticed a couple of black kids across the water and loudly asked, "Who are those kids over there?"

Tommy's father replied, "Oh, those are just some black niggers."

My brothers hadn't heard that word before, so they didn't know it was offensive.

Then, Hughie, always the jokester, shouted to them, "Hey, black niggers!"

"Who called us black niggers?" fumed the boys, running over ready to fight.

Hughie pointed at Johnny, blaming him for the racial slur. Larry Smith, the older of the two boys, was stocky, strong, and knew how to take care of himself. He flung himself into Johnny like a bulldozer, punching him until he fell to the ground. Tommy's dad came running over and shouted, "Get outta here!" And they scattered.

The next day, Hughie and Johnny went to their new school. There was Beaver Smith, the younger of the boys, tall and strong. Johnny ran into him in the hallway, but Beaver was friendly, just like nothing had happened the day before. They were in the same class and instantly became best friends. Beaver invited Johnny to his house after school. While they were playing, Larry walked in the room. Johnny almost ran out the door because he was afraid of Larry. After all, he had hit him pretty hard the day before.

Beaver said, "Hey, Larry, this is a good guy," putting his arm around Johnny's shoulder. He continued, "He's my friend now." So, Beaver and Johnny introduced their older brothers to each other. Larry and Hughie also became friends by the end of the school week. Later, Larry married my sister, Rosanne. Not long after their friendship commenced, I met their little brother, Chuckie, who was only three days younger than I was. We did almost everything together and became close friends.

When Chuckie and I started kindergarten, Mrs. Smith baby-sat me after our half day of school. She loved on us and fed us the greatest grilled cheese sandwiches I had ever tasted. She made them with good ol' government cheese and butter. I will always remember her big smile and pretty dress as she sat at the kitchen table snapping green beans. She introduced us to soul food. Besides fried chicken and mashed potatoes, she made delicious sweet potato pie, collard greens, grits, pigs' feet, black-eyed peas, and old-fashioned cornbread.

This began a loyal friendship with the Smith family that has lasted to this day. Each of our families had nine children. They had seven brothers and two sisters, and we had four brothers and five sisters. The interaction between the families—barbeques, swimming parties, horseshoes, cards, and mutual baby-sitting solidified our relationship. We were so close that we would get "the switch" just like the Smith boys. One of Mrs. Smith's favorite discipline techniques was to say, "Go fetch me a switch so I can whip yo' behind." There was amazing psychology behind that kind of discipline. It kept all of us in line, except for my brother, Johnny, who often got a good whipping because he was hyperactive. But Mrs. Smith loved all of us like her own.

The Grand Union Supermarket was just down the block on the border of the black and white communities. Both communities shared the supermarket with no major problems. The "good people" shopped "up the hill," so we called it the "all-white supermarket."

My mother shopped regularly at Grand Union. With our home so close to the projects and her interaction with the black families at the supermarket, she saw, heard, and felt the oppression of the black community in our town. She was deeply touched by the need to bring the hope of freedom into their lives and social equality to our community.

My mom's involvement in the Civil Rights Movement came with a cost. Because we opened our home to the black and Spanish families in dire need, our family was labeled "white trash" or "nigger lovers." On the outside, all of us shook this off with a smile, but on the inside, it hurt. The more my mother fought for civil rights, the more rejection came from our neighbors. As a young boy, I was not allowed in my friends' homes. While my friends went into their homes to play or go into the swimming pool, I waited outside, trying to find something else to do, pretending everything was normal.

We also became friends with the Shy family who lived directly across the street. They were half-Italian and half French-Moroccan. The five big, athletic sons were wild and always looking for adventure. They weren't afraid of anybody and fit right in with the kids in our family, especially my black friends. Mr. and Mrs. Shy were like an aunt and uncle to my family. Together we experienced the pain of prejudice. We watched out for each other, unified by our shared rejection.

The white families in the neighborhood didn't want their kids to associate with us. So, we sought out more black friends. We struggled with the rejection of the community and Mom and Dad's mental breakdowns. They were always sedated with prescription drugs, so we hung out with no parental guidance. We "chilled" in the black community in the place we called "down the way." Today, they call it "the hood."

We hung out by the corner market called Jack's Store (no relation). We entered that dilapidated corner store through the squeaky screen door that always slammed shut with the volume of a sonic boom because of the rusty spring that held it secure. We entered a wonderland of treats—racks of chips, candy, and soda that our treasure of recovered soda bottle deposits could purchase. People ask where addiction starts. For us, addiction started with Penny Candies, Mary Janes, Squirrel Nuts, and Bazooka bubble gum. That led us to Clark Bars, Milky Ways, and Bomano's Turkish Taffy, all for a nickel a piece. We all wore the same kind of white, high-top Chuck Taylor Converse sneakers. We dyed them different colors to step out in fashion. When the triple-striped Pro Keds and Adidas came out, we bought those too, at the very affordable price of about $10. We went through all the style changes together in the sixties and seventies.

We became even closer to the Smith family as the years went by. When Mrs. Smith died of a sudden heart attack, the nine Smith children became an even bigger part of our family. Some lived in our house for a time. Mom and Dad went to great lengths to be sure they were cared for. Their dad, Otis Smith, who we all called "Pop," began to drink to sedate his loneliness after Mrs. Smith passed on. With Mr. Smith out of the home a lot, Mrs. Smith's sister and brother-in-law, Aunt Perline and Uncle Elsworth, would come on weekends to cook and try to give some supervision.

We ate some type of greens with every meal, but collard greens were my favorite. I ate everything Aunt Perline cooked, except chitlins (hog intestines). I could smell the chitlins cooking from down the block. To me, they stank. But to the rest of the family, they were one of Aunt Perline's specialties. I preferred her pigs-in-a-blanket (miniature hot dogs wrapped in dough) over chitlins anytime. While Aunt Perline cooked, Uncle Elsworth played cards with us. That's where I learned the fine art of poker. As soon as they left, we did as we pleased.

Bonnie Smith was the oldest sister. At the age of 14, she took on the role of mother for the entire family. She did most of the cooking and had her plate full trying to finish high school. They had no washer and dryer, so her brothers and youngest sister, Janie, would often fill up a rusty Grand Union shopping cart laden with the dirty clothes of nine brothers and sisters. Everyone loved the wobbly-wheeled squeaking symphony as it rolled down North Village Avenue to the Laundromat, full of school clothes, athletic socks, shorts, and basketball gear. One thing the Smith's taught us that went beyond color was how to work together, because everyone always chipped in. We had to in order to survive.

After Mrs. Smith died, my brothers and I practically lived over at their house. When we hit our teens, we began to party. Even Pop would hang with us and drink his favorite Muscatel whiskey. We would ask him, "How're ya doin', Pop?"

He would laugh and joke, answering, "Musk ah tell ya?" as he shared his street-wise insights. "See now, uh, don't you be no 'uh-uh', and don't you be no fool."

A MISSION TO PARTY

June, the oldest Smith brother, turned me on to marijuana when I was only 10. My partying days were born in 1968. With my parents mentally and emotionally comatose and Aunt Perline going home to her own apartment after she cooked dinner for the family, we had our choice of homes in which to hang out and party. Before the "Urban Renewal Program" started that tore down all the old homes in the black community and built apartment housing called "projects," the Smith's lived in a two-story, old colonial house with six big bedrooms full of beds and large dressers.

Bonnie and Janie and the rest of the boys kept the house neat and clean. Outside was a porch that wrapped around the front. In the evening, when Aunt Perline went home, we would take the white bulb out of the light fixture in their living room and insert a red one. Then, we would drink Bali Hai Ripple and Boone's Farm Apple Wine until we were "ripped," listening to music, dancing, and getting crazy and funky.

Our social mission at this phase in our lives could be defined by Sly & the Family Stone's song:
We're gonna have a funky good time
I want to take you higher.
The Smiths' house was open to most of the young people from the projects who joined us, as we built our friendship around two common denominators—partying and basketball. Once in a while, Aunt Perline would just pop in and bust us for drinking and partying. I was like her nephew, so she included me when she yelled at us.

As soon as she would leave, we put the red light bulb back in and continued to party and dance the night away. We would slow dance with music from Smokey Robinson, The Temptations, Marvin Gaye, and The Four Tops. I learned how to slow dance (we called it "slow dragging"). By age 11, I got so high on wine sometimes that I started dancing with everyone. I danced with Janie, Bonnie, and other relatives. If no one was interested, I danced with the pole. Even when a white friend, Billy, came into my life, he was accepted by the Smith's as family because he excelled in basketball and had a passion to hang out, dance, and get high.

My brothers and I smoked pot (marijuana) from little joints that we made to monster bongs. Then, we would go upstairs to sleep. The morning activities were not about partying. They were about playing basketball and running in the hood or going swimming and fishing at the pond. We also loved mouse chasing. When a mouse got trapped in a garbage can in the house, we would take the grocery paper bag out of the can, close the top, and take the bag outside. Each of us would get a stick and let the mouse loose in the middle of the street as we beat on it with our sticks.

A BOND BASED ON BASKETBALL

The Smith boys and I played basketball by the hour—outside the house, inside the house, in the rain, sleet, ice, and snow. They were superior athletes; in fact, most of them had the potential to become professional basketball players. Because they dominated every sport they played, the trophy case in their home was filled to the ceiling with trophies from all their accomplishments. All of the brothers mastered at least two sports, but their passion for basketball took priority.

June was probably the most talented all-around athlete. He mastered anything round that could bounce. There was no doubt he was headed for the pros. He played against Julius Erving ("Dr. J") in the streets and even schooled NBA players who came his way. Unfortunately, women, wine, and weed were his downfall.

Larry, the second oldest of the family, played football and basketball and later joined the army. After his army days, he came home, married my sister, Rosanne, and had a daughter named Tonya. When Larry moved into my parents' home with Rosanne, I became very close to him. Many evenings we would stay up late, listen to music, and shoot the breeze. Larry had great insights and a serious outlook on life. He tried to guide me away from my criminal activities, especially when he had to pick me up from the police station and bail me out after I got arrested for robbery. When I was homeless, Larry gave me a place to stay until I could get on my feet or find another place to squat.

Larry always seemed to be there for us in times of trouble. With the reputation of a tough athlete and street fighter, he protected any of his family members—the Jack family, too. When a couple of the black kids from the projects came down and stole one of our bicycles, we immediately told Larry. Within an hour, he was walking up our driveway with the bike in his hand. We asked how he got it back so fast. He simply said, "Don't worry about it. Nobody messes with my family."

Beaver and Greg Smith were the next younger of the brothers who lived, ate, and influenced my life in terms of basketball. Beaver became one of the all-time great high school basketball players in New York City. He and Greg led our high school, South Side High, to victory in many championship games. There was no match for Greg's smooth dribbling and Beaver's pounding the boards (blocking shots by pinning the opponents' shot to the backboard).

Beaver broke scoring records and won every award possible in high school. He then played ball at St. John's University and was drafted by the New York Knicks. Because of an injured hand, he went on to play in Europe and then in the Dominican Republic where he became a legend and paved the way for other American basketball players. In the providence of God, I, too, would go to the Dominican Republic years later and help pioneer a Teen Challenge program, meeting people that Beaver helped and influenced during his career.

During Beaver and Greg's high school careers, my mother and father were somewhat coherent and our entire family supported them at every game. Beaver and Greg ate breakfast at our house before games and my mother gave them vitamins to keep them "healthy and fit," as she would say. During one championship game, Beaver won the "Most Valuable Player" award, and my father received an award for founding the championship tournaments in which the boys played.

I grew up close to Chuckie and Jeff Smith, the next of the brothers. Chuckie's physique resembled his older brother, June. His nickname was "Atlas" because he was built like an Olympian. Jeff's nickname was "Rock Bottom" because he was built like a brick house. They played high school basketball together and led their team to the championship like their older brothers.

Chuckie won every award, as did his brothers, and was sought out by scores of recruiters from Division One colleges across the nation. Chuckie went on to join Beaver in the Dominican Republic and played professional basketball there for a season. I played basketball with Chuckie during his senior year in high school; but because of my desire for drugs and lust, I broke into and robbed a house for money and drugs before practice one day. When somebody spotted me, I was arrested and kicked off the team. I thought my basketball dreams were over.

David, the youngest of the Smith brothers, had superior athletic talent in many sports as well, and became a great basketball player. More important, he became a great father, faithful employee, and well-mannered man, despite all of the obstacles and demons he had to overcome in his childhood. Two other close friends of the Smith family became like brothers to us. Ralph Bruce we called "Cuz" and Barry Hazel we called "Bazel." Barry was one of the first people to turn me on to smoking cocaine.

WE ARE FAMILY

I grew up learning the skills of the hood. Because of the relationships with our cross-cultural friends, there were times my brothers and I thought we were black. We wore black high-top Chuck Taylor Converse All-Star sneakers, double-knit pants, beaver caps, and slick shirts, just like our "brothers," the Smith's. When fights broke out, it was often white against black. There was no role confusion—my brothers and I were usually the white guys fighting alongside our black brothers.

I went out of town with the Smith's to play a basketball game in an all-black community against an all-black team. One of the ball players looked at me and started to elbow me. Without hesitation, the Smith brothers turned on him, ready to jack him up, and warned, "Brother, don't mess with him—he's family." That was the kind of affection and loyalty we had for one another. We stuck together through thick and thin. We often rented out the Martin Luther King Center in the projects for parties with our family and friends. The songs we sang during our heydays at the MLK Center or the local disco to testify to our family unity were "It's a Family Affair" by Sly and the Family Stone and Sister Sledge's "We Are Family."

After our all-day basketball games, we would end up at the "crib" (our nickname for the Smiths' house). Bonnie and Janie cooked for us, and the music would be blaring with some sporting game on the television. Then, we broke out the liquor and the poker began. We played cards all night long into the wee hours of the morning, sipping wine and going crazy. I would sniff some cocaine and continue playing till the afternoon. It was at this time I began to use my slick card moves. Larry or Bonnie always caught me cheating. They never got mad at me, but laughed with me and called me "Crazy Jim."

Bonnie was like an older sister. She taught me how to make grits and pigs-in-a-blanket. Every Christmas, Thanksgiving, and Easter, the first place I went to was the "crib" to hang out with the family. I loved coming into the house and smelling the roasted turkey with gravy simmering, collard greens boiling, and the pigs-in-a-blanket baking. I often snuck into the oven to get some pigs-in-a-blanket and Janie told Bonnie on me.

Bonnie would yell at me, hit me with the wooden spoon, smile, and say, "All right, Jimmy, go ahead. Just take one."

We played practical jokes on each other, and I was one of the worst of the jokesters. Once I called the Smith house and said in a deep voice, "There's a bomb under your table," and hung up, thinking surely they knew who it was. Five minutes later the entire Smith family was rushing into our house screaming, "There's a bomb in our house—there's a bomb in our house!" My father took several of us with him to search for the bomb, but of course there was no bomb. I knew I had to tell the Smith boys what I had done so they would not live in fear. So, I took them aside and confessed, but I begged them not to tell my parents. They never did—and today we still joke about it.

KICKING IT WITH THE BOYS

My experiences growing up in the black community went with me wherever I went. While my mother and father were trying to recover from shock treatment, we moved to Tampa, Florida, and I went to Webb Junior High School. I made friends with all the black kids as well as the white kids. I made friends easily because I could relate to people in different social and economic cultures and connect with them with my crazy stories from growing up in the hood. I knew just how to "kick it" with anyone as I communicated in their times, ways, and daily lifestyles.

During that year in Florida, as soon as I enrolled in school, I began to play basketball and showed the black brothers from Florida some New York ball. The brothers gave me immediate respect and I made some good friends. Race riots occurred in my school. One day I was walking home after school with a group of white kids when a bus full of black kids drove by. Three or four of the white guys with me started throwing big rocks at the bus and broke several windows. The bus driver pulled to the curb, opened the door, and told the kids in the bus, "Go get 'em." About 20 to 30 black boys and girls started running toward us. All of the white kids took off running, but I did not run. I just stood there and watched as the gang of black kids approached me. They stopped when they got close and asked, "Jim, where dem white crackers, man? Where is those blankety-blank white dudes?"

I pointed saying, "Man, they went that way," and they chased them. The black boys and girls understood where my heart was and the type of person I was. They knew I did not have a prejudiced bone in my body. They realized I was their friend, transparent, and not about racism. My mother taught me to resist prejudice. Even as a man, I experienced white racism because of my love for the brothers.

LOVE CROSSES COLOR BARRIERS

I was insecure in a lot of areas, but I was always confident of where I stood in the neighborhood, with my family, and with my friends from the projects of New York. I managed a Laundromat in my hometown when I was 14. One day a black guy started wising off to me. He was messing with my girl so I hit him with the pipe I had in my hand. He ran to the projects, making all kinds of threats. Some of my white friends warned me that he would bring the whole black community to retaliate. I knew better. I told them, "Look, if they know it's me, they won't come down here." His brother might come down, but I knew my brothers—the Smith brothers and Jack brothers—would handle it. Nothing happened.

In my senior year of high school, I tried living with my brother Johnny. Within a year, though, we lost the apartment. Then, I moved in with the Vann's, another black family in my community. Lee Vann was a great guy, and I felt comfortable there. Lee was a close friend in high school and was on my basketball and football teams. When we went away to camps, we stayed together. I lived with them for over a year with all his brothers, sisters, aunts, and uncles.

The Vann's and I would throw down some incredible pigs' knuckles, spareribs, ox tails, and other soul food. We enjoyed an intimacy that crossed all racial and ethnic barriers. We laughed together, cried together, partied together, ate together, worked together, failed together, and succeeded together. This family embraced me and loved me as much as I loved them.

When Lee and I graduated high school, Lee's older sister grabbed me, gave me a big kiss, and said, "You're the first white boy I ever kissed." This was normal for me. I was a homeboy who was just socially color-blind.

A unique aspect of our lives was that all of my brothers had a best friend who was black. Our connection with the African-American community was not just through racial stereotypes like basketball, dancing, and drugs. Russell's best friend was Superfly Bobby Lloyd, a handsome, broad-shouldered street gangster with a goatee. They loved to race cars. Bobby became a special member. Although Bobby was one of the most notorious cocaine and heroin drug dealers in the projects, he kept it away from Russell.

When Russell left home to get married, Bobby stopped racing cars and began to transport drugs. Bobby became the protector of our family. Whenever we had a problem, Bobby was there. We had a lot of problems, so he was there a lot. My father nicknamed him "Black Knight" because he always came after midnight and was a faithful defender of our family.

I could name many other friends that were a part of my world. There is one guy I cannot leave out. They called him "Mad Dog Mooney." George was his birth name; but the director of the recreation center where we hung out as kids, playing pool and basketball, called him "Mad Dog" because of the cheap wine he loved to drown himself in... that old street wine called Mad Dog 20/20.

His big front teeth showing as he smiled and the smell of cheap hooch and cigarette smoke—that was "Mad Dog." Even though he was a black man in a black community, I was his white shadow, trying to keep him out of trouble. People laughed because I always had to cover his back, especially whenever things went down. We were two kids whose roles seemed reversed because we could not fit the racial stereotype each was expected to play. He had a great jump shot but could not punch too well. We hung out, getting high together in high school, but then we drifted apart. In 1991, I was able to get his back again. I snatched him off the streets and brought him into Long Island Teen Challenge when I first started our program. He eventually became one of the staff at our men's program.

TAUGHT TO LOVE

From the perspective of a white man, I am always touched by how loving, warm, and understanding black people are. There is an emotional affection that is unique, shown by their special hug and handshake. This demonstrates a special bond of loyalty with one another, coupled with a competitive spirit that was born out of years of social oppression. Loyalty, sensitivity, empathy, understanding, and caring are some of the characteristics that I have experienced through my interactions with my black family. When people can fellowship together in mature love, these character traits will not be identified by a particular culture, but by the loving nature that God has created within us.

Nowadays when people talk to me on the telephone or I share my culturally diverse background, they wonder what nationality I am, especially with my name being Jimmy Jack. When they meet me, they are really confused. Italian? Spanish? Greek? No. I tell them that inside I am black, Spanish, and Italian; but, outside I am full Scottish—James Macfarlane Jack is my full name. I was raised to love arroz con pollo (rice with chicken), plátanos (fried bananas), spaghetti and meatballs, ham and cabbage, collard greens, potato pancakes, ham hocks, and black-eyed peas—although I never could get the courage to taste chitlins because I just could not get them past my nose.

But most of all, I was raised to love all people.

Chapter 4
We Shall Overcome

*"Momma Jack" receiving an appreciation plaque from me
at our annual Long Island Teen Challenge banquet.*

An ambulance appeared out of nowhere. As the paramedics began to work on Billy, I went around the side of the van, shaking with fear and emotionally in despair. I lifted up my hands and cried out to God. The only thing I knew to do was to pray to the God of my mother—the One that she had trusted all of her life despite rejection, addictions, and mental breakdowns. The One who gave her supernatural strength—Jesus Christ

CAUGHT IN THE WHIRLWIND OF CULTURAL CHANGE

With nerves of steel, yet a tender heart of compassion, my mother worked harder than anyone else I have ever seen. With the responsibility to raise nine children and compassion for a hurting world, my mother faced many obstacles as she entered the turbulent 1960's. The nation was caught in a whirlwind of change.

The Civil Rights Movement led the multiracial landscape from segregation, desegregation, to integration. The Beatles transformed our generation through rock and roll. This prepared the way for the Sexual Revolution. An era of love and peace was ignited by protests against the Vietnam War and fueled by Woodstock that produced flower power hippies, sit-ins, and love-ins. Coupled with the tragic assassinations of President John F. Kennedy, his brother Robert, and then Dr. Martin Luther King, Jr., we were all embroiled in this tumultuous period of American history. It distorted our family's security.

Mom was in the center of this whirlwind. She placed her life proudly in the middle of it all, standing up for what was right. She was a dynamo, a tiny white woman that stood ten feet tall against the bleak world of hate, segregation, and separation. Change came slowly because of generational trends and loyalties. This did not alter my mother's mission; rather, it motivated her. She was a woman ahead of her time.

COMPASSION AND ACTION

Witnessing prejudice and social injustice, my mother embraced people in need. In the sovereignty of God, even before I started kindergarten, Johnny, Hughie, and Rosanne attended the largely African-American Floyd B. Watson Public School. Our cross-cultural training began. My mother's heart began to beat to help marginalized African-Americans to claim their civil rights, so she joined the Civil Rights Movement.

In the early 1960's, African-American community groups were concerned about the educational decline in the school district, especially in their predominantly black schools. This sparked a fire in my mother, even though she was white, because her children attended Watson School. The group took steps for open enrollment, calling for students to be bussed to other schools to move toward a racial balance. To accomplish this, they started a local chapter of the NAACP (National Association for the Advancement of Colored People) and CORE (Congress of Racial Equality). My parents, along with Zeddie and Nashti Brown and a young student named Ernestine Small, all African-Americans from our community, headed the local NAACP chapter.

My parents were also active with the CORE chapters headed by Lincoln Lynch. Today, Ernestine Small still works at CEO (Center for Equal Opportunity) in Rockville Centre and attends our church, Freedom Chapel. Her daughter Donna graduated from our Teen Challenge program and is a leader in the Missionettes program for young girls at our church. Donna's daughter is an inspiring talent in our youth group.

These activist groups also realized the need for revitalization in the minority area of Rockville Centre where other injustices took place. In 1969, The State Housing Authority became involved with the Urban Renewal Program and planned to condemn and demolish the shabby houses in the black community, deep in the back of town. They planned to build projects to confine and condense the families to provide affordable apartments for them to rent.

On the street that faced the white community, architectural plans called for the rear of the houses to face the white community. The homes were constructed so that the black community would live in a circle. It was designed to hide them from public view as they came in and out of their houses. Plans were to erect a 10-foot fence to create a definite separation from the white community. However, unbeknownst to the activist group, the town wanted total demolition. The original plan was only for 160 apartments to be built on Meehan Lane in Rockville Centre, while there were over 300 families. That meant well over 150 families would be relocated. Many people lost their homes.

My mother saw the plan and recognized the resulting injustice and led the fight against the town all the way to Albany, the capital of New York. However, the mayor and town board fought them back. In the end the town board lost. The resistance resulted in major changes: the barrier fence was eliminated and the plan was revised and redrawn to better meet the needs of the black community. The town's new plan added 80 more apartments on Old Mill Court, built town houses on Center Avenue for families to purchase, and changed the whole architectural layout of housing projects. The houses no longer pointed in a circular fashion; instead, the front of the houses faced the community. It took over 10 years for this small group of civil rights pioneers to see these changes.

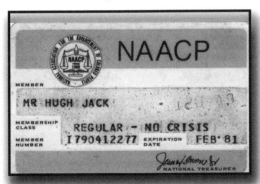

The NAACP, CORE, and The NAACP, CORE, and the Poor People's Campaign made plans to take a group to the March on Washington, D.C. The first organizational meeting in Long Island for the march took place in our dining room. My mother and the Rockville Centre contingent made hundreds of bologna sandwiches in our kitchen to feed those who traveled to march with Dr. Martin Luther King, Jr., for what proved to be his historic "I Have a Dream" speech on the steps of the Lincoln Memorial. Mom marched on Washington with a mission of hope, healing, and freedom.

Following the August 28, 1963 "March on Washington," Dr. King came to Rockville Centre. My mother's civil rights team invited him to speak at three of our towns in Long Island.

The final meeting, in which Dr. Martin Luther King, Jr. attended, was scheduled to be in my home, but it grew so large they had to move it to the Junior High School. When he came and spoke, he challenged the audience to continue the fight for equality. As he finished his speech, he mentioned he would be going to Memphis in just a few days. On that fateful trip, he was shot and killed on the balcony of the Lorraine Motel. A plaque hangs in the hall of South Side Middle School, the school we all attended, to mark the date Dr. King visited Rockville Centre just days before his assassination.

My mother often took me with her when she and her coalition were on one of their missions. They protested and picketed for equal rights as they stood against the injustice and the oppression the black people in our community and nation were facing. As we marched up and down train stations, town halls, and other strategic places, my mom held a picket sign in one hand and me in the other. The first song I learned to sing as a young boy was the theme song of the Civil Rights Movement: the Negro spiritual, "We Shall Overcome."

Throughout her life, my mother did more than hold up a sign or speak out against prejudice and discrimination. She endured the pain, experienced the victories, and celebrated the dream. Even with her intense involvement with the CEO and the NAACP and the mocking and rejection that came with it, somehow even as a young boy I knew deep inside that what my mother was doing was right, and I admired her. The more the white community rejected us, the more the black community embraced us.

OPEN DOORS FOR ALL PEOPLE

When a black family in the projects lost their home to fire, Mom had the entire family move in with us until they had a decent place to live. Because my mother was known for helping needy people, she was told about a father and son who were Cuban refugees, lost and stranded in the subway system of New York City for three days in need of shelter. Roberto, the son, and Manuel, the father, could not speak much English. My parents moved Roberto into our home for a year, and his father stayed with another family until he was able to get his own place.

When Roberto moved out, we had many other people from the projects live with us: Joanne Foster, a young black girl who was homeless; Thomas Lindsey, a young black man; and the Smith's, a family that lived with us on and off for years.

When we had barbecues, my parents opened our doors in our all-white neighborhood and invited our black and Spanish friends to swim in our pool and eat in our dining room or picnic table. This fueled more rejection from our community. But it only increased my mother's desire to love and help needy people of all colors. She taught us that God created people equally.

Some in the white community snubbed us and branded the Jack family as "white trash" or "white niggers." Even though this rejection and ridicule hurt deep inside, later in life I learned that although standing up for what is morally right can be difficult and painful, but the rewards are great.

Social rejection can cause deep wounds and result in a survival defense mechanism that often manifests itself in rebellion against authority. This is an attempt to produce self-esteem and social acceptance within one's own family or community. This survival mentality became a part of our everyday lives and was only sedated by drugs and alcohol. It led to a vicious journey of pain for me.

As we grew older and our lives continued to fall apart, most of us cursed my mother, blaming her for all of our problems. During the painful years of the breakdown of my family, my siblings often told her that she had sacrificed our family for her cause. Looking back, I realize that sacrifice is always the foundation for change and freedom. The sacrifices my mother made were actually an investment in humanity.

The ridicule my mother experienced came not only from friends, family members, and society, but also from her own children. She was mocked for fighting for civil rights. She endured constant abuse, attacks on her life, continuous dishonor, and consistent disrespect. In spite of this, she was able to exemplify the love and forgiveness of Christ in her daily life. In Romans 5:8, the apostle Paul declares, "But God demonstrates His own love toward us, in that while we were still sinners, Christ died for us."

When I argued with my mother or disrespected her, I would go to her later to ask forgiveness. She always told me she had already forgiven me. She had the unique ability to give unconditional love and forgiveness. She could love the unlovable and see the good in every person. She consistently forgave us and loved us through all of the wounds we inflicted on her and our family. The Bible says, "Love will cover a multitude of sins" (1 Peter 4:8). My mother lived this out.

MENTAL BREAKDOWNS

If you hear a lie long enough, you eventually begin to believe it. Society can convince you of almost anything. My siblings and I began to believe we were white trash. When we hit the 1970's, drugs infiltrated our lives and we rebelled in a greater way. My sister, Marianne, dying at 17, other sisters getting pregnant young and having abortions, my brothers being sent away, my arrest, and my father's rage all caused my mother to begin to experience mental breakdowns. However, in spite of her pain and suffering, she continually quoted Psalm 23:5: "My cup runneth over" (KJV). Through it all, my mother was able to cling to this promise of God. She trusted in Jesus.

Mom suffered five mental breakdowns and was admitted into hospitals each time. After being released, the doctors prescribed unlimited Valium and other psychotropic drugs. They rendered her almost comatose but it was the only remedy the doctors offered. These episodes continued for years.

She was so mummified by the medication that her immune system weakened, resulting in an infection on her face that developed into open ulcers on her cheeks and ears. With her hair unkempt, smoking three packs of cigarettes a day, and shoving pills in her mouth that kept her sedated, she became a walking zombie. For several years, she suffered from marching syndrome (standing in place with uncontrolled walking).

I made fun of her with my friends. I often took the cigarette out of her mouth when the ash was 2 inches long, flicked it, and stuffed it back in her mouth as my boys howled with laughter. The joking helped to cover my embarrassment. Deep inside I loved my mother, but I did not know how to handle her mental breakdowns. The only thing I knew to do when my mother was shaking severely was to wrap my arms around her and hug her, whispering in her ear that I loved her.

Mom got worse until I thought she was going to die. So I partied more and more. I helped myself to handfuls of pills from the prescription bottles of Valium in her night table. Many times, after I consumed the pills, I would sit in the living room half unconscious with my mother on one couch and my father on another, all sedated from medication. As we nodded in and out of consciousness we pretended to watch TV. The psychiatrist told her there was no hope. He gave her more pills and tried different psychotropic medications without offering any real relief.

AN UNFORGETTABLE DAY—AN UNFORGETTABLE MIRACLE

Deep in her heart, my mother was hungry for God. Throughout her life, she had joined many different churches that offered only cultural, traditional religion. My mother and her family needed more than a religion. We needed a personal encounter with the One who created it all. He was the only one who could heal her sickness, forgive our sins, and change our lives.

Trembling in her bedroom one night, my mother stared blankly at the dim glow of a tiny 13-inch black-and-white TV with a piece of aluminum foil wrapped around the tip of the antenna. Fighting the relentless roar to surrender to despair, in a final desperate grasp for hope, she tuned in to a Billy Graham crusade.

She heard him speak about a healing Jesus, a personal Jesus who "was wounded for our transgressions. He was bruised for our iniquities, the chastisement for our peace was upon Him, and by His stripes we are healed" (Isaiah 53:5). Those words penetrated her heart. He was not directing her to a religion or even a specific church. He pointed her to Jesus—the only One who could set her and her whole house free.

Suddenly, deep within the recesses of this compassionate mother's heart, there was finally a glimmer of hope. When Billy Graham gave the altar call on the television, she knew that the only chance she had was to act on this truth she had heard. She bolted out of the house to cry out to the open sky for a miracle.

She burst out of the front door of our house with her ulcerated face, scabby lips, and matted hair. There at the curb, she knelt down in the street crying out to God with her hands up to the heavens as Billy Graham had instructed. She cried, "Help me, God! Save me and save my family."

At the time, I was hanging out at the end of the block. One of my friends came running up to me and told me my mother had gone crazy again. He said she was kneeling on the street, praying, and crying out to God.

When I heard this, I ran down the street screaming, "Stop, Mom! Stop it right now. Get back in the house and don't ever embarrass me like this again!" At that age, I could not comprehend her desperation. I just thought she was humiliating me.

At the same time, I thought my mother was going insane and would have to go back into the hospital. As I look back, I can see the truth. Our miracle began when my mother's knees hit the pavement of that street to cry out to heaven. It was prayer without human words that defined her inner pain.

"Travail" is when a prayer becomes a cry, breaking through the heavenlies, and is heard in the inner chambers of the throne room of heaven. Throughout the Bible, Jesus is pictured sitting at the right hand of God the Father, but on the day Stephen was being stoned to death, Stephen looked up to the heavens and saw Jesus standing at the right hand of the Father (Acts 7:54-56). On the day my mother knelt on that curb, I believe Jesus stood again as He heard my mother's prayer.

TEN MIRACULOUS DAYS OF CHANGE

With sheer determination, my mother picked herself from that curb and struggled back into the house. Dragging her battered body up the stairs, sensing a power greater than her own, she re-entered that dimly lit bedroom. Closing the door and locking it behind her, she knew it was time to take action. In a personal, spiritual call to arms, she declared war on the devil.

In that room, she did more than kick the Valium and psychotropic drugs. No one in the family knew what was taking place there, except her and God. Later, doctors told us that while detoxing from the number of medications to which she was addicted, she could have gone into convulsions and possibly died during withdrawal, but the power of God kept her.

For ten days, she tarried in that room, the sheets of her bed soaked with sweat and tears, a testimony to her determination to break free for her family. On day one, she fought death. On day two, she battled despair. On day three, she confronted depression, and on day four drug and alcohol addiction. On day five, she faced down mental illness, and on day six physical infirmity. On day seven, she clashed with divorce and its hold on her family. On day eight, she conquered rejection and on day nine, our rebellion. On day ten, she interceded to overcome prejudice, pain, and poverty.

At the end of the tenth day, Momma Jack emerged triumphant. She was a changed woman. She stepped out of that room in resurrection power, delivered, set free, and on a mission to save her household. The circumstances in the Jack family had not changed, but she had. A neart of faith in this tiny woman of God had been re-formed as God renewed her mind. She strode out of that room a spiritual dynamo with a confidence that God would change everything as a result of her warfare during those ten miraculous days of change.

A MISSION OF COMPASSION

My mother kicked all of her drugs cold turkey. Now, miraculously healed from her own addictions, she was able to pray for our family more powerfully because she truly knew God and His promise. She read the Bible and stood on Joshua 24:15, "As for me and my house, we will serve the Lord." My sister Dianne responded first. When she gave her life to Christ the following year, my mother dedicated her heart to Jesus in an even greater way. Together they began to witness to the whole family. The light and love of Jesus that shined through Mom and Dianne eventually penetrated all of our hearts.

Adele Jack went back to Empire State University a few years later to finish her bachelor's degree. She immediately went on to earn a master's degree from Stony Brook University and became a certified social worker. Then, she went back to work and again picketed in front of soup kitchens when administrative "pencil pushers" wanted to close them down. Ever the activist, standing up for what was right, at age 69 she attended Christ for the Nations Institute to become a licensed minister.

My mother showed me that true compassion is being touched by the sufferings of others, giving them aid, and showing them mercy. As Mother exemplified the message of Christ, "Love your neighbor as yourself" (Mark 12:31), our course was set. God was after us.

I cried out to God by the van, then looked over to see the paramedics finally beginning to try to resuscitate Billy. The situation seemed hopeless, but then, didn't my mother's life teach us that nothing is hopeless when we trust in God?

"For with God, nothing will be impossible." (Luke 1:47)

Chapter 5
A Cub Scout Gone Bad

My innocence at 7 years old in St. Agnes Elementary School;
Confirmation at 10 years old; then 18 gone bad.

As the paramedics continued to administer oxygen to Billy, they both looked at me at the same time and began to shake their heads. Everything seemed to be intensified, yet in slow motion. I remember wondering, "Were they shaking their heads in disgust of what we were—drug addicts, hoodlums, hustlers? Could it be because they knew he was gone?"

I screamed at them, "Keep working on him!" Where did I go wrong? Where did it all start?

A BUSY BUILDER

I had a passion for building things even as a toddler. I used milk cartons to make small boats that floated in the bathtub. As I got older, I painted the trunks of the trees in the backyard. In every corner of my house and backyard, I built some type of hut, fort, or clubhouse.

When I was not working on one of my clubhouse projects, I was building wooden go-carts using baby carriage wheels, a wooden milk crate for the seat, and two-by-four studs from leftover wood I found in the yard or from a home in the neighborhood that was being built. I made a skateboard using one of my sisters' old roller skates and built my own bicycle from parts of my brothers' bikes that were passed down to me. Though violence and destruction were all around me, the activity of building things kept me busy. I was a pretty good kid.

At the age of 9, I joined the Cub Scouts, and it brought focus to my life. Our Cub Scout den had a positive atmosphere and was an outlet for my creativity. I was excited about belonging and learning things.

In Cub Scouts, a manual outlines the achievement requirements and also tracks accomplishments. A cub scout receives bronze, silver, or gold arrow pins as assignments are fulfilled. My scout shirt was quickly covered with arrows. During our weekly den meetings, I noticed other boys with only a few arrows, while I had many. It actually made me wonder if I was cheating. I reviewed the manual with my mother to be sure my calculations were accurate. They were because just about every day I was building something.

Jimmy at age 8

I started out as a faithful, energetic scout, actually excelling in the group. I should have advanced in Boy Scouts, but I never made it to that level. I lost focus and had no one at home to guide me. Not only that, but the hunter from hell—Satan himself—was doing all he could to detour my destiny.

I was inspired for adventure and building by the stories of Huckleberry Finn and Tom Sawyer. I even built a raft out of several empty 55-gallon oil drums my friends and I rolled down to the lake in our town. After we tied some tree limbs on top of the metal drums, it floated enough for us to drift out to the middle of the lake.

Then I began to build motorized bikes and go-carts with lawn mower engines. Things became more serious when I started experimenting with electricity. I rigged my bedroom so I could flip one switch and turn on the stereo, while another switch turned on all the lights in the room. I built an alarm system that sounded if anyone came into my room. I wired a speaker into my sister's room and snaked the wire under her rug to a microphone in my room. When my sister tucked herself in bed that evening, I began to speak into my microphone, calling her name in a deep voice. The speaker was under her bed and I scared her so much that she jumped up and came running into my room, white as a ghost. I burst out laughing, and she joined me in relief that it was me and not a ghost.

I built a small darkroom with a photo lab in my bedroom closet where I could develop my own pictures. This gift for creating and building came from God. It was an early sign of my gifting to build for His kingdom. I was called to dream big. Unfortunately, to get to that place, I took a detour that led me on a painful journey of crime, drugs, and alcohol addiction. It all started with telling little lies, stealing candy, and smoking cigarettes.

THE MISCHIEF BEGINS

When there are nine children in one household, everyone quickly learns to do what it takes to survive, especially when it comes to food. My acts of thievery actually began at the age of 7. My sister Joanne and I often accompanied Mom on her shopping trips because we were the youngest. Mom was health conscious, so she always bought the brands of cereal that had no added sugar. Joanne and I would slip some Frosted Flakes and Sugar Pops into the shopping cart under the pile of other foods.

When we got home, we got the boxes out of the grocery bags and snuck them to the basement. My siblings and I had such fun eating that forbidden food. When we saw how easy it was to sneak the cereal, we expanded our efforts to Ring Dings, frosted cream-filled Devil's Food cake. Imagine stealing a Ring Ding from your own kitchen. My parents bought one box of Ring Dings—12 to a box—so there were three extra for the nine children. I hurried and put the box of Ring Dings in the cupboard and then, when everyone was asleep, I robbed the Ring Ding box. It seemed innocent, but stealing is never innocent. We eventually began stealing cigarettes from our parents and sneaking into one of my clubhouses to smoke them. My world of mischief and thievery began to grow.

At age 8, I created a boys and girls gang on my block. We called ourselves the "Black Butterfly Gang." We took a large refrigerator box and put it on one girl's porch. We built our little clubhouse by cutting holes to make a door and a window, and then we drew a large black butterfly on the front with crayons. We started stealing candy bars from Norman's Candy Store a block away from our home. It was easy to steal, and I enjoyed it so much that my vocation as a thief began to be established. I could also be quite persuasive. One girl's family was well off, so I talked her into stealing cash from her father. I never stole money from my parents because they had very little. My friend got the money, and we bought more candy. We thought we were really having fun as we took the candy to the clubhouse, ate our chocolate, laughed, and with our sugar rush ended up playing tag, red-light green-light, or ring-a-leaveo.

A CRAZY, CHAOTIC LIFE

I started kindergarten at Floyd B. Watson Public School and then transferred to St. Agnes, the private Catholic school behind my house. I attended there from first through fifth grades. My parents' mental and emotional breakdowns made things increasingly worse at home. I began to rebel and goof off at school. I could not concentrate.

Most of the nuns who ran the school were rigid disciplinarians. They hit us with rulers. If they caught anyone chewing gum in class, they would take the gum and stick it on the student's nose and make the student wear the gum through the remaining school day. I was always in some type of trouble due to my chaotic life at home and my inability to concentrate. I quickly disconnected myself from school.

With the diversity of our upbringing and society's rejection of our family, my siblings began to fight with each other. My sister, Marianne, was the peacemaker of the family. She had the ability to disarm contention and bring unity to the family. But that all came to an end when she was diagnosed with acute leukemia at 17. Married and pregnant with a beautiful little girl, her husband, Israel, agonized along with our family, until their daughter, Eva, was miraculously born healthy. Our joy was interrupted as the leukemia continued to ravage Marianne's body. We watched helplessly as the cancer slowly consumed her. She died within 6 months. It devastated everyone in my family, but none more than my parents.

With Mom and Dad in the throes of mental breakdowns and my siblings being placed in reform school or moving out, I lived in turmoil. Three months later, I was hospitalized for 30 days with a severely ulcerated stomach. During this hospitalization, an inexperienced nurse tried to give me an intravenous injection in the back of my hand but kept missing my vein. She missed about five times. I became frantic, fighting her with all my strength. They strapped me down, and finally a doctor

My sister Marianne was the peacemaker of the family.

inserted the needle properly. Something important happened that day. Because of my memories of that horrendous struggle with the IV needle, I never used a needle to inject drugs. This was the providence of God and probably the reason I am alive today. Most of my friends who used a needle for drugs are dead today as a result of overdose or AIDS.

After I was released from the hospital, I was introduced to marijuana by Hughie, Johnny, and June Smith. One Thanksgiving, June came to our house and brought his joint (marijuana). He was a role model to us because of his great athletic skills. We snuck out to the garage and smoked a couple of joints.

That day I opened myself up to a demon that would eventually destroy the potential of every area of my life. Smoking reefer (joints) was considered the norm during the hippie era of the 1970's. Marijuana was accepted as a harmless drug, but it was anything but harmless to us.

THE JAMES GANG IS BORN

I was 10 and on my second time in the fifth grade when I met Billy. We were outside on the basketball court running up and down when I "shook him" (today they call it "crossing him over") and broke for the hoop. Billy pushed me from behind, and I still remember landing on the hard asphalt court, tearing my new jeans. I was angry because they were my only new jeans for the rest of the year. I got up quick with Chuckie Smith on my right and grabbed Billy, ready to punch him in the face.

Billy was from Yonkers, a city boy who thought he was cool. Chuckie was right there, encouraging me to lay into him and take him out. I remember looking at Billy with his baby face as he pleaded, "No, no, please, no."

For some reason I let him go and looked at him as I shook his hand, asking, "Are you OK?" Billy and I just hit it off. We were so much alike— same mannerisms, same way of thinking, same way of joking around. We became inseparable. That is when the "James Gang" was born.

Marijuana gripped my soul, and my true addiction to drugs began. Billy, a couple of other friends, and I were walking near our neighborhood park. We found a little plastic sandwich bag with joints in it. We ran into the park, smoked the pot, began to hallucinate, and broke out in uncontrollable laughter. Our mouths became dry (an expression pot users call "cottonmouth"). Then, we began to experience insatiable hunger we called the "munchies." We stole drinks and food from the picnic tables, ran into the woods, and gorged ourselves, all while laughing hysterically. That day we were convinced drugs helped us have the most fun we ever had. Because I had so much pain and no idea how to handle it, smoking pot seemed to help me forget.

Although I had a passion for basketball, I liked to play baseball, too. I played in Little League. My second year on the team I began to hit the ball really well. I had great athletic ability and led the league in home runs. I played in the all-star game at Hickey Field in Rockville Centre with my father on the sidelines watching me play and coaching me. That was the only span in my life that I felt like I had a normal father, because he was somewhat alert before his last breakdown and subsequent shock treatments. I played well in that game with a broken-bat triple and several diving catches. Although my team lost the game, I won the MVP award.

Despite my athletic gifting and potential, my baseball career was cut short.

After Billy and I met our first girlfriends that summer (identical twins Donna and Denise), we never played again. My baseball days were over.

LEFT BACK AND EMBARRASSED

I had taken a severe emotional hit when I was told that I had to repeat fifth grade. My parents transferred me from St. Agnes back to Watson Elementary School to repeat fifth grade. All of my friends were still there, who had attended that school since we were in kindergarten. I was delighted to be back in public school, but I was embarrassed to be held back. It hurt me deeply because I felt like everybody thought that I was dumb. This planted a seed of profound insecurity in me. All my friends had been promoted to sixth grade. Being held back reinforced my insecurities.

Because I was limited academically and struggled to read or retain information, I devoted my time to athletics, assuming this was where I could excel and gain self-worth. At the end of fifth grade, the school had a field day. The fifth and sixth graders competed in track and field competitions. The individual with the most points (the best athlete of the events) received a trophy at the sixth grade graduation service. The trophy was always given to a sixth grader. There were some really great athletes in the sixth grade. Chuckie Smith was one of them. About 10 sixth graders fully expected to receive the trophy. I worked extremely hard in all the competitions and truly believed that I could win the trophy. All the sixth graders sat anxiously expecting to hear their names called. Suddenly, I heard my name. I had won the trophy.

The other guys were happy for me because they were my friends. As I walked up to get my trophy, I thought, "That's right, man! I can whip you guys even though I'm in the fifth grade." What a happy and proud day.

In sixth grade, I continued to act out and get failing grades. However, a great teacher, Mr. Kelly, took a personal interest in me. He knew I had lost focus since I failed fifth grade. He saw potential and recognized my natural gift in woodworking. He took extra time training me. Once, he actually went down to a lumberyard and got some wood for me to work with. This had a positive effect on me. That year, I achieved passing grades and again won the most outstanding athlete award for the entire school. I even broke June Smith's basketball scoring record. However, that would be the last trophy I would win for the rest of my school years to come.

At 12, Billy and I spent our summer with Donna and Denise. There was an abandoned hospital near my house that became our secret meeting place. We rode our bikes to meet the girls there every day. We hung out in front of the building about 100 feet off the road. The large overgrown hedges in the front kept us out of sight. We continued smoking pot and began drinking there along with all of the lustful pleasures that go along with it. There we cultivated our taste not only for girls, but also for beer and apple wine. We started making out with our girlfriends. There were no boundaries.

Born with an untamed inner zeal, Billy and I became thrill seekers, constantly looking for excitement and challenges. The James Gang was now eight strong, hanging around our block. One afternoon we went to see a movie about Evel Knievel, the stunt man who jumped his motorcycle off huge ramps. After I saw him jump his motorcycle, my gift for building took over. We constructed our own ramps on an empty lot. With our stingray bikes that had V-shaped handlebars and long banana seats, we jumped off one ramp and landed on another. We smashed into things, cut ourselves, and even broke some bones. We built fires between the take-off ramp and the landing ramp and would leap over the inferno with the spirit of Evel Knievel. We even had seven kids lie down, side by side, as we jumped over them. Before long, an ambulance came to the lot regularly just in case someone got hurt. We seldom disappointed them. This was in the mid-1970's, before today's skateboard and bicycle ramps became popular. The James Gang may have been the original pioneers of extreme sports and bicycle ramp jumping.

A GOOD WORK ETHIC

In spite of all this playing around, I had a good work ethic. At 13, I got a job emptying the garbage for the residents of the apartments down the street. I also started my own lawn service. I passed out flyers outside my neighborhood, so people would not recognize that I was a Jack boy. I landed a couple of contracts that supplied me with some cold cash to support my developing alcohol and drug use.

My sister, Dianne, was the manager of a Laundromat down the block from our house. She gave me a job cleaning the floor, the washers, and the dryers. Joe was the owner of the Laundromat and a drug dealer. He recognized I was a good worker. He let me run the place by myself when he went on deliveries and away on weekends. I loved it because I invited all my friends to the Laundromat after work. We partied all night long with beer, wine, and pot. All through my childhood, I desired to gather my friends together and hang out. I finally had everything a wild kid dreams of: a good job, a fine girl, a place to party, and no curfew because my parents were "out of it." I thought I had it made.

THINGS ALWAYS CHANGE

Though I worked hard, by 13, I was a wild adolescent testing my freedom, while my parents were getting shock treatments and addicted to prescription drugs. They were like walking zombies. Their psychiatrist advised them to get out of the unhealthy environment where they lived. This meant moving away from our family and New York. At the same time, my parents received a financial windfall, a retroactive check from the Veterans Administration. They rented our house in New York to the older children, loaded up Joanne and me, and we moved to Tampa, Florida. This was supposed to be a time of rest and healing for them. Joanne and I did not know what to expect. I just knew I did not want to move because I had to give up my girlfriend and leave Billy, my other buddies, and the rest of my family.

I helped load up the two cars. Russell drove one car and my mother drove the other. We picked up my dad from the psychiatric hospital and were on our way to a new life in Florida. As we drove away, Billy rode alongside on his bike as long as he could keep up, waving and yelling, "Hurry up back." I placed my hand on the car window, and we both had tears in our eyes. Beyond the empty pain in the pit of my stomach, I promised myself I would be back.

A CRAZY MOVE TO FLORIDA

We moved into a double-wide mobile home in a newly established trailer park in Tampa. When I first arrived, I was bored. My mom bought me a new motorized mini-bike. Riding my mini-bike around the park and woods kept me busy for a while, but my urge for mischief and excitement took over. I became friends with a few boys from the trailer park. With my New York hustle, I began to school them in the art of getting high on alcohol and pot. A corner grocery store located at the entrance of the park sold wine. I taught the boys how to steal bottles of wine and buy pot from the local dealer. I became the leader of our Floridian gang and led them into their first experiences with weed, women, and wine.

I realized we needed a place to hang out. One of my friends in our gang, Phil, was from the woods of Tennessee. He told me he and his brother used to make log cabins by cutting down trees in his backyard. This inspired me. We got an ax, marched into the woods, began to chop down trees, and built a log cabin for our hangout.

We chopped down 40-foot trees, cut them in two, cut out wedges on each end, and began to secure them on top of each other. When we stepped back and viewed for ourselves the beginning stages of this great challenge, a rush of adrenaline shot through my body. We continued to chop. After getting other friends to embrace our vision, we would race into the woods every day after school and chop and build till our hands were blistered and the axes were broken.

We lifted huge logs on top of each other and wedged them together with the sheer determination of young pioneers. When we finished, there stood before us a 2-story log cabin—15 feet wide and 15 feet tall, surrounded by 70 tree stumps from all the trees we chopped down. We were elated that we made our own place for the gang to hang out. And, hang out we did! On the first floor, we had a hanging couch secured on the ceiling logs with chains, a coffee table, and a couple of chairs. The second floor was our bedroom loft. Many nights there were up to 20 kids from the park partying all night.

Although this was a way to channel my ambitions and drive, deep inside I longed to get back to the neighborhood in New York and hang out with my old buddies. I was homesick for my brothers and sisters. It all came to a head with the log cabin we had worked so hard to build. Rumors started to fly throughout the neighborhood about our mischief at the log cabin. When the director of the trailer park found out about the log cabin, he was angry. One night he, some parents, and some of the staff poured gasoline on the cabin, lit a match, and set it on fire.

One of my friends ran up to me and screamed, "They're burning down our cabin." As we watched our log cabin burn from a distance, I was furious. I could not understand why someone would burn down our cabin. All of that work and all those good times were gone in a few minutes.

HITCHHIKING BACK TO NEW YORK

That did it! I told my mother and Joanne that I was going back to New York. They thought I was kidding. But they did not know that I had met a kid from Islip, Long Island, who wanted to go back also. Shortly thereafter, at 13, the two of us layered on our thermal underwear, filled our pockets with apples and oranges, snuck out of our homes early in the morning, and hit the road with our thumbs out. We were determined to hitchhike back to New York. We made it all the way to Baltimore, Maryland, before our last ride dropped us off in a winter snowstorm.

Sludging through the driving snow, hitchhiking with no luck, we decided to find a place to sleep through the night before continuing our journey to New York in the morning. We were getting ready to sleep in an abandoned car when we noticed a gas station across the street. When we realized the bathroom was heated, we went to the manager and asked, "Sir, can we sleep overnight in the bathroom of your station."

He said, "Sure. Fine with me." I was so proud of myself. This was going to be a warm night. Before I could finish congratulating myself for my wisdom and smooth line, I found out he had set us up. In a few minutes, a state trooper was pounding on the bathroom door. He took us to the police station and locked us up.

I thought, "He set us up!" As an adult when I think of what could have happened to two 13-year-old boys in the rest room of a gas station, I realize that was anything but a set up. It was compassion in action, God's protection.

When the police called my family in New York, they came to Baltimore to pick us up. I did not care because I had made it home. My friends came over, and we hit the streets and partied. My joy at being back in New York did not last long, because my brothers sent me back to Florida.

DAD'S WAKE-UP CALL

When I walked in the door of our trailer in Florida, my father looked up at me and said, "Well, here comes the wanderer."

I was expecting a violent rage or a beating. I was unsure what his reaction might be, but he stunned me when he asked, "You want to go home, don't you?"

Then, a strange thing happened. It was like my dad could really see me—something I had not experienced for a long time. I looked into his eyes and pleaded, "Yeah, let's get out of here, Dad. Let's go back to New York."

As he glanced around the room, Dad looked like he had suddenly awakened from his shock treatment. "What am I doing here?" He asked.

My mother explained why we were in Florida. He looked at Mom and said, "You mean I worked my whole life to get you and the kids a nice, big home, and you have me living in this shoebox!" He looked at me and stated flatly, "I want to move back home." They told the bank they could have the trailer and abandoned the property in Florida.

When we moved back to New York, I was in my element again. I was welcomed back by my homeboys, and the James Gang was reunited with a drive for more mischief than ever before. We started partying, experimenting with many drugs, robbing houses, and doing dangerous things. I became more and more rebellious. I did not care what happened to me.

A MAZE OF CONFUSION

Our family was becoming absolutely drug-crazed. When my parents moved back from Florida, the doctor gave them a fresh prescription for unlimited refills of Valium. For an up-and-coming young drug addict, this was like a free candy store to a sweet-crazed kid. With my parents heavily sedated, my house was a dope fiend's dream; we all ate pills like candy.

Some days each bedroom in our house had its own little party going on. I would sneak in and steal pills, acid, cocaine, and bags of pot from my brother's room and then share it with my friends. We sometimes had 50 to 100 people partying throughout our house. The police came frequently to check out our neighbors' complaints. My parents never knew because they were strung out on prescription drugs.

All of the promise born in that young Cub Scout was now just a maze of confusion for a young teenager. My life had taken a major detour from a high-achieving Cub Scout to a strung-out alcoholic, thief, and manipulating hustler. I was desperately looking for love in all the wrong places.

CHAPTER 6
LOOKING FOR LOVE IN ALL
THE WRONG PLACES

Miriam and I when we first met in 1978.

DISTORTED PASSION

Billy and I were going steady with identical twins, Donna and Denise. Donna was my girl. I thought, I will love her forever. My heart was vulnerable to distortion, rebellion, and perversion. I was a teenage train wreck looking for a place to crash. Worse than that, my older brothers were telling me that life's only real enjoyment was found in drugs, theft, violence, and sex. My older friends and brothers had one goal: to break my virginity and prove I was now a man.

Sexual experimentation releases an appetite that cannot be satisfied. I unleashed that distorted passion with Donna, which we called "love." We were together a year and a half. As I was entering seventh grade, we learned that Donna was pregnant at the age of 13. I was relieved when her mom helped her get an abortion, but that relief turned to guilt, and guilt turned to pain. It became just another excuse to hide behind booze and drugs. After the abortion, our relationship deteriorated and we drifted apart. I lost my passion for her because of the emotional trauma we experienced. The relationship ended in frustration and despair.

I was entering a crucial time in my life with no real parental guidance. In my family, no one feared God except my mother. I thought the world revolved around me, making me feel good, and meeting my emotional and physical needs. This lie caused me to abuse scores of young girls. I was curious about women and furious at how life had treated my family. Confused, highly emotional, and without conscience, I was tormented by lust. So, I started having relationships with many girls. More of them got pregnant, and more innocent lives were aborted.

DRIVEN BY INSECURITY

I was driven by insecurity. These relationships gave me a false sense of accomplishment, acceptance, and self-esteem. I had no concept of what love was, so I thought I was in love with any girl I was with. This often resulted in jealous rages. I could not see beyond the moment. How could I think about tomorrow when today was not finished? All I cared about was my own selfish gratification.

With the influence of my older brothers, I was destined to become a gigolo. I listened to them talk about their sexual activities and even watched them at times. My brothers were handsome and had reputations as being tough and wild. They were womanizers. Like me, they found their social acceptance and security through their ability to pick up girls at their convenience. From the summer after I finished sixth grade until I met my wife, Miriam, I lived this way. I was so driven that, even after I had fallen in love with Miriam, I could not remain faithful to her.

Billy and I frantically searched for hiding places to hang out with girls. The basement storage room of the apartment building where I worked emptying garbage became a favorite spot. With access to couches and old beds, we made a secret room. Eventually, we were caught.

Our next hangout was the laundromat where I worked. Since I had no curfew, I invited my friends over to do drugs all night and we slept there with girls.

We brought girls to the Laundromat to hang out all day. After indulging with our girlfriends, we talked them into getting in the large gas dryers. As they were spinning around and around, we counted each revolution, laughing hysterically until they passed out. It was a joke to us and our desire for fun blinded us to the reality that they could have been seriously hurt or even suffocated. These uncaring, selfish acts continued as we used many girls for a cheap laugh. We treated girls as objects to play and joke with. When you cross the line of abstinence, you sacrifice your self-respect and begin to believe immorality and insecurity are love.

FOX IN A HENHOUSE

Even our move to Florida did not slow me down. At first, moving to another part of the country seemed like a big adventure and I wanted to end my relationship with Donna anyway. Though I was not faithful to her, my jealousy did not want anyone else to have her either.

When I moved to Florida, Mom and Dad bought a nice mobile home in a community for mostly retired people that also allowed families with children. Joanne and I quickly made friends in our new neighborhood and school. Even though we had new surroundings, things had not changed. My parents continued taking so many prescription drugs that they were not able to supervise us and we had far too much free time.

The girls in the mobile home community were as curious as I was, so I was like a fox in a henhouse. This environment fueled my appetite for many girls. With so many empty model mobile homes throughout the park, they became my hideaways for these naïve, young Floridian girls. To me they were a new challenge to seduce and manipulate with my New York charisma. The possibility of getting caught fed my appetite for danger.

The log cabin we built in the back of the trailer park was another hangout. During my year in Florida, I was with many girls until I met Desiree, an attractive French girl. We were close until her mother found out I was the trailer park gigolo and split us up.

I was a discontented, jealous, confused kid. Even though I was in relationships with so many girls in Florida, I got furious if I heard that Donna, my girlfriend back in New York, was seeing someone else.

Looking at my life through the eyes of a wild, worldly kid, it appeared that I had everything—a brand-new double-wide trailer, my own room, a dog, and a mini-bike. The trailer park had a built-in swimming pool with a recreation center. After the log cabin burned down and I broke up with Desiree, I became bored. I began to think that the Floridian culture and mentality of the other kids were slow and dull. I yearned for my homeboys, girls, and family in New York. I was not doing well in school. My search for love had only left me empty. When I ran away back to New York, it caused my mom and dad to move back home to Long Island.

IF WE COULD ONLY FLY AWAY

Before we had moved to Florida, my brother, Hughie, and I built a pigeon coop in the attic over our two-car garage to raise homing pigeons. My dissatisfaction and insecurity was reflected in my love for those birds. It started as a hobby because it provided an escape from the crazy world we lived in.

The pigeon coop offered more than aimless recreation to lost city boys. I had enough church to know that providing for something that God created had to be good, and I needed all the points in heaven I could get. More than that, I loved to care for them. I loved to raise them with the nurturing I had always longed for.

As I observed the pigeons, all they represented seemed unattainable to me. Homing pigeons are amazing birds. Our birds were intelligent, loyal, and free. Unfortunately, I was put down by teachers, struggled for identity, and felt trapped. As far as loyalty, I lived in a world where everyone watched out for number one. My pigeons had an innate sense of direction. I had none.

We could leave Long Island, drive to Jersey, release the birds, and they would be in the loft on their perch when I got back. We could release these birds anywhere, and they would find their way home. As we released them they would circle, stretch their wings, find their freedom, and fly.

The longer I worked with the pigeons, the more I was certain that I would never find the freedom and direction I saw in them as they spread their wings. Until we left Florida, I wondered if I would ever find my way home.

PIGEON COOP BECOMES A HENHOUSE

When I arrived in New York, all of the old gang's energy, imagination, and creativity were channeled toward our appetite for crazed fun, drugs, and girls. With our growing drug abuse, burglaries, gang fights, and womanizing, we needed a place to hang out and hide when the police were chasing us. My apostolic gifting kicked in, and I rallied my friends to build a clubhouse in the attic of my garage. The upstairs of our two-car garage was spacious and separated from my house, so it provided privacy.

Since this had been a pigeon coop, the first task of our building process was to scrape off an inch of gooey, slimy, stinking pigeon droppings from the floor. Some of my friends had a difficult time catching the vision. Even though they all drifted off when it came time to scrape pigeon poop, Billy was there with me. We were determined to build our new home for the boys. After the floor was clean, the rest of the gang caught the vision and chipped in. We turned the pigeon coop into our clubhouse.

We constructed two bedrooms and a living room with stolen wood and insulation from a local building site. My friend, Vito, also had a clubhouse for his gang, and we called the two E-13 and E-14, which meant Escape Thirteen and Escape Fourteen. My clubhouse was E-14 and was a perfect place for bad things to happen. With bedrooms in the back, our girls could stay overnight. We also had a large living room with a console color television and sectional couch. Sadly, our little clubhouse became a flophouse as my older brothers also used it for their lustful pleasures. With no supervision, no one to watch over us, and no one to tell us that what we were doing was wrong, we were consumed with partying. Hanging out with my homeboys and home girls became more important than school, work, our future, and even basketball.

ON THE PROWL

I was still looking for love, though, in all the wrong places. I was enrolled at South Side Junior High School for ninth grade and on the prowl for a new relationship. I met Olivia, a black jazz dancer who was one of the most attractive and popular girls in my grade. She became my high school sweetheart. With her bright personality, good looks, and focus, we became very close. Unfortunately, within a month of our new relationship we were arrested for stealing a bicycle.

It was the first day of spring and the police set up a bike in the front of the school to try to stop a rash of bicycle thefts. Olivia and I saw the bike and jumped on it together for a quick, innocent, romantic joyride. As soon as we left school grounds, a black, unmarked police car skidded to a stop in front of us. Immediately, two plain clothes detectives jumped out, grabbed us off the bicycle, and slammed us up against the car. We were both stunned as they handcuffed us and threw us in the backseat of the police cruiser.

Olivia was released and, as usual, I was charged with the crime. She testified on my behalf during the proceedings. Following the trial, even though the district attorney made an issue of the fact that we were an interracial couple, I was acquitted. It was probably the first time I

Miriam Navarro-Jack, age 21

was innocent, but it was not the last time I was handcuffed.

This was the beginning of many other arrests. For a short time, Olivia was able to keep me to herself. My clubhouse was our meeting place, and our relationship grew serious. I was never satisfied, though. With my lustful drive and insecurity, a legitimate, committed, caring relationship did not satisfy me.

Julie was half-Italian and half-Jewish. She became my next girl. When I wanted a break from Olivia, Julie became my main squeeze in high school. For a while, I even dated both of them at the same time. I did this with many other girls. None of them knew I was cheating on them. I actually thought I loved them both.

THE LOVE OF MY LIFE

After graduating high school, I met the love of my life. Billy's pretty Puerto Rican girlfriend, Annie, had a fine sister named Miriam. She was a beautiful, petite girl with a slim dancer's body. She was one of the top Latin disco dancers on Long Island. Nobody could dance like Miriam. Even though she had a boyfriend, the first time our eyes met, we fell for each other. I was not about to try to steal this guy's girl, but I knew I had to see her again. One evening when I was hanging out with Billy and Annie, Miriam was there. She whispered in my ear that she wanted me to call her. I was floating on cloud nine. When her boyfriend found out, he was mad, angry, and crazy. But he knew I was crazier than he was, so he left us alone. The story is best told by an entry in Miriam's diary:

FREE-FALLING FOR JIMMY

It was a hot summer day today and I was out with my boyfriend, Antonio, bike riding. I love riding my bike. I love to go as fast as I can, pedaling faster and faster until the houses and cars just whiz past me. I love that feeling of free-falling, almost like I can fly. Maybe that is my problem— my love of free-falling. Is that what is happening to me?

I was whizzing down the road just missing cars by an inch on my ten-speed racing bike. My feet were locked into the straps of the pedals. I always wondered what those stirrups were for. Hmmmmmm. Anyway, I was in tenth gear, going faster and faster until, without warning, I began to lose control.

My handlebars began to vibrate, then to shake and wiggle. I tried to jump off because I knew it was going down, but could not get my feet out of those d—n straps. The vibration got worse and I felt the bike wobble as it began to go down. It was like in slow motion. The bike hit the curb and kept going. Not able to detach myself from the bicycle, I slid across the sidewalk on my right side. Finally, I skidded to a stop and for an instant just lay there.

I wasn't sure what was going on. Antonio helped me to get out of the pedal foot restraints and slowly lifted me to my feet. Dazed, I stared at him for an instant, and for a moment time stood still. Shakily, I said to him, "Does everything look OK?" as I stood there staring at him.

He looked at me quietly and slowly said, "I think you need to go to the hospital."

I took a deep breath wanting to panic, but knowing that I couldn't. I said, "Yes, let's go."

We rode our bikes to the hospital. I was afraid to look and see what was wrong, but the stinging pain on my face, legs, and chest told me this was more than a brush burn. I wiped the blood from my chin as I sat waiting for the doctor to see me. Seemed like forever until, finally, my name was called and I went in. They cleaned up the blood and bandaged me with gauze. I was wrapped up like a mummy. I looked ridiculous.

Now, here is why that's important. Coming back from the hospital, going past the high school at the pond where we hang out and smoked pot....This is crazy, but I met this incredible boy at the pond after the hospital. His name is Jimmy Jack and he sat on a park bench. He looked like Adonis. Wavy, shoulder-length, light brown hair with blond streaks and he wore this brown leather vest with no shirt underneath. He is so handsome with a beautiful smile. He has that rugged look, kind of a bad boy thing about him. I wonder, am I free-falling again?...I am somehow intrigued and mystified by his deep sullen voice. He was with Billy. I hear he's his best friend. Billy goes to my school and is going out with my baby sister.

I stared at Jimmy, forgetting that I was all patched up like a mummy. I watched as they smoked their weed, passing the joint around. I want to know him better, but without anyone knowing, especially Antonio. Even though he and his mother escaped from Cuba trying to find a new life in the states, he can be so jealous. I wonder?

Miriam and I planned our first date in New York City. She lived two towns away from me, and I planned to meet her at the Long Island Railroad station in my town. Miriam accidentally got on the nonstop train to New York City and passed me. She had to come back, and we finally met at my station. We never made it to the city and hung out in the waiting room at the train station talking, laughing, and getting to know each other. We were both 18-year-old kids just out of high school with three life-goals: to have fun, get high, and dance. Miriam and I dated often, but I was still seeing Olivia and Julie. My thinking was so distorted that I honestly believed I loved all of them at the same time.

SNEAKING AROUND

There was a time in the early stages of my relationship with Miriam that I was seriously involved with all three girls at the same time. So, I would sneak around with one or the other. Many times they suspected that I was cheating on them and tried to catch me. I manipulated and convinced each one I was with that she was my main squeeze.

I remember one incident in my first apartment when I was with Olivia. I had a chain lock on the door when Julie came over unexpectedly and knocked. Olivia answered the door. As the chain lock caught the door, Julie caught a glimpse of Olivia. I reached over and slammed the door. While she banged on the door, I snuck Olivia out the back window, drove her down the block, came back, and climbed in the back window again.

I opened the door and said, "Oh. Hi, Julie."

She yelled, "Who's in here? I saw a black girl in here!"

"Nobody's here but me," I sheepishly replied.

"I saw her!" She screamed.

I put on my best innocent look asking, "Whadya mean? What's a matter with you? I was just takin' a shower."

She searched the place as I tried to convince her she was going crazy. I played it off like an innocent kid.

Later that evening, I snuck out and met Olivia. I had no control over my morals and cared only about satisfying my own needs.

After I met Miriam, I did the same thing. One day, when I was staying at my mother's apartment while she was away, I invited Miriam over for dinner. I was still going out with Julie at the time, who came over one day looking for me. Julie rang the doorbell, Miriam looked out the door, and Julie saw her. Julie began frantically pounding on the door, screaming for me to open it. I had Miriam climb out the back window of the second-floor apartment and down onto the roof of a stairwell. I drove her down the block, came back, and snuck in the window again with Julie still banging on the door.

I went downstairs, opened the door and said, "Oh, come on up."

"Where is she?" Julie screamed.

"No one's here. I don't know what you're talking about," I responded innocently.

It drove these girls crazy. She began pulling her hair saying, "I know I saw somebody in here. You think I'm going crazy?" Again I convinced her she must have been seeing things.

DOUBLE STANDARDS

I played all these crazy games and lived these crazy lies like I had a split personality. Finally, Miriam and I moved in together, so I decided it was time to let the other girls go. If I had not stopped seeing other girls, Miriam would not have been willing to stick with me. She was my little Puerto Rican princess. A beautiful, young woman, full of joy, excitement, and zeal for fun. We had a lot of so-called fun—we danced the nights away fueled by cocaine, alcohol, and lust. Miriam was a smooth dancer and taught me how to turn my funky dance steps into classy, slick disco moves. Following the movie *Saturday Night Fever*, we spent our weekends at the disco. We won dance contests and this brought a superficial sense of self-worth. Yet, at the end of the night, we were fighting because I was flirting with other girls or her with other guys.

We were still teenagers and I had no concept of faithfulness in a relationship. I lived by a double standard. I was always flirting, but if anyone tried to talk to Miriam, I would fly into a rage and start fights. I gradually let go of Olivia and Julie to concentrate on Miriam. She became the focus of my desire but I was never successful at being faithful to her until I met Christ. I was so driven by my lustful desires that I went back to wandering in and out of discos, bars, and the streets looking for a girl. Even though I was living with Miriam, who was so beautiful in every way, nothing could satisfy me.

When my drug and alcohol abuse grew more extreme, the love I thought I had for Miriam became even more distorted and perverted. I remember the fights Miriam and I would have over stupid things—just jealous fights about who we were with on the phone and other petty insecurities. In the end, I would throw her stuff out on the lawn of our apartment.

By the time I was 21, the honeymoon was over, even though we weren't even married. For the next 5 years, the fighting progressed beyond quarreling and verbal abuse. I became physical with her, smacking her, then her hitting me. She would run out of the house, and I would grab her and pull her back. We always made up, only to repeat the same pattern over and over again.

On one particular drug binge, we came home from a bar and fought till daybreak. When Miriam ran out of the house, I was so jealous and angry that I got in my car and jumped the curb with my 359 Skylark chasing her. She dashed into the park, and I pursued her with my car. She was inches away from the front of the car, sprinting for her life as I tried to run her down. I realize now that my own unfaithfulness was the root of the jealousy. I figured if I was cheating, then she must be cheating too. Often we separated, but we always ended up back together. We moved into a number of different apartments over the next several years, only to be evicted from each one.

STAND BY ME

Even through all of my unfaithfulness and drug addiction, Miriam stayed with me and forgave me. I began to see that this was true love. Miriam became close with my mother, and Mom taught Miriam to be patient with me. Miriam, like my mother, was able to see in me what I could never see—that there was a good person inside created by God. Miriam was able to love me, even though I was not able to love her.

Through all the pain, rejection, and abuse, Miriam stood by me. With her beauty and talents for modeling and dancing, she could have chosen many other established men. But, she stuck it out with me—a loser. She believed in me before I believed in myself. After we were evicted from many apartments, Miriam moved back home with her parents, and I ended up living in my car with my two dogs, Chi Chi and Dillinger. Chi Chi was a beautiful, short-haired, tan dog. Chi Chi gave birth to only one puppy, Dillinger. He was ugly and shaggy. He was a mutt, but Miriam loved him just like she loved me.

I usually parked my car in a parking lot and slept for a few hours. Then, Miriam would sneak me into her basement early in the morning, and I would sleep on the cot next to the boiler to get warm. When her parents went off to work, I came upstairs and she cooked breakfast. Afterward, we hung out until she left to go to work. Then, I drove around to find Billy to go get high. This empty cycle continued for 12 agonizing months.

DREAMS TURN INTO NIGHTMARES

One day I got a ticket for having the dogs in the car. I knew they needed to go even though Miriam complained bitterly. I wanted to keep her happy and give them a nice place to stay. Since we wanted the best for them, we decided to take them to the shelter to find them a nice home. We headed for the pound in the middle of the night. In the darkness, the dogs looked at me with such innocent eyes as I gently dropped them over the fence. It was not until we drove away that we saw the sign, "All dogs dropped off will be destroyed in 72 hours." I tried to rationalize that there was nothing I could do. They were better off dead there than sleeping in the car with me. It seemed like everything in our lives was dying.

I could not seem to find real love anywhere. Because my world revolved around buddies, girlfriends, family, and self, all of my relationships ended in disappointment. Now, I even lost my dogs. All that was left was the pain of shattered dreams. The dreams we once had turned to nightmares.

Chapter 7
Jimmy Jack, When Are
You Coming Back?

The beginning stages of gambling with my life.

THE GANG GROWS

Do you remember the song by Martha Reeves and the Vandellas: *Jimmy Mack*? The song mirrored my life:

Oh Jimmy Mack, when are you comin' back?
Jimmy, Jimmy, oh Jimmy Mack, you'd better hurry back.

During the early 1970's when this song came out, just about everybody I knew sang it to me jokingly because the actual song sounded more like "Jimmy Jack" than "Jimmy Mack."

Well, I am not Jimmy Mack, but I was lost, searching, and desperate. When I moved to Florida with my parents, my buddies and girlfriends had a going-away party for me. The theme song of the party was, of course, "Jimmy Jack, when are you coming back...?"

When I returned from Florida, my appetite for action was on fire. Jimmy Jack was back and worse than ever. As my dad began to recover from the shock treatments, it placed him in an almost comatose state and I had no supervision from him or my mother.

One day, my friend Tony and I got into Dad's meds. We thought if this stuff got my father numbed out, it should do the job for us. We grabbed only two of his red pills and went into my clubhouse to get high. When we took the pill, we were like zombies. We could not laugh. We could not move. It was a horrible high. I began to realize what my father was going through. This experience only caused me to seek a better high.

After moving back home to New York, our little gang added even crazier, more energetic boys and girls. Jamie, Joey, and Jackie were three brothers who loved to party. The chemistry among us ignited a level of rebellion that accelerated my destruction.

Two other brothers, Chris and Jay, were from a family of intellectuals. Their parents were college professors. There was not even a TV in their house. When we were with their family, they talked about what was going on at Yale or Harvard. Their idea of pleasure was discussing poetry, Hamlet, and Shakespeare. Chris and Jay became a personal project of the gang. We had to teach them to live street smart, so we did everything we could do to corrupt them.

When we robbed houses or cab drivers, Chris and Jay would walk away. We thought they were lightweights with no nerve. At the same time, I could see that they had a disciplined nature that I lacked. I liked that about them, and yet I also hated it because I felt they broke our unity at times when they did not join us in certain crimes.

There were other crazies in the crew. Tony was a crazy, smart, wise guy who had a natural build like a weight lifter. He had no fear. When a fight broke out, he was the first one to whip out his belt that had a razor-sharp buckle and whack anyone in his way. Brendan was a smooth dude who liked his women more than fighting. He also had some sense when it came to breaking the law. Although Brendan ran with us in the streets, he had some sensible boundaries that kept him out of jail. Vito was a short, stocky, hot-headed Italian who had the other clubhouse, E-13. We used it as another place to escape when we needed to hide from the cops. Vito had his own gang, but he often joined us when we planned to rob someone.

Helping me hold things together was Billy. We were like twins. Whatever I did, he did. And whatever he did, I did. This was the "James Gang," a bunch of wanna-bes with five daily priorities. Every 24 hours needed to have time for girls, drugs, breaking the law, a fight, and playing basketball.

A RAMPAGE OF ROBBERY

My ninth grade year was explosive with a higher level of violence and thievery to support my growing addiction to drugs and alcohol. When my homeboys and I finished building our clubhouse, E-14, it became our home for our sexual pleasures, getting high, and planning our next robbery. We quickly went from robbing rolls and milk at 4 a.m. from the local delicatessens to robbing houses.

We went on a rampage of robbery. We even robbed our girlfriends' houses when their parents were away. Our girlfriends told us when their families went away. Within minutes of them leaving for vacation, we would break in and tear their homes apart looking for money.

At one house, we brought our own cases of beer and ate barbecued steaks from the freezer. We drank beer out of huge flower vases and smoked pot all night. When the munchies set in, we ate their food, made ice cream sundaes, and, then, searched the house for money. We gathered up the cameras, stereo, televisions, silverware, and anything we could sell. With the volatile chemistry of Vito, Tony, Billy, and me, all hell broke loose. Tony started breaking windows and throwing cans of paint all over the living room walls and floor. Vito got the electric knife out of the kitchen, plugged it in, and began to cut the living room leather couches. Billy was the pyromaniac, so he tried to light the house on fire.

When we were done, we called a cab from the house and headed to the diner. At age 15, with excessive pot smoking and racing metabolisms, we were always hungry. After wolfing down a cheeseburger deluxe and fries, we got bored. We were frustrated that we had taken so little cash from the big robbery. We only had merchandise and a few jars filled with change to show for our efforts. Since we had no real money, we decided to rob the cab driver in hopes of getting a couple hundred bucks to buy enough stuff to get high.

We called for a cab. The plan was for me to sit in the front; Billy, Tony, and Vito were in the back. Vito's job was to grab the driver around the neck with his belt, Tony was designated to spray mace in his face, and my job was to grab the guy's money. Billy was to open the doors for us to make a quick getaway. We got into the cab and told him to take us to North Village Avenue, a few blocks away from my clubhouse.

When I yelled, "Now!" the boys executed the plan. As they subdued the cab driver, I grabbed his leather money pouch, and we took off for E-14. We got there out of breath and flushed with excitement. We huddled to count the loot. We realized we had done everything perfect except grabbing the money. Instead of getting the money pouch, I had grabbed the leather cover for the cabby's advertisement board. We laughed and joked thinking the whole thing was hilarious...until I was arrested.

A few nights later, I called a cab to meet my girlfriend, Olivia, at Michele's house, one of our home girls who was having a sleep over. Imagine my amazement when the same cab driver picked me up. As I jumped in the front seat, we looked at each other. I did not have much of a prayer life at the time, but that was one moment I asked God to blind his eyes, hoping he did not recognize me. I had the same jacket on with the same paint stains from the other robbery. All I could think about was my rendezvous with Olivia. The cab driver dropped me off at Michele's house, and I was sure I had gotten away with it until the pounding on the door interrupted us at 4 a.m. I did not even have sense to climb out the window.

When the police asked if the young man who took a cab was there, Michele said, "Yes." I was arrested, charged with five felonies, and in the end sentenced to 7 years of probation. If I was 16 years or older, I would have been charged as an adult and spent several years in jail. My mother fought with the court system not to send me away to a juvenile detention center. She was determined to keep me home while all my brothers had been sent away when they were younger. However, her determination to help me did not change my delinquent character.

BEER BASHING

One of our youthful traditions became detrimental to my health, my academics, and my athletic career. It was getting high before school every morning at our clubhouse, E-14.

As I mentioned before, I was tall and looked older than I really was. On one particular morning, when I was in the ninth grade, I bought a couple six packs of Heineken beer. Tony, myself, and some other friends decided to meet before school to get a buzz. I went to the delicatessen at 7:30 a.m. in the morning and by 8 a.m. we met at E-14. We knocked off a couple of bottles and got a quick high. Often when we drank beer, it seemed that a violent streak would come upon us, especially Tony. We called it getting "Beer Muscles." We decided to walk out of E-14 and head toward the school.

I can't imagine what it looked like to see a group of teenage boys walking around at 9 a.m. with beer bottles in their hands and cigarettes hanging from their mouths.

Tony had an incredible arm. He could have been a professional baseball pitcher, but the early morning "get high" meetings detoured his athletic gifting. Tony took a rock and whipped it at a school bus that was driving by. The rock hit the bus window and it broke. Now, the bus was full of kids at the time, but that didn't stop the bus driver from slamming on his brakes and immediately turning into the parking lot. He jumped out of the bus carrying a fire extinguisher and stormed toward us in a rage. Tony and I both had beer bottles in our hands.

I told Tony to hold my bottle. Now he had two bottles of Heineken in his hands, and I was ready to take the driver out. The driver approached and I grabbed him by his shirt and reached out to hit him, but before I could there was a crash and a flash. I felt something running down my neck—I didn't know if it was beer or blood, but I didn't really care. Tony had swung to hit the man over the head with one of the bottles of beer but missed him and busted the bottle over my head. Even then, I was so "hard-headed" the bottle didn't even break the skin.

I looked at Tony stunned and so did the driver.

Tony said, "Oops, sorry Jim," then instantly took the other bottle and smashed it over the bus driver's head. The bus driver crumbled in my hands, unconscious.

Meanwhile, all the kids on the bus were sitting there looking at us, so we made a mad dash for the school. Since I smelled like beer, I ran straight to the bathroom to wash my clothes and hair.

At 9:30 a.m. I heard a loud noise in the hallway and kids running. I came out of the bathroom to ask what was going on. Someone began to tell me that another bus driver saw the beer bottle fight in the parking lot and followed two boys to our school. They continued to say that the bus driver was inside telling our principal that the two boys who hit the other bus driver over the head with a beer bottle ran into the school.

I came out acting like I had no idea what was going on when all of a sudden, about 50 kids on the bus started yelling "There he is, there he is." Immediately, the bus driver grabbed me and identified both Tony and me.

The police station was right down the block from our school so they called the police. We were picked up and brought to the police station. But the bus driver knew my family's reputation for being tough street fighters—especially my older brother—and was afraid that if he pressed charges, we'd get him back.

The driver dropped the charges and the police could do nothing. There we were in the police station, with the principal and assistant principal who now had to walk us back to school. This was one of our "morning devotions" from our junior high days.

Later we played basketball, bragged, and laughed the fight off, not realizing that "youthful traditions" like these were leading us down a road to destruction.

NON STOP TROUBLE

My life was a vicious cycle of nonstop trouble. I was in and out of court and subjected to years of wasted therapy. I mastered lying to my therapists, counselors, and probation officers. When I felt that my creativity and potential were beginning to diminish, I embraced the only life I knew. I went back to selling drugs and hustling people for chump change to support my alcohol and drug addictions. Life was all about feeling good, being happy, and having fun in an effort to block out my past. I was just destroying myself, though.

My high school years were as full of turmoil as my younger years had been. Even though I was using drugs, drinking, and carousing, I managed to attend some classes. I also had an obsessive desire to play basketball. The Smith boys took good care of me and we played basketball in the street, in parks, and inside and outside our homes—any place with enough room to bounce, pass, and shoot.

If it were not for basketball, I would have quit school. It was impossible for me to concentrate in class, so I fooled around and messed up every day. Our pot dealer lived down the street from the school, so we had easy access to drugs at every break during the school day. It never occurred to me that what I was doing was physically, emotionally, and mentally damaging. In fact, I thought the jocks and others, who did not live like my friends and I were living, were really missing out. Looking back, it is hard to imagine how much I could have achieved both academically and athletically without the dulling effects and powerful influence of drugs and alcohol.

CAREER CUT SHORT

In tenth grade, I went out for football. Even with my vices, I was quick and fit. But, I could not concentrate or focus enough to remember the plays, so the coach stuck me in as a defensive end where I could just charge and tackle. I also played wide-receiver because I had good hands to catch passes. Trying to be the life of the team, I stuck with the same ol' shenanigans. I brought vodka, beer, and pot to football camp during pre-season conditioning. After three practices I would invite many of my teammates to my bunk to celebrate. Because of my reputation as a tough and crazy guy, I was able to manipulate many of my teammates to shave their heads and promised each one I would shave mine. My word and plans were always deceptive. I never cut one strand of my own hair, yet most of the team shaved their heads.

The coach rarely called plays that threw me the ball because he heard rumors about my influence and mischief at the camps and had little confidence in me. The rumors were accurate, but with my distorted desire for fun, it was the only way I knew to relax with the other players when we were bored after practice. With my natural athleticism, I eventually started on varsity but never reached my potential.

Along with my athletic side, there was an artist in me. I really enjoyed sculpting. It provided an interesting insight into the eternal fight for my destiny and my own internal conflict. In the tenth grade, I made two sculptures in art class. One was the face of Jesus and the other the body of a naked woman. I was so proud of them. I sent them both into the kiln to be glazed, ready to reveal my genius. When they came out of the kiln, the statute of the naked torso was destroyed and but the Jesus sculpture fired correctly. The face of Jesus was intense. Since I knew Dianne was into "God stuff," I gave it to her. She was kind enough to put it in her home as she continued to pray for me. This was not the only time that God tried to reveal His power to me by shattering my lustful illusions. The lustful statue was shattered, leaving only the face of Jesus as a reminder of *His Love*.

In eleventh grade, I excelled in basketball, although I was not a disciplined player. I was often late and sometimes missed practice altogether to make a pit stop with a girl at E-14 or the school basement. I would con my coach into letting me continue to play by telling him that I missed practice because I had to see my probation officer. Like my influence on the football team, I turned my basketball teammates on to getting high. I was a terrible influence on the team but did not realize it because I was always high on drugs, too.

DAD SOBERS UP AND WAKES UP

I began getting high even more with my friends in E-14. Smoking pot was not giving us the high it used to. So, we began to smoke powdered hashish until we passed: out. We practiced a crazy method of smoking hash that could have killed us. We filled a hash pipe full of crushed powdered hashish and inhaled it through the pipe. We held our breath while one of us wrapped our arms around the other person's chest, squeezed until that person passed out, and then dropped him on the floor. This is what we called a "mean hash rush." No one died, but millions of brain cells did.

During this time, my father slowly decreased his use of antidepressants and began to sober up. When he finally came to his senses, he decided to put me on a curfew for the first time in my life. What a shock! He set my curfew to be in the house by 10 p.m. during the week and 1 a.m. on the weekends. Then, my father ordered me to stop hanging around with Billy and bringing him over to our house, because he was getting arrested all the time. I thought both restrictions were impossible. Even though I tried to comply, Dad and I had violent conflicts over the new arrangements. I came home drunk and got into fights with my father, screaming and arguing, until he chased me upstairs.

I did not quit seeing Billy. After all, we were a team. We were good-looking young guys. We had a smooth line and played ball, so it was easy to pick up girls and make the other guys jealous. We thought we had it going on, but we were really just a couple of hoodlums hanging out and styling with slick threads. Even though I loved Billy like a brother, he was not a good influence on me—and I was certainly not a good influence on him. We fed into each other's weaknesses.

If an outsider touched one of us, our household had a loyalty that was incredible. But, we also had lots of fights within the family. Dad joked around with me often in front of my friends, saying things like, "Hey, I know you're no good because you're hanging out with my son. He isn't any good, so if you're hanging out with him, that means you aren't any good."

Another of Dad's favorite sarcastic comments was, "Hey, Jimmy, I stuck up for you today."

"You what ... what did you do, Dad?" I grew more and more excited. Did Dad really stick up for me? Could it be true?

"Oh, your friends told me you weren't fit to sleep with pigs, and I told them you were." Then, he would laugh and slap his knee, enjoying himself. I grew numb to his sarcastic humor and learned to laugh with him. The truth was, he was right. At that time in my life, I was no good.

Finally, our arguing got out of hand. I had been trying to keep the 1 a.m. curfew. One early morning I slipped into the house, and my father heard me. He started yelling and reached out toward me. For the first time in my life, I grabbed my father by his shirt and pushed him against the stairs. I shoved him to the floor and screamed at him, cursing, "Don't you ever touch me again. I'm fed up with you!"

My father returned my stare, stunned but fearless. "Oh, this is how you are now, huh? This is how you are? You're a tough guy, huh, a tough guy?"

I let go of him and ran upstairs to sleep. When I awoke in the morning, I almost felt sick. I never felt so bad in my life because I had laid my hands on my father. I wrote him a long letter and told him I was sorry. He said, "OK, let's try it again." But, I still could not keep the curfew.

The time came for the Mayor's Trophy Game between my hometown's rival teams. Everyone was talking about the clash between St. Agnes, where I attended first through fifth grades, and South Side High, the public high school for which I was to be the starting guard. Both teams were recognized as the dominant squads on Long Island. The stage was set for the game to be held at the famous Long Island Nassau Coliseum, the home court of the ABA Nets basketball team and their star player Julius Erving, "Dr. J."

Just before the game, I snuck Billy up to my room to sleep over. My father came into my room and caught Billy there. He screamed at me and Billy, smacked me in my mouth, and kicked Billy out of the house. I did not say a thing. I held in my anger. My father was trying to save me from a life of failure, but it was too late. I was already set in my ways.

During the game, I was full of anger at my father, but I was also in the zone. I scored the first 12 points in the first quarter, six straight jump-shots that in today's game would be three-pointers, and the crowd roared. My father was in the stands. I glanced up at him as I scored another basket, "Take that, Dad! In your face—!" There he was in the stands, clapping like nothing happened. He was actually right, but my blame-shifting rebellious mentality was set.

We won the game in double overtime. The game made the headlines in The New York Post the next morning, featuring a big picture of me driving to the basket. It was an incredible game, but my father and I never said a word to each other about it. He did not seem to have the ability to say, "I'm proud of you," or even "Good game." He could verbally express his criticism when we fought and even protected us when needed, but because of the torture of the war, he had a hard time affirming me. He never spoke of this incident until he lay on his deathbed.

THE FIGHT CLUB

Even though I was able to camouflage my inner anger with humor and crazy stunts, it often came out when I got into fights. Although my brothers were fierce street fighters, I was the one who tried to defuse the situation and stop them from fighting. I knew their potential for killing someone. Yet, their fighting instinct wore off on me, especially when I was challenged by many people due to my reputation. When I was 15, an Asian kid strolled into town, threatened my friends, and then came looking for me. He was an experienced karate fighter on a mission to prove himself. When he ran into me, his karate stuff did not help him. I had learned a lot of techniques from watching my brothers fight, and this gave me an advantage.

Lesson number one: hit your enemy first before he hits you. Lesson number two: hit him with anything and everything you have. As he came karate-kicking toward me, I picked up my bicycle, whacked him with it, and punched him in the head several times until he started crying. I felt so bad for the kid that I invited him into our gang. After he joined us, I taught him how to break into restaurants and rob their liquor cabinets to fill our bar at E-14.

In every town, there is always a bully who intimidates everyone. Frankie, a 6-foot, 4-inch, 240-pound, solid muscle tough dude, was the big intimidator in our town. In high school, he was a tough football player and sergeant of arms for one of the local fraternities. As the sergeant of arms, he led the violent initiation process new recruits were forced to go through. This gang initiation was called "dogging." Chris, one of my homeboys, had been beaten so badly by Frankie with a paddle that he collapsed in my arms when he came over to my house. He showed me his backside that was completely black, purple, and blue. I told him I was ready to run out and bust Frankie's head. He pleaded with me not to because he had been inducted into the fraternity and might be kicked out if I went after Frankie. I did not go, but kept this incident in my heart.

A couple of years later, I was working in a gas station. Frankie came looking for a fight. He pulled up to the self-serve gas pump and stepped out of his van, angry and drunk. He yelled at me to pump some gas in his car—now!

I took the gas nozzle out and said, "Here, you pump your own gas. It's self-service."

He said, "You pump my ---- car, you ----."

So, I handed him the nozzle and said, "You pump your own gas."

He threw it at me. I caught it and immediately tossed it back at him. As he went to catch it, I served three right hooks and a couple of round houses to the head. As he crumbled to the ground, I reminded him of what he did to Chris. My boss grabbed me and took me inside the station. Frankie took off and threatened to come back.

Later, it was time to close the station. We turned the lights off and I was outside in the cashier booth, counting the money, when Frankie's van pulled up on the side of my booth. His driver-side window was open, and he was telling his buddy how he was going to kill me with the thick, long chain in his hands. I was literally 2 feet away from him, but he could not see me because the lights were out in the booth. If he saw me, he could have cornered me in the booth and killed me. So, I slowly snuck out of the booth.

As he was winding the chain around his hand, ready to hunt me down, I approached his van window without him seeing me. With every ounce of my weight and strength, I punched him in the face through the open driver's side window and walked back into the station. When he finally awoke and came to his senses, he took off. The police came looking for me and told me he went to the hospital and had called them, asking them to talk to me. When he sobered up, he realized what had happened and feared my older brothers would come after him. After this incident, we ran into each other, but his intimidation tactics were all gone. We became friends.

I began to realize that I had a hidden rage like the rest of my brothers. I believed it had been transferred by my father's explosive anger and would ignite when provoked. Although I always tried to avoid a fight, there were times I felt I had to retaliate when someone crossed the line of respect, especially concerning my girl.

While walking into a bar with Julie, two thugs sitting in their car began to make disrespectful remarks about her. I knew they were from out-of-town. I walked Julie into the bar and grabbed two of my buddies. I told them just to watch while I took care of both of them. If they had a weapon, they were to jump in. I called both of the thugs out of the car. As soon as they were shoulder-to-shoulder next to each other and an arm's length away from me, I hit both of them instantaneously—one with my right hand and the other with my left. They were both knocked out with one punch each. My tough-guy reputation was elevated to my own demise. Now that my peers thought I was the undefeated street fighter of the town, I was driven to a new level of craziness.

COMING TO THE RESCUE

When I was in twelfth grade, my dad kicked me out of the house. I moved into my own apartment with my brother, Johnny. The partying increased to a new level. My brother helped me out at this time in my life, but my athletic career was about to end because I had no control of my desire to get high.

I heard that a schoolmate who lived near the school had some drugs stashed in his room. Just before practice one day, I decided to steal his drugs. I burglarized his house, but a neighbor saw me and turned me in. I went to basketball practice like everything was normal. The next thing I knew, boom! I was busted. A detective came and dragged me off the basketball court.

After the arrest I was thrown into jail, charged with breaking and entering. I simply laughed because I had another felony under my belt.

During this time, a friend of our family, Mike Globinger, was a private detective and the bodyguard for the bishop of the St. Agnes Diocese. Mike took an interest in me to try to help me get my life in order. He watched me grow up since I was a young kid and busted me several times with petty crimes. He knew my family and our plight well, and respected my father. When he heard I had been arrested, he used some connections to get a judge out of bed to arraign me at 1 a.m. in the police station to keep me out of jail. By 8 a.m., I appeared before another judge.

Another friend of our family, Rev. Frank Robinson, was the local Baptist pastor in the projects. He came to my rescue and represented me in court. Mike was also there to represent me. They obviously saw something in me I could not see in myself.

Before I was to appear in court, my father gave me some instructions on how to behave before the judge. Although Dad had plenty of his own problems, he knew the right way to behave. Just before we entered the courtroom, my dad said, "Spit the gum out before you go inside, Jimmy."

As usual I ignored him. I went into the courtroom, and the first words out of the judge's mouth were, "We are going to start this session right and proper." He pointed straight at me and said, "You! Spit that gum out."

My father was absolutely furious and his body language let me know it. As my case was being heard, the judge asked my father, "Mr. Jack, how is your son's behavior at home?"

With the gum incident and my father's integrity on the line, he responded, "Very disobedient, your honor."

The judge's next words, "Lock him up," took my breath away. The minister, the bishop's bodyguard, and I all looked at Dad like he had two heads.

Later, Mike and Frank asked Dad, "What did you say that for? Why do you think we're here? We were trying to get your son out of jail."

Dad sternly replied, "Sir, I don't lie in the court of law." That was just how Dad was.

Somehow, I was bailed out later that afternoon and continued playing basketball as well as everything else that was destroying my life.

JUSTIFIABLE LIES

I continued getting high and missing basketball practice to be with my girlfriends, until finally my coach called me into his office and yelled, "Jimmy, let me tell you something. You're the worst influence I have ever had on my team. You have such talent, but you are poison to this team. I'm kicking you off the team—today! Get your things and get out of here."

I cursed out the coach and stormed out of the room thinking he was the biggest idiot in the world and had no clue what was going on. My victim mentality was so deeply embedded that I always blamed others for everything. I was never the failure. I was always the victim. I rationalized another failure by convincing myself that getting kicked off the basketball team was great because now I had more time to get high and run around with girls.

Somehow, I managed to get through high school using my talents as a hustler to pass classes. I had a plan. I always sat behind someone I thought was smart—usually girls who wore glasses. My rationale was: first, girls are smarter than boys. Second, if they wear glasses they must read a lot because if you read a lot, you burn out your eyes. My assumption was the thicker the glasses, the smarter the girl. I would cheat off their papers to get through high school.

Sometimes we were put in cubicles to take tests. I maneuvered my chair so I could see through a crack in the wood or a hole in the pegboard to cheat. The fact that I graduated is a miracle... or maybe they just wanted to get rid of me. After high school graduation, I was more concerned about girls. The more women I had, the more I needed to get high. Even when I found my true love, Miriam, and moved in with her, I did everything I could to sabotage the relationship. I had no idea what real love was.

HUSTLING FOR A HIGH

Because my father was a 100 percent disabled veteran, I was able to receive child of veteran college benefits. With that money I went to Nassau Community College. I majored in hotel and restaurant management because that was the lifestyle I loved—sleeping, eating, drinking, and partying. My hustling tactics went into full gear at college since I did not want to study and could barely read. So, I befriended a security guard who had the keys to the teachers' offices. I conned him into getting me all my exams a week before the tests. I scheduled a study time at my house with some of my fellow classmates and gave them the tests to review. They found all the answers. This was the only way I passed some of my courses. I did go out for the college basketball team, but was cut because of my drug abuse. My body could play, but my mind could not. I ended up quitting college after a year.

I got a job in New York City working in a hotel on 55th Street and 7th Avenue. I was contracted to wallpaper the hallways of the hotel's 200 rooms. This job provided my chance to daily sleep off my hangover. After the owner found out I only wallpapered half the rooms I submitted payment for, I was fired. Billy worked in the city at this time and stayed at his sister's apartment downtown during the week and spent the weekends with Miriam and me. Because Billy was dating Miriam's sister who still lived with her mother in Long Island, our apartment was their hangout as well. Billy and I roamed New York City till the wee hours of the morning. We fit right in with the street hustlers. After work and before heading home to Miriam, I often jumped on a subway to 42nd Street and learned street scams so I could hustle extra money.

One particular scam I learned was Three Card Monte. The scam consisted of a dealer who shuffled three cards over each other on top of a cardboard box or table. Two of the cards were a ten of hearts (red) and a ten of diamonds (red). The third card was the ace of spades (black). The red tens were the losing cards and the black ace was the winner. The colors were used to manipulate the eyes. The game was illegal because it was street gambling. As such, it was virtually impossible to win because the shuffle of the cards was so quick and tricked the eyes so that a person was convinced he picked the winning ace every time.

There was always a partner working the scam. He was usually dressed in a suit with a newspaper under his arm. When the shuffle was done, the dealer showed the ace and where he placed it. However, with a quick shuffle, the ace was switched with either the ten of hearts or ten of diamonds. The partner's job was to immediately bet and place $100 down on what looked like the ace of spades. This bet reinforced the sucker and with a great confident smile, the victim would throw his $100 down. As the dealer turned over the losing red ten, the smiles turned into anguish, and the sucker usually continued until his money was all gone.

I mastered this game because I had been one of the suckers. I lost my whole paycheck one evening and had just enough money to take the subway home and buy a deck of cards to learn the scam. And learn I did. A month later, I went back to the city with a vengeance and set up my own scam with a cardboard box and a partner. I won my money back, brought the game into the bars I hung out in and drank for free all night. My Three Card Monte days ended, though, when the cops caught me hustling in midtown Manhattan, slammed my head against the police car a few times, knocked some sense into me, and made me an offer I could not refuse.

At this time in my life, I could not keep a job because I was always out on the streets hustling with the boys. Any money I did make was spent on drugs. Miriam worked, and we lived off her income. But, it was not enough to sustain us as we got evicted from one apartment after another.

THE CALL OF THE WILD

To avoid the responsibilities of providing for Miriam, I escaped by going on wild binges with Billy and the boys. One evening as the bars closed at 4 a.m., we still wanted to party. We hit the after-hours club and continued our binge there. When they ran us out, the James Gang was in full force. For excitement, we went to an adult group home where mentally ill patients were housed.

I told the boys, "Let's go wake up our friends and have a little party for them." We arrived at the group home full of expectation. We went room to room awakening the residents. They did not know what was going on. They knew they got medication in the morning, but there was some confusion as we were quite early.

With a bottle of vodka in my hand I shouted, "Get up! It's time for meds." I laughed with glee as they responded, as though I was the director. A line of patients came down the steps and filled the downstairs foyer when the house manager awakened. I grabbed him and slapped him on the back of his head. "We've got this covered," I said. One of the boys grabbed him and locked him in his room.

As I was shouting instructions, a resident snatched the vodka bottle out of my hand, guzzling it. Imagine that, he seems to have an alcohol problem, I thought, clinically.

I wrestled my bottle back and reminded him, "This is not good for breakfast and certainly not with your meds."

I always loved the movie *One Flew Over the Cuckoo's Nest* starring

Jack Nicholson. He faked insanity to get into a hospital for the criminally insane. He manipulated the staff and took the residents on an ill-fated fishing trip. Nicholson's character portrayed a man who knew how to function on the borderline of insanity. Yet, in the movie he inspired a bunch of mentally ill men and took them on a normal outing, which was one of the most exciting days of their lives. I really identified with that. I guess deep inside of me, I had a calling to help hurting people, but it was twisted and perverted.

As one of the residents began to distribute the meds, I decided to jump on line. I figured I could use a couple of psychotropic drugs to keep me going. As we were joking in the line, the police burst into the house. They knew immediately that I was the ringleader of this crazy gang. After they found out I had a warrant, I was back in jail for another one of my crazy missions.

CONNING CONTRACTORS

During this season I connected with two of my older brothers' friends, Jerry and Ricky, who were hustlers and master manipulators. They wandered all over the country conning people. I was drawn to them because of their sarcastic humor, energy, and wild lifestyle. I started spending a lot of time with them in bars where they hustled people out of their money shooting pool. We all started using cocaine and heroin and hanging out in the city with Billy, getting drugs and roaming in and out of bars, streets, and parks.

Sometimes I was away from home for days at a time. My relationship with Miriam became worse than rocky. Miriam liked cocaine, but every now and then I would slip heroin in with her cocaine without telling her. I do not know how we survived.

When Miriam and I were evicted again, she moved back home, and I was left homeless. Ricky and I went to a broken-down, 6-story apartment building in Long Beach, Long Island. A number of drug addicts hung out in the place, even though it was not really fit for human occupancy. Ricky and I hustled the owners of the building. We told them we were contractors capable of renovating the entire building.

We walked out of the meeting with a job and a free 2-bedroom apartment. The next day a company brought us a scaffold, bricks, mortar, and jack hammers. We climbed up on the scaffold and started hacking away at the front of the building. We were supposed to be renovating it, but we had no idea what we were doing. We worked all day drinking beer and wine and did cocaine and heroin at night. It was a crazy time.

After living like this for a while, the owners figured out we were hustlers and kicked us out of our apartment. Ricky and I moved into Jerry's house. Billy and Hughie ended up moving in, as well. Jerry's dad lived with us and treated all of us like his sons. But, we turned the house into one of our drug havens.

After Miriam found out I was so strung out on drugs, I checked myself into a detox program for the second time, hoping to get some sympathy from her, only to be kicked out for smoking pot. Again, my victim complex kicked in as I made excuses for myself and blamed others for my setback. The truth was that I was a failure at everything I did. I needed a miracle that could only start in my heart.

JIMMY JACK IS BACK - IN SEARCH OF A MIRACLE

My sister, Dianne, was a severe heroin addict. One day she gave her life to Jesus. She sincerely had a genuine encounter with God. She experienced a spiritual rebirth. She shared with me for years a prophetic reality that I often mocked: "Jimmy, God loves you and He has a plan for your life."

I would laugh at her, "Plan? Yeah, right! What plan?"

She repeatedly invited Miriam and me to church, but we thought she was crazy and I did not hesitate to tell her so. I called her a born-again freak.

Miriam and I had been living together off and on for about 7 years when Dianne's husband, Bobby, entered Brooklyn Teen Challenge, a Christian, faith-based program for drug addicts and alcoholics. We had been kicked out of our last apartment, and Dianne wanted to give us a place to stay while Bobby was gone. She consulted her pastor about our situation, and we moved into a spare room in her home.

Living at Dianne's was nice. Miriam and I thought we were pretty slick. We had a routine of eating chicken wings in our room, drinking beer, vodka, and using drugs. We watched *The Honeymooners*, *The Twilight Zone*, and *The Odd Couple* on our little black-and-white television. We hid everything from Dianne; but being a former drug addict herself, she knew we were dabbling. So, she just prayed for us with more faith and determination. She prayed just outside our bedroom and was bold in her witness for Christ. Once in a while she would pop her head in the door and say, "Jimmy, God's going to transform your life and raise you up. You are going to preach the gospel one day."

"Sure, Dianne, sure. You're out of your mind, you know," I would respond. "You need to come on in and get high so you can get back to reality."

One Tuesday night, I needed $200 and asked Dianne for a loan. She said to me, "Jimmy, this is church night, but I'll make a bargain with you. I'll give you the money if you'll come to church with me." I did my best to get her to change the terms, but she stood firm.

Dianne attended Sheepgate Assembly of God and always had positive things to say about Pastor Joe Cedzich. She regarded him as such a sincere, faithful man of God. So, I felt a little more comfortable to go.

"OK, what time does church start?" I asked.

"7:30 p.m.," she replied.

I then asked, "And what time is it over?"

She said, "9 p.m."

I promised to be there at the starting time, 7:30 p.m., but got there at 9 p.m. sharp. While I planned to get there at the end, the service had just begun as it was a Pentecostal church. Pentecostal church services start at the end of the service with heavy-duty prayer. They had an altar call where the pastor invited people to the front of the church for salvation and prayer. When I entered the church, I looked down at the altar and saw a gray-haired man laying hands on some people. People were falling backward to the floor and ladies were placing blankets over them.

Oh, oh, I'm in big trouble, I thought, because I realized what Dianne was trying to do. She wanted to get me under the blanket. I was a hustler, and hustlers always try to figure everything out so they can counteract what the other person is doing.

My mind was racing. Dianne was at the front of the church praying for people. I caught her eye, as if to say, "See? I'm here, just like we agreed."

When I waved at Dianne to come to me, she waved back and called me down to the front. Well, she had the money (and I wanted the money), so I figured I had better play along. I was a little nervous when I reached her. "Listen, Dianne, I don't want to disturb anything that's going on. Just give me the $200, and I'll get out of here," I offered, cooperatively.

This was not going over with my sister. "First, we've got to pray for you," she replied with authority and faith. Now, I had done a lot of things for $200 in my life, but this was way beyond anything in my experience. I assumed Dianne wanted the pastor to push me down on the floor.

Dianne then turned to Pastor Joe and said, "This is my brother, Jimmy, who we've been praying for."

Right then, I thought, *What did she tell this guy? I know what he's thinking. He's saying to himself, 'This kid's going down.'*

At the same time I was thinking, *The kid ain't going down.* Looking the pastor straight in the eye, I dug my right foot into the carpet and put my left foot a little behind me to brace myself and thought, *Go ahead—give me your best shot. I ain't going down.*

Sure enough, the pastor placed his hand on my head and began praying with a little pressure—so I pushed him right back with my head. As we were rocking back and forth, Pastor Joe was using lines similar to those I had heard in the movie *The Exorcist:* "Satan, I rebuke you in the name of Jesus of

Nazareth. Come out of him, you foul demon of hell!"

As he prayed I thought, *Man, what's he talking about? I'm not like that girl in* The Exorcist. *I've just got a little drug problem. I don't have demons.*

The pastor kept praying, and finally I said a prayer, "OK, Lord, show me that You're real. If You show me that You're real, I'll give my life to You." By this time in my life, I felt sure I was going to die soon and I really did want to live.

I know God touched me that night, but I was more eager to get my $200 than I was to change my way of life. I felt something, but I didn't realize what had happened or what lay ahead. I left the church service thinking I had added hustling God to my list of accomplishments. I had no idea that I was about to experience one of the most terrifying nights of my life.

TRAGEDY IN MANHATTAN

I know I have woven some of this tale throughout the book, but now that you know me more, allow me to share the rest of the story. After church that night, Billy and I returned to the Lower East Side of New York City to cop four bags of heroin. That was all we could afford. We got set to use. We parked near Norfolk and Houston Streets. I snorted one of the bags, and then we cooked the other three bags so Billy could shoot the dope in his vein.

We got water from a leaky fire hydrant on the corner and poured it into a carbon-charred spoon to liquefy the powdered heroin. I held a lighter under the spoon while Billy cooked it up. Straining it through a cigarette filter to keep the impurities out, we drew the potent mixture into his syringe. Most of Billy's veins were already destroyed, collapsed from constantly sticking needles in his hands, feet, and arms, so it was hard to find a good vein. I helped Billy tie off his upper arm with a belt as he frantically searched for a good vein. I held his bicep to get a vein. He finally penetrated a usable vein and then shot the three bags of heroin into his arm.

Within seconds the very thing I always feared came upon us. Billy looked at me in panic and utter shock exclaiming, "Jimm--...!" He fell out of the van before he finished getting my name out. I realized he had overdosed. The bags we bought must have been uncut, pure heroin. I knew that this was how people often die.

Billy was on the street turning blue; he wasn't breathing. I jumped out of the van and began mouth-to-mouth resuscitation. With my hands on his chest, over his heart, I was doing my own clumsy version of CPR. I pumped his heart up and down, crying and screaming, "Come on, Billy!" His heart stopped beating and he stopped breathing. I lifted his limp, lifeless and held him close.

I slapped him, hugged him, and tried to make him walk until we both fell to the ground.

Billy was closer to me than a brother, and now it looked like I had killed him. "Billy, wake up! You can't die! You can't die!" I screamed. "Don't do this to me, Billy! Wake up!"

We were in lower Manhattan with no help, and I thought my friend was dead. I was sobbing hysterically and began to cry out to God, "Please don't let Billy die."

I looked at Billy's lifeless body one more time when, out of nowhere, a paramedic's van pulled up. I still have no idea where they came from, but the older paramedic asked coldly, "What's going on here?"

Their question was short, and my answer was even shorter as I screamed, "Heroin overdose!"

Another junkie walking by on the street, realizing we must have gotten some potent stuff, excitedly asked, "Wow! Where did you cop the stuff?"

There was no urgency in the efforts of the paramedics, barely older than Billy and I, as they backed their van up and opened the rear doors. Years of rescuing the casualties of drug infestation made them callous to my cries. They reacted as though he was dead and there was no need to rush.

I lifted Billy's limp, lifeless body up into the van with all the strength I had. I yelled, "Now, you work on him. You get to work on him!" There was no way I was going to just let Billy die without at least trying to get help.

The paramedics began to run fluids into Billy's body and pumped oxygen into him. After a short time they shook their heads like he was gone and there was nothing else they could do. I stood by the side of the van and got serious with God.

I will never forget that moment as I screamed and prayed. I remembered the God of my mother, the God of my sister—Jesus Christ, the One who healed the sick and raised the dead.

"God, please! Don't let him die!" I cried. After I prayed for Billy, I began to bargain with God. I promised Him that I would do anything He wanted me to. I would stop smoking. I would never drink again. I promised I would never do drugs again or steal again. Oh, I made so many promises and I was completely sincere—because I was desperate. "I'll become whatever You want me to be, God. Just don't let Billy die!"

I turned my head and looked inside the van and Billy's blue eyes opened, at first blankly and then he looked at me. Resurrection power came into his body and he jumped up. He pulled the needles out of his arm, jumped off the stretcher, and out of the back of the ambulance.

Suddenly, I heard the voice of God in my spirit say, "I showed you." God brought me right back to the church service earlier that evening. When Pastor Joe prayed for me, I had asked God, "If You are real, please show me." And show me He did.

Billy asked, "What happened?"

"You just died, man!" I replied, amazed at the sudden change. "I'm all right now, Jim. Let's go get high," Billy said.

"No way, brother. You just went to hell and back—and now we are going home," I responded, my mind, body, and spirit shaken over what had just happened.

As I drove home, I was trembling because of all of the promises I had made to God. I could hear my own words, "If you bring Billy back to life..." God had done what He had promised; now could I keep my promise? I knew deep inside that I could not honor all the promises I had made to Him. After all, I could not keep my dad's simple curfew, keep my dogs alive, or even care for Miriam. I felt like I hustled God big time.

I was so unfaithful to God. Later, however, I learned a divine truth from 2 Timothy 2:13, "If we are faithless, he remains faithful. He cannot deny Himself." I did not understand at the time how faithful God could be. Suddenly, I realized there was one promise I could keep: I would never get high with Billy again. And, we never did get high together again.

THE PRISONERS WERE LISTENING

After that night, my life went lower and lower. Because of my close encounter with Christ, the worse I got, the more I felt the awesome reality of God in my soul. I could not outrun His presence. That is what prayer does—and people were praying for me.

Bobby had entered Teen Challenge. I had a hard time grasping what Dianne was telling me about Bobby. After all, he was 35 years old...and in Teen Challenge? He was anything but a teen, and although I knew he was a challenge, I did not realize he was in the adult branch of Teen Challenge. Knowing Bobby, I thought he was hustling everybody. Dianne said he was singing with the Teen Challenge choir at her church, so she invited Hughie and me to come to the service. Being curious, I told Dianne, "Yeah, sure, I'll come." But I thought, *I can't miss this—I have got to check if Bobby's hustling or not.*

Dianne was a determined, strong-willed woman, and she had plans for her brothers that evening. She put Hughie and me right in the front row, so it was a little hard for us to make fun of Bobby without everyone looking at us. God had it all planned—and it was truly an unforgettable night.

As the choir got ready to sing, I was recalling how our relationship had evolved from the early days as a boy when Bobby tried to shield me from drugs, to the crazy times partying together later in life. I recalled the night Bobby and I were in a disco, dancing the night away. To keep up the pace, drugs were always a part of the festivities. Our eyes met, and we laughed, and knew it was time. We made our way to the rest room through the pounding music and smoke-filled dance floor as we dodged dancers, lovers, and fools.

We went into a bathroom stall together, and Bobby whipped out dope. As we began snorting the cocaine, a detective came into the bathroom. When he heard us, he flashed his badge over the door and ordered us to come out. I nearly panicked, but Bobby quickly flushed the drugs down the toilet and opened the door. Once we had buried the proof, we chased him out of the bathroom, out of the disco, and down the street because we were so mad he had made us flush our drugs. Suddenly, my daydream was interrupted as Dianne elbowed me in the side.

There was Bobby coming onto the platform with the choir. He was standing next to Ralphie, who they called the "Old Man" even though he was only 42. Ralphie was a colorful, Puerto Rican character. He was missing one front tooth and had a thin, drawn face, accentuating a big indentation in his chin. "H-a- t-e" and "L-o-v-e" were tattooed on his knuckles. When he even slightly flexed his muscles, his chiseled physique was evidence that he had been working out with weights in prison for a long time. He looked almost sinister with his dark black hair and mustache, but his face glowed like an angel's with peace and sincerity.

When he and Bobby stepped out from the rest of the choir and joined two other men to form a quartet, Hughie and I were mesmerized. They began to sing a gospel song by Leon Patillo: Go ye, therefore, and teach all nations... Go, go.

The men sounded like angels. The miraculous change in them was obvious. That night at Sheepgate Assembly of God, I started listening, truly listening, to the message of Jesus Christ. The Bible describes the apostle Paul and Silas being beaten and locked in a Philippian jail for preaching the gospel. In spite of their great pain, they got up at midnight and began to sing hymns and praises to God. Acts 16:25 says, "And the prisoners were listening to them." I knew that Bobby, Ralphie, and the others had been in bondage and were now free. The prisoners, Hughie and I, were listening, deeply desiring freedom. I left the service impressed, but unconvinced that I could ever change. My answer to everything was to get as high as possible and run as fast as possible. But my running buddy was Billy, and now I could not get high with him anymore.

NEARING THE END

At the same time, our lifestyle was catching up to us. Our friends began to die. One of my black friends became quite successful and made it all the way to Wall Street. The rest of us were still getting high on all kinds of drugs, so we were really proud of Bernard. He still lived at home in his mother's house. One evening after work they got into a fight. She told Bernard to go downstairs and just be quiet. He responded, "OK, Ma, I'll be quiet. I'll just kill myself."

"Oh, Bernard, stop it," was her dismissive reply as she continued washing the dishes. A little later when she heard nothing, her spirit jolted within her and she ran downstairs to check on him. To her horror, her son was hanging on a boiler pipe, dead.

We went to Bernard's grave side service that week. As his casket was being lowered into the ground, some friends dropped bags of pot and poured wine and beer into the grave. We thought this was what Bernard would want.

My friends continued killing themselves. Danny was one of my buddies that I often got high with. He jumped off the 85th floor of the Empire State Building and ended his misery. Another friend took a double-barrel shotgun and shot himself in the chest. Another jumped in front of a racing train on the Long Island Railroad. Many others overdosed on drugs. Jerry and Ricky both died from their drug abuse. When I paid my respect at Jerry's funeral, I was so shaken because his funeral was held at the grave site of his father. Ricky's cremated remains were in a shoebox placed on top of his father's grave, adjacent to the tombstone. I remember thinking, "Here lies Jerry, one of the fastest-talking pool sharks with massive potential, destroyed by his uncontrollable desire to get high." What he owned was in his shoebox, and I was next in line. I began to get a sense of the imminence of my own death.

Then, I received a phone call that shocked me: it was from Billy's family. He had been stabbed in the heart and was about to die. I dropped to my knees and began to cry and pray. Billy had been in Spanish Harlem buying heroin when two drug addicts jumped him to steal his dope. Billy refused to let go of the bags of heroin, and they stabbed him in the chest with a 12-inch knife. I wept and began to plead with God. Again, I made a promise. "God," I said, "if Billy lives, I will bring him to Dianne's church for prayer. Please don't let him die, God."

Billy survived, ripped the intravenous needles out of his arm, and left the hospital prematurely. He called me, and I said, "Billy, we are going to church tonight before we die." Because of our loyalty toward one another, good or bad, Billy always listened to me.

That night Billy and I walked into Sheepgate Assembly. I held him up. Together we slowly walked down the aisle and Pastor Joe looked at us. I was ready for anything—the blanket, oil, whatever. That day we were there for one reason—prayer for a new life.

I said, "Pastor Joe, could you please pray for us or we are gonna die."

Pastor Joe laid his hands on both of our heads and gently prayed, "Lord, deliver these boys and raise them up to be soldiers for the Cross." Billy and I left with a little hope, still desiring a miracle for a new life.

A battle was going on inside me. My mother was praying for me, my sister and her church were praying for me, and Bobby and his Christian boys from Teen Challenge were praying for me.

DANGLING IN THE BALANCE OF LIFE AND DEATH

The next week, November 4, 1984, will forever be engraved in my life. It was the day my life dangled between heaven and hell.

It was midnight. I was on an intense drug run and ended up in the projects at Barry's apartment, who was introducing all of us to smoking free-base cocaine.

An empty search for hope at the bottom of a bottle.

I parked my unlocked van in front of the apartment complex with the keys in it. Everyone in the hood knew me, and I never thought anyone would steal my van. I was a makeshift carpenter at the time and all of my tools were in the van, along with my wallet and license. It was not much, but it was basically everything I owned. After smoking some cocaine with Barry, I went outside to roam the streets. To my amazement, the van was gone. I found a screwdriver on the ground and stuck it in my pocket, in case I found the thieves who stole my van. I thought someone was playing a trick on me, so I called a friend who was an on-duty cop. He picked me up in the squad car, and we drove around looking for the van but could not find it. I was about to go crazy, so I told him to drop me off at a bus stop so I could go to Dianne's place in Long Beach where Miriam and I were staying.

Some really crazy people live in Long Beach, but on my way there I was as crazy as any of them. I was growling and moaning like a demon-possessed person. I had the screwdriver in my hand, ready to fight. I noticed passengers moving toward the front of the bus as I made my way toward the back. The bus dropped me off about ten blocks from Dianne's house, and I had to walk the rest of the way.

I saw the Brown Derby, a gun-slinging, knife-throwing bar that I would never go to in my right mind. But that night I was out of mind. I only had $2 in my pocket, but I was determined to buy a drink to forget my misery.

I boldly walked into the bar and said to the bartender, "Give me straight vodka, no ice." I clearly remember guzzling the vodka down, frustrated because I felt my life was over. Darkness surrounded me and I knew something desperate was going to happen. I thought I would probably end up in prison, hurt someone else, be badly hurt, or even killed that night.

There I stood as my life passed by me. I came to the conclusion that I was nothing but a no-good, dirty failure. It was the beginning of the end of my victim mentality, because I suddenly began to realize there was no one else to blame and that this one was on me. What a horrible reality to believe that, at the age of 26, you have failed life. I just wanted to end my life, end up in jail, get stabbed, or shot.

Through the cigarette smoke and blaring music, I glanced down at the end of the bar and saw a crazy dude looking at me. I started to go after him with the screwdriver. In the providence of God, at that same moment, Georgie Delgado, an addict hustling on the streets, walked by the bar and saw me through the window. (Georgie told me years later, after he became a minister, that God told him to help me that night).

Ironically, just two weeks earlier, I was playing bodyguard for Dianne when she tracked Georgie down to try to get him into Teen Challenge. As Dianne was encouraging Georgie to give his life to Jesus and go into Teen Challenge, I was sitting and listening to them, thinking they were both insane. Now, here I was about to confront a crazy stranger with a screwdriver and challenge death. I thought, *"Who is crazy now?"*

Georgie only stayed at Teen Challenge a few days, but long enough to learn that our only hope was Jesus. In a split second, Georgie saw my predicament. He stormed in and jumped in front of me. He said, "Jimmy, stop! Don't do anything. There is someone who can help you."

"Who, Georgie? Who can help me?" I asked, looking at him hopelessly.

"Jesus and Teen Challenge. They can help you, Jimmy," he answered.

Instantly, something happened to me when I heard those words. I threw the screwdriver to the floor. For the first time in my life, I was truly broken. When Georgie spoke those words, things were put in motion in a way that only God could orchestrate. My heart opened, I looked down at my hands, threw them up in the air as a sign of surrender, and started to cry. I felt like my hardened heart melted out of my eyes.

I said, "Georgie, call Dianne. She'll know what to do with me." As I stood there crying like a baby, it seemed like only seconds later that the door burst open and Dianne and Miriam came inside. They grabbed me and threw me into the backseat of Bobby's Cadillac as Dianne drove to Brooklyn Teen Challenge. I did not know where I was going. I huddled, lonely in the backseat, as only my uncontrollable sobs broke the darkness.

RESCUED FROM THE PIT OF HELL

Dianne brought me to Brooklyn Teen Challenge at 1 a.m. At that point in time, I was anything but a willing candidate. The rage over my hopelessness was now focused at everyone who was trying to help. I was swinging, cursing, and resisting everyone. But the guys who had been in the Teen Challenge choir at my sister's church were there. Some comforted me and others prayed for me. Finally, I slipped into a restless sleep as Dianne and Miriam left.

This was not a regular intake time at Brooklyn Teen Challenge, but they kept praying for me anyway. Bobby was in the second phase of the program at Camp Champion in upstate New York. He was interceding for me, too.

At 4 a.m., I awoke and did not know where I was. I suddenly felt trapped and heard something telling me, "Run. Get out! Get out!" I did not know if it was the demons of lust and addiction speaking into my mind, so I ran out of the house. I immediately started hustling money for beer and drugs.

Without question, the war in heaven and hell for my life was raging. I am so grateful that God's power overcame the power of hell again as God drew me back to Brooklyn Teen Challenge.

I'M CLEAN! I'M CLEAN! I'M CLEAN!

As I wandered back to 444 Clinton Avenue, I found the doors open and walked back in. When the staff found me, I had cigarettes behind my ear and in my mouth. I was delirious from the alcohol and drugs. I again began to fight, curse, and wrestle with the staff, but they just started holding me, praying, and speaking words of love. They shared the compassion of Jesus. I finally fell asleep.

When I woke up, I went down to the chapel, and there were about 20 guys kneeling down and praying. I saw the glory of God on their faces. I knelt down in the little chapel, put my head on the seat of a chair and for the first time in my life asked God to forgive me. Finally, I was really sincere. I was not running from an arrest or getting away with a hustle. I just wanted God to free me from my torment.

I had cried out to God many times before, especially in the back of a police car or in the police station. There are two very spiritual places people pray—in a church sanctuary and in the back of a police car. I remember my own prayers when I got busted. I prayed as though I was Billy Graham. As soon as I was released, though, I forgot about God until I was busted again.

The prayer I prayed that morning was different. I wanted to live. I wanted God to truly forgive me. When I was young, I would seek forgiveness from the priest at my former church during confession. I never told him my full sins because I thought I would have to go to the altar and pray 1,000 "Our Father" and "Hail Mary" prayers. So, I was never honest with myself or him in my repentance. But this was different. I desperately wanted to change, and I did not want to be dirty anymore. I wanted to be free, and I wanted God to save me.

In that split second, kneeling at a folding chair before God, I realized that only He could forgive me and change me. When I got up from that place of prayer, I felt like my sins, bondage, and all my vices stayed in that chair. I was free. I knew instantly that I was a new creation. I was forgiven. All the men stood in a circle, holding hands and praying. There, even though I was filthy, stinking like a gin mill, and wearing grimy, ripped-up pants and clothes, for the first time in my life I realized I was clean—*really clean.*

I was dirty on the outside, but a good hot shower could take care of that. It was not about my clothing. I did not care. I could throw the clothes in the laundry or the garbage. I knew that I could do sit-ups and pushups to sweat the stench out of my body as I did in other drug programs. But, I could never get the stench of sin out of my heart. For the first time in my life, I was clean on the inside by the precious blood of Jesus. I knew that my sins had been thrown into the sea of forgetfulness, never to be remembered again. I committed my heart, soul, and life to the lordship of Jesus Christ that day. My heart cried out, "I'm clean! I'm clean! I'm clean!"

On November 4, 1984, God restored the dream and the miracles began.

"Therefore, from now on, we regard no one according to the flesh. Even though we have known Christ according to the flesh, yet now we know Him thus no longer. Therefore, if anyone is in Christ, he is a new creation; old things have passed away; behold, all things have become new. Now all things are of God, who has reconciled us to Himself through Jesus Christ, and has given us the ministry of reconciliation, that is, that God was in Christ reconciling the world to Himself, not imputing their trespasses to them, and has committed to us the word of reconciliation."

2 Corinthians 5:16-19 (NKJV)

CHAPTER 8
"BOY, YOU HAVE A MESSED UP FAMILY"

The Jack family head count - I'm in my mother's arms.

NO TRUER WORDS

One time at Brooklyn Teen Challenge, I had the honor of driving David Wilkerson, the founder of Teen Challenge and Times Square Church, from a crusade in Manhattan to the Brooklyn Teen Challenge office. I felt so privileged to be with him and wanted to thank him personally for being used by God to start Teen Challenge. I was excited because after 15 divorces, children born out of wedlock, and addictions of every kind in my family, over 60 members of my family and friends had been transformed by Jesus Christ through Teen Challenge. As we parked, I was thinking of words to say because Brother Dave does not really like accolades or compliments. I asked him if I could just share something with him before he got out of the van. He looked at me with his piercing, greenish-blue, prophetic eyes, and I was suddenly empowered to share my heart.

"Brother Dave, I want to thank you for your obedience in starting the Teen Challenge ministry many years ago. Because of your faithfulness in the establishment of this great ministry, not only have I been delivered and saved from a life of crime and drug addiction, but 60 members of my family have been miraculously transformed. My brothers, sisters, and I were all messed up on drugs and alcohol in some way or another.

We all had some type of drug dependence. Even my mother and father were addicted to prescription drugs. I know my mother would have gone through the Teen Challenge program if she knew about it at the time of her need. Thank you for being obedient, Brother Dave. Because of that, my whole family has found salvation."

He fixed his eyes steadily upon me and I waited in great expectation for some powerful utterance, for a divine message, or a prophetic word from him. Finally, through the deafening silence came the response, "Boy, you've got a messed up family, don't you?"

I shook my head, "Yes," as he stepped out of the van, heading to the center to resume his busy schedule. That was my prophetic word from Brother Dave. He is such a humble man, he could not take credit for what God had done. As I reflect, no truer words could have been spoken of my family.

MANY MIXED EMOTIONS

When my parents moved from Levittown to Rockville Centre, I was 2. Next to our block was St. Agnes Cathedral. Mom joined the Roman Catholic church and brought all of us to mass. This was our introduction to Christianity, and every Sunday was a holy war. Trying to dress, clean, feed, and deliver nine kids to church on time, made the Crusades "small potatoes," but Mom was determined. Add my father to that volatile mix, one of us was going to be yelled at or slapped upside the head every Sunday.

First Holy Communion

I know Mom was trying to get us into heaven, but I often thought, *I sure hope heaven is better than this.*

I remember entering the church. I was awestruck by the edifice, the towering cathedral ceilings, the colored light streaming through stained-glass windows, and the smell of incense that rose from the altar. The statues of Jesus and all of the saints surrounding us as the choir sang music from the rear balcony gripped our young hearts. I had such mixed emotions. One part felt holy awe, one part fear of God, and one part fear of my dad if anyone got out of line. I loved and hated it because we went through so much pain to get there, but then I honestly did not understand what was going on when we got there. My emotional state made it almost impossible to see the love God had for us. We would get into our seats as my mother sang loud and high. I was embarrassed because I felt like everyone was looking at how loud she sang. She was a charismatic Catholic ahead of her time.

WAR ZONE AT HOME

Our home was not always a war zone. At times we all gathered in the living room, laying around our sectional couches or carpeted floor with the fireplace burning with leftover wood from around the house. We watched Bonanza, Mutual of Omaha's *Wild Kingdom*, and Disney movies. We were normal in many ways—often eating together in the dining room at our long walnut-stained pine, colonial table with benches on each side. Mom and Dad were seated at each end, training and refereeing. During my adolescent years, we had some peaceful times with only the normal turbulence any large family would experience. Even when the nine members of the Aggleston family from the black community lived in our home for 3 months after their house burned down, our family was still somewhat stable.

The breakdown began with a combination of our rejection by the white community and the cultural whirlwind that our country was experiencing. The love movement, drug movement, Vietnam, and assassinations of President Kennedy and Martin Luther King, Jr., as well as my sisters and brothers seeking peace and security through multiple relationships, all contributed to our demise.

My parents were consumed with helping the poor and needy. At the same time, they were just trying to make it with nine children of their own. Arguments and fighting were an everyday routine. Having three kids of my own now, I can only imagine the stress on my parents, especially as I consider the pressure of all nine of us running wild.

The breakdowns in an environment of rage, with both parents emotionally checked out, medicated beyond caring, created an atmosphere that drove most of us out as quickly as we could. Some left home early which led to illegitimate children, abortions, and broken marriages.

Another thing that contributed to our terrible reputation was the bias against interracial marriage. I have six African-American, three Hispanic, one German, one Polish, and one Irish brothers-in-law. I have only five sisters. Marianne, who passed away, only married once. I have Jewish, Spanish, Polish, Italian, and German sisters-in-law, and all kinds of mixtures between. Add to that our two Moroccan and two Chinese cousins and an assortment of religions from Presbyterian, Methodist, Baptist, Assemblies of God, Pentecostal, Catholic, Jewish, Muslim, and Buddhist. At present, several of my brothers and sisters are single, and I am sure the "Jack United Nations" will continue to grow.

Add to that chemistry, alcohol and drug addiction, eating disorders, rage, lust, promiscuity, and fear, and there was a combustible mixture that led to the dysfunction of our family. The consequences of our lifestyle not only affected my immediate family, but also 37 nieces and nephews, some of whom are racially mixed.

LEAVING HOME—MARRIAGE, THE WAY OUT?

I was 4 years old when my oldest sister, Sandy, graduated from high school. She immediately left home and got married at 18. She had four kids with her first husband and added four more step-kids with her second husband. I loved to baby-sit for them. They saw me and my crazy brothers as role models. Consequently some of them followed in my footsteps.

Russell also left home right after high school to get married. After two divorces and three children, he moved away from Long Island, married again, had two more children, and separated himself from our family in the Pocono Mountains for 20 years. But, his problems followed him.

Marianne left school prematurely when she was diagnosed with leukemia. She immediately got married and gave birth to a little girl at 17.

Dianne quit school at 16, got married, and had a son just before she turned 17, but quickly divorced her husband. Then, she married a heroin addict and soon joined him in his addiction. She then married Bobby Lloyd, who had five girls of his own from previous relationships.

Hughie (known also by his first name Alex) quit high school at 17 to marry his girlfriend and had a son and daughter by the time he was 19. After several years, he left his wife, son, and daughter, and took off to Hollywood. After years of teaching disco and ballroom dancing, Hughie came home because my father was critically ill with cancer. He married again and had several more children, but that marriage ended in divorce, as well.

Rosanne, Johnny, and Joanne all finished high school and married several times with many divorces. I had many distorted relationships from seventh grade on but never married because I realized I was not responsible for myself, much less for a wife and children. Perhaps I somehow subconsciously feared marriage because I saw what had happened to my brothers and sisters.

REFORM SCHOOL FED THE ANGER

The issues that caused these broken marriages were anger and insecurity. The hotheads of our family were really Dianne and Johnny. Johnny had a violent temper along with my sister, Dianne. They were both crazy street fighters. One time at a picnic in the backyard, they grabbed knives, ready to go at each other until Marianne intervened. When I was ten years old, she was always there, constantly the peacemaker, ever mending conflicts in an effort to keep the family together. When she died, there was no one to stop the fighting.

Johnny was sent away to reform school, and Hughie soon followed. Everyone else was leaving and Joanne and I were the two youngest left at home. Rosanne ran away and was sent to a shelter before she came back home. Because of this, there were a few years that the fighting calmed down.

Amazingly, our dysfunction actually seemed to cause us to bond. We recognized the breakdown of the family and realized the only way to survive was to look out for each other. I visited Hughie and Johnny in reform school. I was amazed that they were allowed to smoke. I asked my mother if I could go to reform school because I wanted permission to smoke. Even though I was only 10, I snuck cigarettes behind my mother's back and thought reform school was a great idea. It became my goal.

THE INNER EXPLOSION

Though violence started in my family before Marianne died, it really erupted afterwards. Mom and Dad began to fight all the time. He began to vent the emotional pain trapped since the war. He often came home from work drinking, angry, and ready to pick a fight with my mother. It didn't take much—the garbage was not out, the food was not cooked, there was too much salt in the rice. He would lift his end of the dinner table up, sliding all the food toward my mother or fling a bowl of food across the room.

We all sat there shaking. He would antagonize Mom, saying, "You like that? Are you happy now?" We all ran for cover.

Another time he ran to the refrigerator, grabbed a bowl of spaghetti and meatballs, dumped the bowl, and began to smash it into the carpet with his shoes, yelling and cursing. When my father got angry, it was like the demons from hell came out of him. Over time, his anger became a part of us.

The very anger we hated about our father became ingrained in us. My brothers began to retaliate and act out. I remember an incident when Russell got in a fight with my father. He was fed up because my father was mocking his wife, calling her a slut. Russell grabbed my father, shaking and threatening him. When the fury came out, we ran to hide in closets, behind couches, and other places we thought might be safe from a missed swing or errant flying object.

Another time Rosanne wanted to go out with her teenage friends to the school dance. My father asked her, "What kind of girls are going there?" Hughie always tried to take the brunt of the outbursts by pulling the attention to himself. Only 16 at the time, he was sitting on a stool in the kitchen making a peanut butter and jelly sandwich and sarcastically answered my father's question, "Street walkers." My father round-housed Hughie and knocked him right off the stool. Dad was only 5-feet, 9-inches and 155 pounds, but he had that suppressed power so he packed a punch. I think that is how he survived in the concentration camp.

Rosanne vanished. I was frozen in fear, unable to run. Hughie jumped up and started wrestling my father. Then, while he had my father's arms pinned, my hotheaded, 14-year-old brother, Johnny, saw his chance to release all of his frustration. Hughie would never hit my father, but Johnny punched Dad right in the mouth. Hughie and I were stunned; I think even Johnny was stunned.

When Hughie let go of him, Dad looked Johnny in the eye, took out his wallet, throwing money on the floor, and screamed, "Come on, why you don't rob me? Now that you're big enough to jap me, why don't you take my money from me now? Come on, you yellow-belly..."

Johnny and I both ran upstairs, locked ourselves in our rooms, as Hughie ran out of the house. These types of incidents happened often, but we never talked about them. No one ever apologized. No one dealt with the pent-up anger. Just like my dad, we never knew how, where, or when it would explode.

THE FIGHTING CONTINUES

My brothers came back from reform school as street fighters. They began hanging out with wild friends and became more experienced in fighting. Along with the sense of betrayal from my parents putting them in reform school, the anger and abuse they encountered while being away fueled their rebellion. The community and even the police feared my brothers.

There was constant conflict, especially between the black and white communities. Any dance or sporting event was an excuse for a fight. When a fight broke out on the basketball court, Johnny started swinging. Once I was in the stands with Johnny at one of my high school basketball games. A fight started on the court. The next thing I knew, Johnny dodged out of the stands, ran onto the court, grabbed a player and then a referee, and pounded them in the face. It was like a frenzied shark attack when he smelled blood. You had to hold him back because he would just black out and start punching.

I remember the first time I was suspended from school. I barely made it to junior high and was caught smoking in the bathroom. Johnny was in the eleventh grade. As soon as he heard I had been suspended, he went back to the school, grabbed the teacher who caught me smoking, and threatened to kill him. Johnny was arrested that day and thrown in jail for threatening my teacher, but they let him go. That was just how we were. My brothers always had my back, and they were always there when something happened.

Hughie later became a DJ and a dancer. He had moved to California during the disco fad but later came back home. Right up the block from our home in Rockville Centre was a new disco called the Vertigo Club. They hired Hughie as their first DJ. Hughie called himself "Automatic Jack," in honor of Dad. We passed out flyers all over Rockville Centre and half of the projects came to the club. I do not think the owner expected the place to be filled with black people. It seemed he wanted to focus more on the white clientele. He did not know Hughie had a black family.

We were all in the club on Hughie's first night. Johnny and I were on the dance floor, along with the Smith brothers, when Johnny bumped into a couple accidentally. The guy cursed at Johnny and made a wise crack. Johnny pushed him, telling him to get away. I was dancing and suddenly saw Johnny fall on the dance floor out of the corner of my eye. I thought he had just slipped on the floor. But, then I saw Johnny grabbing the guy by the throat, shoving him in the corner, and pounding his face. I found out that the guy punched Johnny when he was not looking as he was dancing. The Smith brothers also jumped in and started beating the guy.

I picked up Marianne's mantle of peacemaker after she died. I knew the potential of a violent, deadly fight that could erupt. When I was with my brothers, I was ready to disarm a fight when it got out of hand for fear of a potential death. The fight at the disco club was growing deadly. In my heart, I knew they were going to kill the guy. So, I ran over, jumped on Johnny's back, and tried to pull him off. He just kept fighting as I kept trying to break it up. Hughie jumped out of the DJ booth and joined the frenzy. I felt bad for Hughie—that was his opening and closing night as a DJ at the Vertigo. When we left that night, they told Hughie to take his DJ stuff and family and, "Just go!"

Johnny cared little who he hit in his rage. One night when Billy, Johnny, Miriam, and I were living together, Johnny complained about the food. Billy made a wise remark, and Johnny turned around and hit him in the mouth. I jumped on Johnny to break it up, but then we all started fighting. My mother came out screaming, "Cain and Abel, stop! It's just like Cain and Abel." In the end, Billy had several chipped teeth. We got up, got some beer and pot, and got high. Nothing interrupted an opportunity to party.

When we walked into the local bars, our reputation as womanizers, fighters, and thieves went with us. Men would hold their women, the women would hold onto their pocketbooks, and the bartenders would hold onto their tips and a bottle because surely a hustle or a fight was coming.

RAPIDLY GOING DOWNHILL

We lived as though dysfunction was normal. Even though we did our own thing independently, we loved each other, bonded, and existed together. There is still an incredible bond in my family today. We tried to encourage one another even though we knew no one was excelling and we were all going downhill.

Our family partied all the time either in the projects, at the Martin Luther King Center, or at my house. We partied wherever we were to make us feel good and to attempt to satisfy a void that only God could fill. But we did not acknowledge God in the mix at this time. Through all this turmoil and mess, constant separations, divorces, and the breakdown of the family, deep down inside I began to realize the devastation that was taking place, but I just kept getting high to mask it.

As we grew, we began to reproduce. We grew up and married early. Some also became alcoholics and drug addicts. My mother always looked upon us and continued to love us. She accepted us as we were and prayed for us. In her mind she could see us through the eyes of Christ. She quoted Scripture to us and told us how much God loved us and how good we were even at our worst. She was a testimony of God's grace and mercy.

THE TIDE BEGINS TO TURN

I could go on with stories about my brothers and sisters, but I would rather share how God turned the direction of my family. It is a miracle that I am the only living Jack that has never been divorced. Without God, Miriam and I were on an inevitable collision course with destruction until God taught us to dream again. I praise God for my wife and children. My children have not had to battle the pain of divorce because Christ has made our marriage secure.

When my mother was miraculously healed through her faith in Jesus, one by one the rest of my family came to Christ. Dianne surrendered her life to Christ. Together, my mother and Dianne began to pray for our household.

First, Bobby gave his life to the Lord and was the first one to go into Teen Challenge. Seeing the change in him, Miriam and I, along with Billy, gave our lives to the Lord and also entered Teen Challenge.

After this, Rosanne, her daughter Tonya, and husband José entered Brooklyn Teen Challenge's family ministry. Today, Rosanne is a deacon at her church and works as a teacher in a Christian day care center.

Russell moved back home to Long Island and began attending our church, seeking the true peace that only Jesus can give. Russell turned his life over to Jesus and married a Christian woman named Rose. Together they have worked for Teen Challenge.

Eventually, my oldest sister, Sandy, gave her heart to the Lord and became a volunteer at Teen Challenge and Freedom Chapel. She and her husband, Phil, have been a part of our hospitality ministry, sharing their gift of helps with the needy of our congregation. Through her influence, her sons entered our program seeking salvation and healing. The rest of her family visits our church—that usually turns into a family reunion.

Hughie entered Teen Challenge a couple of months after I did, and God turned his life around. He now attends Freedom Chapel with his wife, Linda, and is a licensed minister. I had the privilege of leading his oldest son, Alex, to the Lord and then officiating his marriage to Lenore, a young Christian woman, in 2004. They now attend our church faithfully.

Through the consistent testimony of my life and other family members who went through our Teen Challenge program, my hard core brother, Johnny, entered our program, where a great work of God began. Today, Johnny is working in a Methodist church in Denver, Colorado, serving the Lord with his son, Anthony.

Joanne also turned her life over to Christ and has ministered with me at Teen Challenge and Freedom Chapel for many years. Her son, Eric, graduated Teen Challenge. He fulfilled his dream and enrolled at Central Bible College and played basketball. Eric also has a beautiful wife and family.

IT WAS THE WAR, IT WAS THE WAR, IT WAS THE WAR

Unfortunately, before the miraculous transformation took place in my family, my father was rushed to Mercy Hospital. My father was diagnosed with cancer at age 60 and refused chemotherapy. The doctor said he had cancer throughout his entire body.

He gave up the will to live. He could have had many years left, but the inner pain caused by the war, the deep wounds of his children and their painful choices, as well as the appalling future ahead of them, left him exhausted and stole his will to live.

He deteriorated quickly, called the whole family in, and put us all around his bed. It seemed like he was giving up. He was tired and in so much pain. After all he endured—Marianne dying, the humiliation of my sisters getting pregnant and married at young ages, and everyone breaking the law—all his hopes for his children were gone. Two sons had been sent away to reform school, and now I—his last hope—was breaking the law and destroying my athletic future. Having been separated from my mother and now diagnosed with cancer, my father had a broken heart. Dad basically gave up his will to live.

Dianne was the first to receive Christ and was set free from her heroin addiction. During the nine weeks Dad spent in the hospital, she had the opportunity to lead him to the Lord. She spent time with him daily, reading the Bible and praying. Then one day, he received the baptism in the Holy Spirit. God whispered to him that he was forgiven for all his war casualties from his B-17 bomber.

He was instantly set free! The next day, he called us into the hospital room. One by one, from Sandy all the way down to me, like an Old Testament patriarch, he spoke powerful words of securing love and forgiveness over each one of us. When he got to me, he paused momentarily, looked at me lovingly, and said, "Jimmy, you played a great basketball game at the Coliseum." He finally spoke the words of affirmation I had waited my entire life to hear.

There on his deathbed, Dad's last words were, "It was the war... It was the war... It was the war."

We all bowed our heads and left the room. They were the last words Daddy ever spoke to us. It meant so much because it was his way of saying he loved me and was proud of me. Speaking of the war was his way of saying, "I'm sorry, I'm sorry. The pain that I experienced in the war I laid on you. I'm sorry." My father passed away just days afterward on October 10, 1981.

A HIDDEN SPIRITUAL LEGACY

Years later, after my father died and I was in the ministry, a hidden spiritual legacy was revealed. This revelation took place at a Baptist church in my hometown, adjacent to a movie theater that was one of our favorite hangouts. When we were not sneaking into the movie theater, we were trying to break into that church. At a young age, we thought we were invincible. We had no fear of God or man.

Twenty-five years later, in 1999, the pastor of the church heard of my miraculous conversion and invited me to preach. A few days before I was to minister, my mother found an old brochure in my grandfather's archives. To our surprise it was a church bulletin from a Sunday service in 1933 from the same Baptist church. On the cover was a black-and-white photo of the church with a model-T Ford in front. The church had not changed in 66 years. I had never met my grandfather. To our amazement, there on the bulletin was the name we shared, James Jack. They called him James, but his given name was Duncan Macfarlane Jack. He was a deacon in the church. In 1933, my destiny was being bathed by the prayers of my grandfather.

When I preached at Rockville Centre Baptist Church, I brought my son, David, in his Royal Rangers uniform. As I introduced my son, I shared how David's great-grandfather had prayed for us. There was a hush as I showed the congregation the bulletin from 1933 and they grasped the reality that it was the power of answered prayer that had brought us there. The prayers of my grandfather in the early 1930's helped usher my father into eternal life in his last days and influenced my life, as well. And just to think, your prayers for your children and grandchildren are just as powerful.

A MOTHER'S LEGACY

My mother supported and encouraged me all through Bible College. When Miriam and I graduated and returned home to pioneer the Teen Challenge program, she continued to help by editing the newsletter and serving at our coffeehouse. She became our certified social worker and was my greatest fan.

My mom lived radically for Jesus for over 20 years, faithfully serving the Lord at Teen Challenge and Freedom Chapel. She never missed sending a card or gift for birthdays, anniversaries, graduations, or any occasion. She provided gifts for her children, grandchildren, great-grandchildren, friends of the family, and even strangers in need. She was the designated baby-sitter for all 33 grandchildren and 22 great-grandchildren until she became ill.

She suffered congestive heart failure in February 2000. I was doing a crusade in India in February 2000 when my sister called to say the doctor gave Mommy less than 24 hours to live. Securing a standby plane ticket, I rushed from the crusade to New York. As I flew over Italy, in deep intercession, the Lord confirmed to my heart that she would recover. When I arrived at her bedside, Mom shared that Jesus had appeared to her in her room to tell her that her time was not up. She was released from the hospital within a week and the whole family had time to spend with her as miraculous family restoration continued to take place.

Eight months later when Mom was taken to the hospital, each of us came to spend the last days with her. The night before she passed away, I was alone with her. She appeared to be going into a coma. I shook her vigorously and cried out, "Mommy, Mommy, wake up!" I just wanted to hear her voice one more time before she slipped into eternity.

I shook her, pleading, "Mommy, say something." Finally, she turned with her last bit of strength and last breath and said, "I love you," and went back to sleep. I sat back in the chair, overwhelmed as I witnessed once again the love of this great woman.

I replied, "I love you too, Mommy." She laid back and rested. I sat back pondering her expression and praying that God would make me a giant of love like my mother. Those were Mom's last words. What a way to leave this earth. Love defined Mom's legacy, even at the moment of her death.

She went to be with the Lord with her family by her side. All the family that had once hurt her and put her through hell stood weeping as this tiny giant of a woman, this incredible warrior, slipped into eternity. Some of my sisters and brothers were not able to recognize her greatness until after her death. We all had a deeper understanding of her greatness on that day. Her memorial service was held at our church, Freedom Chapel.

Families for whom she had prayed for years, who had never ventured through the doors of a church, were at Freedom Chapel for her funeral. The Smith family was there. My mother's sister and her husband and her cousins were there. Everybody gathered to say goodbye and farewell to "Momma Jack."

I preached her memorial service. It was a highlight of my ministry. I preached about the compassion and love of Jesus that I saw in my mother. I saw Jesus in my mother. Through the perseverance, shame, and the pain she endured, I cannot think of another person on the face of this earth that represented Christ like my mother.

Mom died in peace knowing her household was saved. Hebrews 12:2 says, "Looking unto Jesus, the author and finisher of our faith, who for the joy that was set before Him endured the cross, despising the shame, and has sat down at the right hand of the throne of God." Mom experienced a little pinch of what He bore for humanity.

As she was laid out in her casket, all of the Smith family gathered around "Momma Jack." It was such a testimony of her life as Otis Smith, the oldest of the family, known to us as June, leaned over the coffin and kissed her goodbye. This African-American family that she helped to raise and loved so much, held one another, wrapped around the coffin, weeping. At the grave site we stood over her final resting place with scores of people she had touched from every culture and society.

People of every race, color, and creed gathered to show their respect for this wonderful woman of God. The bagpipes played "Amazing Grace" through the crisp autumn air. Then, her African-American son-in-law, Bobby Lloyd, stood and sang that old Negro spiritual: "Swing Low, Sweet Chariot, Comin' for to Carry Me Home." It was a memorial to her fight for civil rights and the grace of God that had brought her through. I stood before her coffin and saluted her, "Mom, you were a warrior for God's kingdom. I take your mantle and salute you. We will continue the fight, the good fight of faith."

My mother was looking down that day. I do not know if Jesus was sitting on His throne or standing to welcome her like He did the martyr Stephen when he was stoned to death in the Book of Acts. But, I know Jesus was looking down. On that day, surely "Momma Jack's" cup was running over.

My mother stood on two verses that were the bedrock promises of salvation for our family. I stand on these today and pass them on to you for your family:

"Believe on the Lord Jesus Christ, and you will be saved, you and your household." (Acts 16:31)

"But as for me and my house, we will serve the Lord." (Joshua 24:15)

Chapter 9
Look What the Lord Has Done

*Receiving my Bachelor of Arts degree in Bible
from Central Bible College.*

PRESERVED FOR A PURPOSE

November 4, 1984 was a miraculous day for me at Brooklyn Teen Challenge. I had been spiritually blind for 26 years when I knelt by that chair in the chapel and asked the Lord to come into my life. I awakened to the spiritual realm of the kingdom of God. When we went out in the yard to exercise early the next morning, I was hung over and could have stayed in bed, but I got up because I was a different person. Something had touched me—God was in my life. The workout consisted of stretching, jumping jacks and jogging around the house several times. As I joined the men, I looked around and saw everything with new eyes.

For the first time in my life I could truly see. I saw people walking by and said to myself, *Look, there's people! I wonder if they know God?!?*! With new vision in my heart, I rejoiced at everything I fixed my eyes on... the tree (there was just one of the property), the brick buildings, a pigeon, a rat (remember, we were in Brooklyn).

The greatest revelation exploded in my heart when I realized that God had saved me and preserved me for a purpose. Right then, I realized that life was more than just eating, drinking, getting high, having sex, making money, owning a car, a boat, a business, or a house. Life was about purpose and restoring broken dreams. I knew God had a specific destiny for me. Suddenly, I had a burning desire to press on to embrace everything God had for my future.

The Brooklyn Teen Challenge men's center is a large, brick home with a carriage house in back that was converted into staff quarters. A few trees and a cement basketball court filled the backyard. The building faced a street that was relatively quiet during the day, but when the lights went out, it was like a war zone with drug dealing, gunshots, and street crime.

One of my favorite memories is the little back bedroom on the second floor that was used as a kitchen. They taught me to make coffee the old-fashioned way in a huge pot. We put the coffee grounds in a sock-like strainer and then poured water through it. The coffee was delicious and the guys loved it. The students in the program were excited about the coffee because it was the only "legal drug" we could have. The staff often joked with the new guys as they rushed for a cup of coffee, generously spooning in six or seven sugars, "You didn't stop taking drugs; you just switched mugs."

This spacious house had been a beautiful mansion in its prime during the 1950's, when the Clinton Hills section of Brooklyn was an upper-class neighborhood. The ceilings were 12 feet high and set off a large staircase in the center of the house that led up to the third floor. When David Wilkerson purchased this building for the first students, it was a deteriorating structure in a sad state of repairs and full of garbage. Like our lives, God changed all of that. The body of Christ came together to clean up that house and make it a testimony of restoration to the whole world.

Normally about 30 men fit there comfortably. During David Wilkerson's street crusades, we opened the doors to those who were bound by drugs at the street meetings and could squeeze up to 40 guys in the house.

THE FIRST TEST

When I entered Teen Challenge, God gave me a new life, and I found a new perspective. On November 11, I faced my first major test. My brother, Johnny, was getting married and I was scheduled to be his best man. I knew my family thought I would leave the program because my tuxedo had already been ordered and I never missed a family party, especially my brother's wedding. I was expected to be there, but I knew in my heart that I could not leave. Nothing could pull me out of Teen Challenge because I was finally in God's hands. One of my brother's best friends, Joey Spallino, a charismatic rock musician, stepped in to be his best man in my place. Joey was exactly my size, so the tux fit him. He was so drugged out that he filled my presence, as well. The wedding went on without me that evening while I was safe in Teen Challenge.

NEW LIFE BIBLE

Upon entering Teen Challenge, the students received a New Life Bible, written at about the sixth-grade level. This Bible was awesome because I had never read much.

It read like, "See Jesus walk. Walk, Jesus, walk."

Here I was, a 26-year-old man and my favorite books were National Geographic, Sports Illustrated and the Highlights magazine for kids because I loved to search for the hidden pictures in the mosaic scene. (Actually, I still enjoy looking at the magazine when I bring my kids to the dentist.)

Later, Miriam and Dianne brought me a New King James Bible. It was electrifying to me. I could actually understand the Bible and I began to seek God diligently. I began to know Him through His Word because it was exciting and relevant and I realized that God was real. The Bible became my instruction book. It was my passport into heaven. I began to experience hope as God did more and more miracles in my life. As Miriam visited me, she fell in love with Jesus and me in an even greater way.

Brooklyn Teen Challenge is a hub of restoration for all of New York City. We were rescuing dope fiends and drug addicts from Bedford Stuyvesant, Spanish Harlem, Little Italy, Harlem, Red Hook Brooklyn, the Bronx, Queens, and Long Island. The guys who came here were hard-core hustlers from the streets of New York City.

WE'RE IN THE BIBLE

Most of us quit school early and were not good readers. When I first began to read the Bible, I started in Genesis but did not know where to read in the New Testament. One of the residents who had been in the program several weeks before me knew how to read well and would often point out scripture verses that were inspiring. One day Ron called several of us together and shared a passage that would become a foundational truth in my life. Ron yelled, "Hey, check this out. Bring your Bibles!"

We all ran over with our Bibles, asking, "What? What?" Then, he sent us back for our highlighters. When you first enter Teen Challenge, your mother sends you underwear, stamps, pens, paper, envelopes, and highlighters. I always thought highlighters were used just for graffiti, but their real use was to mark words in the Bible for future reference.

Most of our Bibles looked like a graffiti wall in the city.

Ron told us to turn to "First Corn-run-thi-thanz, Chapter One." We could not pronounce Corinthians, much less find it in the Bible. We searched and then asked what page it was on. When one guy found it and announced the page number, we discovered we all had different Bible versions so the page numbers were all different.

Then, someone shouted, "Go to the index." Thank God for the "Book of Index." Most of us remembered where that was and we were on our new journey into the Bible. Within five minutes we were calling out, "I got it! I got it!"

Then he read I Corinthians 1:26-28 where Paul addressed the church in Corinth: "For you see your calling, brethren, not many wise according to the flesh..." This drew an immediate response, "So far, so good, because none of us here are wise. So far, we qualify."

He continued reading, "...Not many mighty, not many noble, are called." We all looked around at one another and nodded our heads knowingly—not much nobility here, not here in this crew as far as what we knew of nobility. Still doing well and qualifying. Then, Ron continued reading this verse that rocked our world: "But God has chosen the foolish things of the world to put to shame the wise and God has chosen the weak things of the world to put to shame the things which are mighty; and the base things of the world and the things which are despised God has chosen and the things which are not, to bring to nothing things that are."

When Ron finished reading and the truth sank in, there were a bunch of ex-dope fiends giving each other double high-fives and shouting, "We're in the Bible! We're in the Bible!"

God uses the foolish and despised things of the world, the base things. Then came the inside revelation on the "base things" of this world (v.28). "Base things" may mean one thing to you, but it meant something totally different to us. When Richard Pryor set himself on fire, he was "free-basing" cocaine. It is called "base smoking" on the street. We had all done it so, we identified with this phrase: One man shouted, "Hey, God is even calling 'base smokers.' That's us!" We shouted some more. When we realized that God had called the foolish things of the world for His mission and that Jesus died for drug addicts, too, we had new hope.

We began to grasp that God was not only interested in great intellectual, grand, and noble people with great gifts. God was looking for those who loved Him. He does not call the qualified; He qualifies the called. When that understanding came, we all knew we were qualified. We started learning the word of God and growing in grace.

SECOND PHASE—CAMP CHAMPION

At Teen Challenge, I bonded with a brother named Wayne who became one of my closest friends. Wayne entered the program a week before I did. He was a crazy, colorful black dude. When his brother threw him out of his car in front of Teen Challenge, he was carrying a .44 Magnum, a pint of Wild Irish Rose wine, and a big marijuana joint in his mouth. He also sported a chain that hung from his earring across to his nose. When Wayne got to Teen Challenge, he began to get his life cleaned up.

Miriam visited me during church services at the program's church, King's Chapel. We heard the preaching of Don Wilkerson, David Wilkerson, and many other speakers. During this time (mid-1980's) Brother Dave returned to New York City to preach in the streets and pioneer Times Square Church. The students and staff of Brooklyn Teen Challenge were a vital part of his crusades. It was there I fell in love with street ministry. In God's providence, He was training me for my future ministry through the Wilkerson family and Teen Challenge.

In the middle of December, Wayne and I were sent upstate to Camp Champion, the second phase of the Brooklyn Teen Challenge program, to finish the program. Bobby had already been there for several months. There my journey to maturity really took off.

Camp Champion is a beautiful property located 100 miles northwest of Brooklyn and a world away from New York City. On the 400 acres of wooded land, deer, bear, raccoons roam freely, often coming up to the lake in the center of the property. On

At Teen Challenge, I bonded with Wayne, who became one of my closest friends.

the south side of the lake were homes for staff and a recreation hall. There was also a large home with ten bedrooms for the family ministry where husbands, wives, and their children in the program stayed.

On the north side of the lake was a huge wooden building with large windows affording a view of the outdoors, called the Lighthouse. The first floor housed the Teen Challenge offices, a library, a dining room, a kitchen, and the chapel. There were classrooms and a recreation room on the lower level. At night we could look out the library windows and watch deer come to eat the toast we had thrown out. Some days we handed raccoons bread from the back door of the kitchen.

Two other large houses were on the property—Alpha House and Shekinah House. They each accommodated 12 to 15 men. Wayne and I were assigned to Alpha House. They also called it Animal House because our group leader was young and hardly ever there. There was far too much opportunity to do our own thing and "test the limits." Bobby was in Shekinah House. Wayne and I would sneak out to raid their snacks when we were running low. As God was healing me from my drug addiction, I fell in love with that place. I felt incredible victory.

BROUGHT TO THE LIGHT

God began to deal with my character as He exposed my flaws. One of the first teachings we had was on Obedience to God. It seemed like after every class on character development, I was personally tested. In my second week at Camp Champion, my obedience was tested.

Although Bobby was a senior student and we lived in different houses, we saw each other often. He looked out for me. Miriam was at home and I had not heard from her for about two weeks. The rules did not permit me a phone call until I had been there for 21 days. One Saturday afternoon, since my group leader was not around and I was missing Miriam, I went down to his office. With a spatula and my old "B-and-E" techniques (breaking and entering), I broke into the office to use the phone and call Miriam. I felt strangely uncomfortable, yet unusually excited.

I called Miriam at her job, the Casual Chick Boutique in Freeport.

As soon as she answered, I said, "Hi, Miriam. How's my baby?"

She said, "Oh, how are you, Jimmy? How are you doing, honey?"

"I'm doing fine," I responded excitedly. "Miriam, I am serving God. I'm being obedient. I'm loving God and I'm doing the right thing for the first time in my life."

I was totally blind to my disobedience. I had disregarded the fact that I had broken into the office, was in rebellion to the rules, and making an unauthorized phone call. I heard Miriam say, "Jimmy, guess who just walked into the store?"

There was excitement in her voice as she said, "Bobby and Dianne." Before I could tell her to keep quiet about me being on the phone, she said, "Hey, Bobby and Dianne, guess who's calling me! It's Jimmy calling me from Teen Challenge."

I did not know that Bobby was on a weekend pass. How could he walk in at just that moment in a boutique 100 miles away from me? I thought, Man, what a bad break!

Bobby did not make a big deal with Miriam about the phone call, but he made a mental note as he said, "Uh huh, uh huh."

Since Bobby did not say anything, I just played it off and said, "OK, honey, gotta go. God bless you." I snuck out of the office. No problem, I thought.

I was in my room in Alpha House when Bobby came home from his weekend pass. He walked into my room ready to talk. He looked me in the eye and said, "Jimmy...."

I said, "What's happening, Bobby?"

He said, "You made that phone call, didn't you?"

I said, "Yup."

"Well, you know the deal," he responded. He seemed to see right into my heart with his deep brown eyes. I saw strength to do the right thing that I had never seen in him before.

I was stunned. "Come on, Bob. It's no big deal," I answered flippantly.

He said, "You need to go and share what you did with your group leader, or I will have to do it for you."

I said, "OK, I know I got to do the right thing." I put my head down and went inside. Part of me felt betrayed because on the streets we always covered for each other. Why would Bobby be willing to betray me? At the same time, the Holy Spirit was speaking to my heart saying, "This is the right thing to do. Trust Bobby. He wants the best for you."

It was a long 24 hours wondering what would happen. We had a LIGHTT session (Living in Group Harmony Through Truth) on Monday night where I confessed my transgression. The staff gave me a scripture project for my discipline. I thanked Bobby and realized if I had not been exposed and guided to walk in truth, I would have started down the slippery slope of compromise. Getting caught was not a bad break; it was actually *the grace of God*, because I was about to face an even greater and dangerous temptation. If it was not for Bobby bringing my hidden disobedience to the light, failure here would have destroyed my future.

A CHRISTMAS TEMPTATION

The next class was Temptation. It was Christmas Eve and the countryside was covered with snow. The fresh scent of the country air was mixed with the fragrance of the pine trees that surrounded Camp Champion. The aroma of the wood-burning fireplaces blending into the winter breeze made the scene refreshing and tranquil. I had been clean from all drugs, alcohol, and tobacco for two months.

The fragrance of Christmas filled my emotions and spirit with genuine joy.

When our Executive Director, Don Wilkerson, arranged for a group of us to go Christmas caroling, I was as excited as a little boy. He announced that our last stop would be a lady's house who had invited us in for hot cocoa. Suddenly, the demon of drugs whispered in my ear, "I'll bet there is codeine in the medicine cabinet." I was shaken by this temptation. I had not faced any temptation like that since I had arrived at Teen Challenge. I was suddenly scared. For years I had a problem visiting people's homes because their medicine cabinets were such a temptation. I could not resist checking out the bathroom and stealing any pills I found.

My brother Hughie and I had a construction business. Our business card read, "Jack Brothers—Honest and On Time." In reality, the only time we were on time was to get the down payment. The honest part was that we were honestly never coming back. The job had one other perk. When I was giving an estimate for the work, the last thing I did before leaving was to ask if I could use the bathroom. Safely behind a closed door, I inspected the medicine cabinet and helped myself to anything I could steal or sell.

One customer must have been a retired pharmacist. When I opened his medicine cabinet, I found jars of Valium. I took all I could stuff in my pockets and made plans to return for another estimate. I thought that we had hit the mother lode. I could not wait to get back to the bathroom to stuff my pockets again. I returned

Me and my brother's original business card to our phony business.

to the house and asked to use the bathroom before leaving. As I finished, he looked in the bathroom and immediately realized what I had done. He chased me down the street yelling, "Give me my Valiums!" As I dove into the van, I threw him a handful of pills and we screeched away with the deposit and our pills. We never went back.

That evening as Brother Don prepared us to go caroling, one of the guys said, "I love hot chocolate; I can't wait to go to the lady's home." Again, I heard Satan whispering, "And she has drugs." I rebuked the thought again as I realized, *I am not the only one that knows about it. I started sweating and shaking, gripped by an unusually strong compulsion.*

The first thing I did when we got to the lady's house was to ask to go to the bathroom. I went in, opened the medicine cabinet, and sure enough, there was a bottle full of pills—Tylenol 3 (with codeine). For years, those were some of my favorite pills. I took eight of those bad babies and stuffed them in my pocket, saying to myself, *Wow! This really is Christmas.*

When you are sinning, you think you know who you can tell and who you cannot. Wayne was the kind of guy I could tell, so I whispered in his ear, "Listen, I got a bunch of codeine; we're gonna get nice tonight. What do you think, last time before the New Year?"

He was excited and said, "You bet!"

We got in the van to go back home to Teen Challenge. I thank the Lord there was a mile-long road from the main road into the woods to get to the house. Wayne was massaging my back all the way home, whispering excitedly, "We gonna get high tonight!"

I had Satan whispering in one ear, "Don't worry about it, Jimmy. You take these pills and it will be the last time you take them. It'll be great. You deserve it."

In the other ear, I heard the Holy Spirit saying, "Don't take them—there's a blessing. Don't take them. Your victory is at hand."

And then there was Wayne... "We gonna get nice tonight."

Finally, the van pulled over so we could all get out and walk up the hill to our house. With temptation vibrating through my body, I began to run up the hill. I outran Wayne to the house with the pills still in my hand.

I could hear Satan, "No problem, last time. Don't worry about it."

The Holy Spirit was saying, "No, no, don't take them. There's a blessing; there's a blessing."

I was tormented as I ran up the stairs into the bathroom with Wayne following close behind. In a sudden burst of conviction, I took the pills from my pocket, threw them into the toilet, and flushed it, breathing hard from the battle I just fought.

When Wayne rushed in, he was so excited, almost yelling, "Where are they, Jimmy?"

I paused for a moment soberly, steadily looking him in the eye, "I flushed them down the toilet."

Then he really shouted, "You idiot!"

Nothing he said could shake the peace I had in my heart at that moment and the joy that flooded my soul as I began to realize I really was changing with God's help. I had never won a battle with temptation before. I got the victory that day. I knew then that I had overcome the enemy. That was the first of many victories that would follow through the power of Jesus Christ.

Wayne was in and out of Teen Challenge about 12 times before he graduated. In fact, after I graduated I went out on the streets to find him and help him back into the program only to have him run again. Every summer when I came home from Bible school, I went on a mission to find Wayne. For six years, this was the pattern. Finally, Wayne fully surrendered and made Jesus the Lord of his life and Master over his addiction. He graduated the program and today has a lovely wife, Stacey, and a beautiful daughter, Nicole. Wayne has a great job, owns his own house and volunteers at Teen Challenge.

THE BLESSINGS OF OBEDIENCE

Miriam visited me often before we got married. During the Christmas season, she brought little gifts. I had such a beautiful woman, so faithful, so nice, always there and very committed. She was slowly recovering from her own addiction, partly because I was not there to lead her astray and partly because she was living with Dianne. While Miriam did her own thing for a while, she experienced victory over drugs, also.

Since Miriam and I had lived together for 7 years and I was now following the Lord, I wanted to do the right thing by her: I wanted to get married. So, I put in a request to my group leader. I was shocked when it was denied. I was disappointed, but by this time I had learned to trust God.

Just after my Christmas test, Brother Don called the entire men's program together during the first week of January. As he led us in prayer in the chapel, we had no idea what was coming down. He shared, "Brothers, I have some sad news to tell you. We are closing the men's program and selling the camp."

We were all shocked and asked, "When?"

"As of today." This was horrible news and some broke down in tears. Wayne was crying out loud. Bobby was about to graduate, so he was not too upset as he was already going home. I had only been at Camp Champion a little over a month and had no idea what I was going to do. Brother Don offered to interview each of us and transfer us to other Teen Challenge programs.

When he got to me, he pulled me into a room and said, "Jimmy, I hear that you put in a request to get married. Would you like to get married and join the family ministry with your wife?"

I looked at him quizzically, the amazement clearly showing on my face, "Miriam in Teen Challenge? Brother Don, I never thought of it. This is my thing, not Miriam's."

He looked at me with concern and compassion and said, "Seek the Lord about this. Let's see what happens."

Before I even got a chance to ask Miriam about it, the next day I received a letter from her that said, "Jimmy, I prayed and sought the Lord. I feel that we should get married and join the family ministry there." I knew this was my answer from God and the blessing the Holy Spirit had spoken to me when I got the victory over those pills on Christmas Eve. If I had yielded to Satan's temptation to take those pills, I honestly believe God would have closed those doors. But I overcame. God was faithful and He blessed me.

Miriam and I were married at Sheepgate Assembly on February 8, 1985. Pastor Joe married us. Annie, Miriam's sister, was the maid of honor and Billy, who was still using heroin at the time, was my best man. It was a stressful wedding because most of our family were not really familiar with our new relationship with Jesus and many were still on drugs. There was no alcohol at the reception in the church's basement, so everyone was making trips into the parking lot and bathrooms to get high and drink.

After we were married, we met with Program Director Pete Rios, a 20-year graduate of Teen Challenge, and his wife, Demaras. They played an important role in our foundational training as students in the family ministry. I asked them if we could spend some time together for our honeymoon. His response was, "Hey, you'll have a one-year honeymoon right here in Teen Challenge."

My mother faithfully came to visit me with Billy. He was heavy on my heart because I knew if he did not surrender to God he was going to die soon. I prayed for him for 6 months. God honored my prayers and Billy entered Brooklyn Teen Challenge and gave his life to Jesus. He was the first of many, as a stream of friends and family members began coming to Christ through Teen Challenge.

Miriam and I on our wedding day (February 8, 1985) with Pastor Joe and Elaine Cedzich officiating the ceremony. We then spent a one year honeymoon in the Teen Challenge program together.

FROM STUDENT TO STAFF

Miriam and I thrived in the beautiful, serene atmosphere of Camp Champion. We learned to love each other on a new level, experiencing a love born out of commitment, not emotion. After my tenth month (Miriam's seventh month in the program), we were asked to become junior staff members. We went home on a weekend pass to pray about our future. While I was at my mother's house, my oldest brother, Russell, called. He had been trying to get in touch with me and thought Mom might know where I was.

Russell was like an idol to me. He loved sports, girls, and race cars. He married young, left Rockville Centre, and lost contact with the rest of the family for many years. He said, "I heard that you just graduated from Teen Challenge and you're doing well. I have my own construction company up here in a private resort community on a lake. I know you're a good carpenter and I'd like to offer you a position. You could be a partner in my business. I'll get you a truck, a car, a house on the lake—and there's a good church up here."

This seemed like the opportunity of a lifetime. I could lead my brother to the Lord, go to church, and have a whole new life. I answered him, "Russell, you might not understand this, but I've got to pray about it."

He said, "Jimmy, remember this: You have a lot to give; don't let those church people just use you up."

I prayed, "God, if You want me to stay at Teen Challenge, speak to Don Wilkerson."

Within one week, Brother Don wrote me a letter that I still have today. He said, "Jimmy, I know you are graduating. If you feel called into the ministry, I recommend you stay on as leadership here at Teen Challenge and then go to Central Bible College or Christ for the Nations Institute. You have been on my heart and that is what I think you should do. Commit this to prayer and get back to me."

I could hardly believe what a direct answer to prayer God had given me. I replied to Brother Don, telling him I intended to finish my internship at Teen Challenge and then go on to Central Bible College because it was a certified college and had a good basketball program. He wrote back, offering me a full scholarship from World Challenge, David Wilkerson's ministry.

I had the privilege of personally ministering to Russell for ten years through many different relationships and trials. He finally settled down and met a great woman named Rose. Rose loved Jesus, and I had the honor of officiating their wedding. He gave up the business he offered me and moved back to Long Island. Both Russell and his wife worked full time at Long Island Teen Challenge: Rose helping to manage our Blessingdales thrift shop and Russell helping to establish our T.C. Auto Repair and Redemption Center. Now they have moved on to other opportunities.

ON TO BIBLE COLLEGE—AIN'T NO STOPPING ME NOW

When we began to get ready for college, Miriam and I purchased a tiny, 2-door compact car—a Ford Fiesta from a worker at Teen Challenge. I bought a make-it-yourself U-Haul trailer and built my own little hitch because I wanted to save money. I thought I could do it myself. We drove it home to Long Island, packed it up, kissed everybody goodbye, and set off for our college adventure in Springfield, Missouri.

As we drove on Interstate 80 in Pennsylvania, the trailer hitch snapped and the U-Haul trailer, which was heavier than the Ford Fiesta, began to fishtail. As we were sliding back and forth, spinning all over the interstate, we screamed, "Jesus!" We almost flipped over before the safety chain broke and the trailer shot into the woods. We skidded off the side of the road and into the ravine. The trailer was in pieces, the tires had disintegrated, and our personal belongings were scattered across the hillside. Thank the Lord we were not in traffic; God protected us and the other traffic.

We got out of the car and surveyed the damage to the vehicle. All we could do was pray. With the help of four passing motorists, we finally pushed the car back up onto the main road. I knew we had to keep going, but I did not want to leave a mess. So, we picked up everything that was littered throughout the woods and on the side of the road, stacked it in a neat little pile, and waited for the police to arrive. After waiting almost an hour, I looked at Miriam and said, "We can't stop. We've got to keep going, Miriam. We've got to get to Central Bible College."

We put the spare tire on the car, stuffed the car with the clothing we had collected from our belongings in the woods, and got back into the Ford Fiesta. We abandoned the shredded belongings and shattered trailer and took off, leaving all of our earthly possessions behind.

Our traveling trials were not over, though. We broke down in Ohio. It took two days to get the water pump fixed, but we kept on trucking. A few days later, we finally arrived at Central Bible College. We drove onto campus and saw the mobile home we had rented. I hugged Miriam, kissed her, and said, "Honey, God will provide for us. Tomorrow I have to go to school, so let's pray." We moved into our new home, and the next morning I walked out the door with my briefcase in hand, eager to attend orientation and start my life at Central Bible College.

REDEEMING THE DREAM

God met our material needs. Because I had never been a real student, I did not have comprehension or retention skills. I had a heart to learn so I worked hard as Miriam faithfully prayed for me. I often went to the library to do my homework. I was so thankful that we had received a scholarship from David Wilkerson because I devoted my time I not only to studying, but also learning to learn.

I saw God restoring so many things in my life and recalled that Brother

Don had said Central Bible College (CBC) had a good basketball team. I prayed, "Lord, You have already given me so much. Do you want to redeem this part of my life?"

I went to the gymnasium the next day. I approached Kirk Hanson, head coach of CBC's basketball team, and shared, "Coach, I'm 28 years old and married, but I would like to play basketball."

He asked me if I had played college basketball before and I told him, "No, just on the streets and in high school."

Coach said, "Tryouts are next week. Be there, show me what you got."

I tried out and made the team. Because I was 28 years old and the rest of the players were 18, they called me Methuselah, the oldest person in the Bible. I may have been the oldest guy on the team, but I kept up with those boys. I outran most of them because for the first time in my life I was clean and in tip-top shape, 6-ft, 2 inches, 185- pounds - ready to play ball.

I found out that in college ball physical fitness was not enough. My mind still needed healing, so Coach took me under his wing and helped me memorize the plays. I will never forget awards night that year (1987). Coach presented me with the award for "Most Inspirational Player." Ten year before, in 1977, my coach had kicked off the high school basketball team for being the worst influence. What an incredible turnaround and a powerful testimony of God's redemption.

NOW YOU CAN—
HIS STRENGTH IS MADE PERFECT IN OUR WEAKNESS

Central Bible College basketball team, 1987; I am number 34 (top row, middle). Check out the shorts!

The following school year I faced another test. Brother Don called saying that my scholarship had to be cut after the first year. My sophomore year was a challenge. With my basketball schedule, employment, and intense classes and homework, there were many times I did not think I could make it. When I felt overwhelmed I often went into the locker room to cry out to God. Sometimes I drove around the campus weeping because I felt so much pressure.

At times I thought I had to quit the team because it was just too much. Coach sensed my heaviness and prayed for me many times. Many times I entered the campus chapel and knelt at the altar, crying out, "God, I can't do it; I can't do it." During those times, when I reached a place of brokenness and total futility, God would whisper in my heart, "Jimmy, now you can do it, because My strength is made perfect in your weakness." This blessed assurance from the Holy Spirit would cause me to rise from that altar with a strength that I knew was divine. God's intervention and intercession continue to strengthen me to fulfill my calling today.

Coach Hanson was a great influence in my growth in Christ and character during my years at CBC. He and his wife Lynn took care of us, and I was so proud of him when he was elected to the NCCAA Hall of Fame as one of the winningest coaches in Missouri college history.

On graduation day, May 1989, Mom came to Springfield. My family surprised me by sending Billy with her to be by our side. Miriam graduated with an associate degree, majoring in Christian Education, and I graduated with a Bachelor of Arts degree with a major in Bible.

THE NEXT PHASE

In 1991, Brooklyn Teen Challenge commissioned Miriam and me to start a Teen Challenge program on Long Island. Billy helped me pack the moving truck and load my new used car onto a vehicle trailer. This time I had a customized hitch from the factory. I learned my lesson on hitches. We rented a house in Lindenhurst. Miriam was about to give birth to our miracle boy, David, and we were ready to give birth to Long Island Teen Challenge.

I called all the pastors I knew, sent out support letters and began to put together our first newsletter. People started calling and pastors started sending drug addicts to our house. I used one room in the house as my office and the basement became an all-purpose room. We folded the newsletters and prepared them for bulk mailing on the ping-pong table. My mother was always in the basement working with volunteers.

When Bobby graduated from Teen Challenge in 1985, he went home and held a job faithfully as a mechanic for a car dealership. He also was a youth pastor and a liaison for Brooklyn Teen Challenge. Bobby sent people to the program through Sheepgate Assembly. Most of the drug addicts he sent were our friends and family.

I invited Bobby to join forces in the mission God had placed in my heart for Long Island. I realized I needed a strong assistant to open this outreach. I shared my vision to start a coffeehouse and asked him, "Bobby, do you want to help me pioneer this outreach? I need your help."

He answered, "Sure, I'd love to."

Bobby was always the leader in the streets. Even though he was like my older brother, I knew I had to ask him to let me be the leader. It was hard for me, but Bobby acknowledged the call of God on my life and graciously embraced his position as my assistant. He has been one of the greatest armor bearers and spiritual giants in my life.

THE FIRST COFFEEHOUSE OUTREACH

Our first ministry was street crusades. We started going to drug-infested areas to set up platforms, sing gospel music, testify and preach. It was the same type of street ministry I had learned from David Wilkerson and had also established while at CBC.

We heard about a little VFW Hall in Amityville on Route 110. We rented it for $50 a night. It was just a small room that held 75 to 100 people and we called it Freedom Outreach. There was such an anointing in that place. We arrived at 6 p.m. to make coffee, which overcame the stench of Pine Sol and Budweiser. We put coffee tables around the room and then went out street witnessing.

We brought addicts in and gave them bagels, donuts, and coffee. When the room was full of people, we began to sing praises to God and give testimonies of His power to transform lives. Drug addicts came from all over New York and we interviewed ladies and men for Teen Challenge. We referred them to centers across the Northeast because we did not have a residential home of our own yet. The place was always packed.

THE FIRST RESIDENTIAL HOME

Miriam and I opened the basement in our home to provide beds for people in immediate need. Our first student was Barry Hazel. The night I gave my life to Christ, I was in his apartment freebasing cocaine. I grew up with Barry, a 6-foot, 5-inch black brother, Now, he came to our makeshift crisis home in my basement. Barry became one of our outreach directors and dean of men at Long Island Teen Challenge. He has moved on to new ministry opportunities and continues to be used by God to minister to young people.

The testimony of our coffeehouse outreach and street ministry began to spread throughout the churches. A Jewish believer called me to set up a meeting. He had heard about our ministry and said he wanted to help us to get our crisis home. His name was Jack Toback. I met with him and Pastor George Nuzzolo from Oceanside Full Gospel Church.

As we sat to meet, Jack quickly asked, "Why don't you have a residential home, yet?"

I shared our vision and confided that we were simply waiting for God to supply the money.

He asked, "How much money do you need to buy a home."

I had no knowledge of real estate, financial statements, audits, or administration. I did not learn that in Bible college. I was about to blurt out, "Two hundred thousand dollars."

Pastor Nuzzolo quickly cut me off and said, "Four hundred thousand dollars."

"How much do you have toward the total amount?" Jack asked.

I told him, "One church has pledged $50,000 toward our ministry."

"No problem," he said. He took out his checkbook and pen to write out a check for $350,000. I looked up speechless as he presented it to us. We were so excited at God's provision. We purchased our first crisis home for Teen Challenge in Centereach and rented another one several miles away.

AS THE NEED GROWS, THE PROGRAM GROWS

After several years, we needed larger facilities. We needed two large homes for men and space for administrative offices, so we prayed about it. God answered our prayers. Vito and Marge Stallone, first cousins of actor Sylvester Stallone, owned a beautiful three-acre estate with two houses and a cottage in West Babylon. When the Stallone estate became available and the real estate agent showed me through the beautiful grounds, I was struck by the serenity of the surroundings. As I looked at the beautiful greenery, flowers, and giant oak and pine trees, I prayed, "God, if You can make a way, do it."

The asking price was $700,000. Every time a guest speaker came to our church, I took him over to the estate and asked him to join me in prayer, asking God to make a way. God did make a way. The Stallone family cut the price in half. We sold our home and purchased the property. They held our mortgage and we moved all our men into those large houses. One house was used as a crisis center—we called it Genesis. The other we used for the training phase—we named it Shekinah (the Old Testament word for the Incandescent glory of God). We renovated the cottage to make administration offices. The miracles were not over because one year later, we purchased the beautiful house next door, situated on one acre, for a women's home.

Hundreds of precious ladies and men have found restoration through the love of God in these homes and have learned that they too can dream again. Over the last 15 years, we have grown from that original coffeehouse to a full-time residential ministry restoring young men, women, and married couples with drug and alcohol addictions. We have established four homes for men housing up to 70 residents and a home for 20 ladies. In 2007, we expanded the Shekinah Home adding 16-20 more beds, a multipurpose room (chapel/classroom/dining room) that can accommodate 75, and a new full-service kitchen.

Miriam and I have had a burden to minister to married couples ever since God used Camp Champion to restore us. We now have Petra House, a home where up to five married couples can live. Their marriages are healed through application of enduring biblical principles and the love of Jesus.

OUR COFFEEHOUSE BIRTHS A CHURCH

When we outgrew the VFW hall, we rented a warehouse to continue our Friday evening coffeehouse. We also started a service on Tuesday evenings. With students graduating and other people committing their lives to Jesus, we finally needed to start a Sunday morning service. We quickly outgrew that facility and were about to be evicted when the Lord intervened. He provided a new warehouse on two acres.

We had been fighting the eviction in court so, when the judgment came against us, we had to move everything out after the Palm Sunday service. The Lord provided $75,000 for the new property; and in 1996, the Monday morning after Palm Sunday, I signed the contract for the new property and the Teen Challenge students, staff, and volunteers from our church came in like a military force to convert that warehouse into a place of worship. The following week, Easter morning, Freedom Chapel worshiped in a beautiful new sanctuary a building that we owned. The glory of God continued to fall on the ministry.

In 2009, Freedom Chapel moved into a beautiful new 36,000-square-foot building with a sanctuary that holds 1,000 precious people of God. The former Freedom Outreach facility is now a multi-purpose youth outreach center. Freedom Chapel has become a thriving, multicultural church on Route 110 in Amityville.

The name of our town was popularized by a book by George Lutz and Hollywood's portrayal of the "Amityville House of Horror" in 1979 with its remake in 2005. This movie recounts the supposed demonic occupation of a home not far from our church and the family's struggle to maintain a house that seems to have a mind of its own.

The Amityville horror began in November 14, 1974, when Ron "Butch" DeFeo, Jr., shot his entire family to death in family home at 112 Ocean Avenue. The reasons he killed his family were far from mysterious. DeFeo was a bully, a liar, a thief, and a drug addict. Shortly before the killings, he attempted to fake a robbery from his father's car dealership to get money to support his drug habit. When he was exposed by his father, he killed them to cover his crime. Drugs and death are still a part of that neighborhood, but by God's grace we are turning the horror into hope.

Freedom Chapel is in the heart of a predominantly black and Spanish community and is home to Teen Challenge graduates, their families, and hundreds of children, young adults, and families from the community who receive Christ through our street ministries. Our church has become a lighthouse, raising up heroes in the faith

OUTRAGEOUS OUTREACH

Evangelism has always been the heart of our ministry. We conduct crusades internationally and Freedom Outreach street rallies and tent meetings throughout the New York City metro area. This innovative, multifaceted community initiative strategically targets troubled neighborhoods for evangelism, providing free meals, gospel music, food distribution, and preaching. After covering the area with invitational flyers, we set up a platform and several hundred chairs. We offer free balloons, basketballs, bicycles, face painting and free food—and the children come. Many of the children bring their parents who hear the gospel for the first time.

From September through December we still return to drug-infested communities for street rallies and bus in over 200 children to our Super Saturday Kids Krusade. We have puppets, games, and lunch, ministering the compassion of Christ.

I love to stand in front of the kids and see hundreds come to know Jesus Christ as Savior.

"How many of you want to be a doctor?" I ask them. Twenty five lifted their hands.

"OK, how many want to be a fireman?" Another 15 raise their hands.

I go on to other professions: school teacher, professional athlete, veterinarian, lawyer, and astronaut. As I see these precious children raise their hands, my heart weeps because I know that without a message of hope, 80 percent would not fulfill their dreams. In fact, their dreams would turn into nightmares.

We are teaching these children to dream and then I challenge them to dream with me. I let them know that their dreams can become a reality because God offers hope, a future, and a purpose. I never had this as a youngster. No one ever told me there was that kind of hope available in Jesus. My heartbeat, my passion is to offer this hope to those that are lost.

Our Super Saturday program builds to a huge climax with a special Christmas Celebration. Hundreds attend as we give away 100 brand-new bikes and stuffed Christmas stockings to every child.

Hoop Challenge Basketball Camp is another valuable tool. Over 100 at-risk girls and boys, ages 7 to 15 years, attend our camps. They are taught basketball and life skills as we minister the love of Jesus. At Hoop Challenge, campers are challenged to resist the lure of drugs, alcohol, and lawlessness and are instead encouraged to pursue their education, purpose, and dreams. In addition to this, we teach them about the love of God. Most basketball camps charge kids $300-$500 per week. We charge only $30; but no one is turned away. We provide scholarships for those who have no money.

Hoop Challenge meets Monday through Friday from 10 a.m. to 3 p.m., and the camp is packed. The campers wear their Hoop Challenge T-shirts. We have guest speakers work with the kids—former NBA players, coaches from St. John's University, Villanova University, Hofstra University and coaches from other Division One colleges. These guest speakers know Hoop Challenge is not a moneymaking scheme. And the kids do not come just because we bring in NBA players. Guests come because they want to help these young boys and girls, and the children come because they want to learn to play basketball.

We couple the basketball camp with a tent crusade every evening. Ministries come from all over the country—youth groups, singles ministries and choirs—to join us throughout the summer for these outreaches. At 5 p.m. under the main tent we have a program for kids with clowns, puppets and activities. At 6 p.m. under the food tent is a free barbecue. At 7 p.m. is a gospel concert with music, testimonies, and the preaching of the Word of God.

The week culminates on Friday night when all the Hoop Challenge campers receive their trophies. They bring their families and we share the love of God. We tell parents how we are showing the children how to know the Lord and giving them guidance and hope. During the altar call, many parents give their lives to Jesus. After the message, we give out trophies to every camper. We also give away basketballs, toys, bicycles, and food. This is our part in fulfilling the Great Commission of Jesus Christ.

Our thrift store is called Blessingdales, a name coined by Teen Challenge students. People often come into Teen Challenge with no extra clothing. Whatever clothing is donated to them they call a blessing. Now we have our own Blessingdales thrift store which provides many products for the local community, other non-profit organizations and our own Teen Challenge students.

God has opened other ministry doors for us. In addition to being an ordained Assembly of God minister, I have been privileged to serve as a member of the Board of Directors for Teen Challenge International, USA, the Northeast Regional Representative for Teen Challenge, and also the inaugural USA Alumni President. I have joined outreaches with Global Teen Challenge and preached around the world.

Never could I have thought that one day God would take me from being a student at Brooklyn Teen Challenge to serving as Executive Director of Brooklyn Teen Challenge alongside one of its founding fathers, Pastor Don Wilkerson, who now is the center's President.

Receiving my Ministerial Ordination with Miriam by Rev. Saied Adour, Superintendent of the New York District of the Assemblies of God.

THE SOURCE OF STRENGTH

Sometimes I feel overwhelmed with the burden of raising finances and the responsibilities I carry as a father to three children, ordained minister, Executive Director, and Senior Pastor. I continue to apply what I learned as a student in Teen Challenge and Bible College. I go to my Heavenly Father and cry out, "God, I can't do this on my own."

God speaks to me by the Holy Spirit and says, "Jimmy, now you can do it because My strength is made perfect in your weakness." I have learned not to depend on natural talents or acquired skills. God reminds me that the "Cub Scout gone bad" is now a testimony of His grace.

"My grace is sufficient for you, for My strength is made perfect in weakness." (2 Corinthians 12:8-10)

CHAPTER 10
A FRIEND WHO STICKS
CLOSER THAN A BROTHER

Rev. Billy Laan at Times Square Church's Upper Room coffee house outreach on 41st Street and 9th Avenue in New York City, across the street from the Port Authority, a ministry David Wilkerson founded.

PARTNERS IN LIFE

The common threads of my story is the relentless call by the grace of God on my life and the companionship of my best friend, homeboy, and brother, Billy Laan.

When I met Billy on the basketball court when I was 10, we became inseparable—partners in crime, partners in love, partners in pain, and partners tempting death. After God's miraculous intervention, we became partners in the gospel through Teen Challenge for 8 years. Unfortunately, Billy's addiction had exposed him to the HIV virus. He contracted AIDS, and dynamics related to his affliction eventually took his life. We do not mourn his death, but we celebrate his life and ministry so we can learn from this dream cut short.

Billy was fearless. He had no fear of heights. In fact, he had little fear of anything. Whether he was balancing on the roof of St. Agnes, holding to the bumper of a moving bus, or balancing between addiction and death, he always pushed the edge. That is why my dad forbade us to be together. Still, I always found a way to meet him or sneak him into my house.

When we were 11 years old, we were watching TV with my brother,

Johnny. Billy was smoking a cigarette, thinking Dad was in bed, but he heard us. When he came downstairs, Billy and Johnny both had cigarettes in their hands. When they heard Dad walking toward the room, Billy quickly stepped on his cigarette. My father came in and asked, "Billy, are you smoking?"

Billy replied, "No," as smoke seeped out from under his sneaker.

Dad kicked Billy out of the house and said, "Jimmy, I told you I don't want you hanging around with that kid."

Dad recognized the same craziness in Billy that he saw in me and the explosive potential for danger. Nothing my dad said made a difference, because we would let nothing interfere with our friendship. Since Billy had no dad or brothers, he kept coming around until my father finally accepted him—in fact, my family emotionally adopted him as one of our own.

Our bicycles were our transportation—Stingrays with the long banana seat. We took pride in them. Billy always had the best one because he was the only boy in his family. If one bike was out of commission, we rode together. He sat in front since I was taller, and we double-pedaled with his feet on top of mine. We raced up and down our block, a baseball card secured onto the rear fork with a clothes pin. The card rubbed against the spokes and sounded like an engine.

We rode up and down the block seeking mischief. One of our favorite pastimes was provoking a dog named Chips. He lived a block away and chased us when we rode by his house. At times we armed ourselves with eggs. When the eggs did not stop him, we lit firecrackers from our cigarettes and threw them at him.

Once, Billy got off his bike, and I started chasing him. He rammed into a parking meter headfirst and almost knocked himself out. I rode him home on my bike. As we entered his home, he started crying, and his grandma and mother put ice on his head. As he was crying, everyone was fussing over him and asking, "What do you need? What do you want?"

Billy was only 11, but answered, "I need a cigarette. Gimme a cigarette!" Everyone felt bad for him, so his mother let him smoke right in front of her. We all joked about how he could get over. He was a hustler even in his youth.

Billy and I were team thieves and Billy had nerves of steel. At 13, we rode our bikes to office buildings or banks, parked out front, went inside, and marked out one of the workers to hustle them. While I told the office manager I wanted to open an account or get a job, Billy would maneuver her pocketbook under the desk with his legs and feet. He pulled it toward him, took out her wallet, and pushed it back again. Then, we left with money to get high. He and I also walked into stores and diners to see what we could steal. Billy never hesitated to steal the transparent containers on the counter used to collect money for charities since we were his favorite charity.

BILLY'S FAMILY

Billy had lived with his sisters, mother, and grandmother since his parents were divorced. Because his father left when Billy was only 6, his mother and grandmother spoiled him. His mother had a good job so his closet was full of nice clothes and the pantry was always stocked with plenty of candy and snacks. I walked or took him home on my bicycle just so I could get some of those snacks. His grandmother, who we called "Grams," cared for him during the day. Because Billy lived down the block from our elementary school, we often went to his house for lunch. Grams made bacon and eggs with delicious, cold PDQ chocolate milk. We always had the "munchies," especially after smoking pot.

Grams loved Billy. She did everything for him. When he came home from school or playing basketball, Grams would take off his sneakers and rub his toes. We laughed, calling it "toey rubbing." I hung out with Billy so much that his family accepted me as their own. Billy's mom was like my second mother.

Even though we were bad for each other, Billy's family never turned me away. Rick, Billy's stepfather, was wild himself and he let us smoke cigarettes. Later, he played cards and hustled with us. Jackie and Marylyn, Billy's sisters, were like my own sisters. They yelled at us but looked after us at the same time. Billy's future brother-in-law, Paul, grew up with my brothers. He tried to guide us in the right direction but it seemed that most weekends our families had to come down to the precinct to bail us out.

Billy and I were closer than birth brothers. When I moved to Florida at 13, Billy promised me he would only smoke marijuana while we were apart. We wrote regularly, and I reminded him not to do any other drugs except pot. I knew that Billy was an extremist. I began getting messages from my homeboys in New York that he was overdosing on pills, a pattern that followed him throughout life.

When I ran away from Florida and moved back home a year later, Billy was there. He helped me build clubhouse E-14. It was our hangout, and we stayed there all hours of the day and night. One night we lit Billy's shoelaces on fire when he was sleeping. He awoke, got up, and tried to take his sneakers off. When they would not come off, he just went back to sleep. We laughed and mocked, "Oh, he's waiting for his grandmother to take them off." Meanwhile, his sneakers were really burning, and we had to undo them for him.

CHANGE OF SCENERY DID NOT CHANGE BILLY

Billy's family moved to Freeport, New York a couple miles away. He began to hang out in the black and Spanish community. Billy easily adapted to the culture because of our diverse family. We continued hustling, smoking pot and many other drugs, playing ball, and womanizing. We went into racquetball and tennis clubs and hit the locker rooms, acting like we belonged to the clubs. We robbed money from the lockers. It was an easy hit for us because there was a string of health clubs on Long Island we could ride our bikes to and easily get away.

One time in Freeport, we hit the mother lode at a racquetball club. We opened a locker and found a wallet containing $1,000—all $100 bills. Billy snatched the money. We were strolling out when a lady asked, "Hey, what are you guys doing in here? You were here last week—now get out!"

"OK," we mumbled as we took off running. A thousand dollars in 1975 for 17-year-old's was like hitting the lottery.

We made it to a friend's house in the hood and used the money to score drugs and booze. Word got out on the street that two white boys were carrying $1,000 they had stolen. That was a very dangerous message in the streets because it was an invitation to freely be robbed. As we smoked our pot, we grew more paranoid and kept checking out the window.

We looked out the window and saw a detective going house to house. We assumed someone had ratted on us and he was coming for us. We snuck out the back door and ran through the woods to the railroad tracks. We kept running alongside the railroad tracks. We could hear people chasing us until we outran them. We thought it was the detectives, but we found out later that some black dudes from the hood were chasing us with guns. God protected us again.

We took our stolen money, hit the shops on Jamaica Avenue in Queens, and bought some uptown threads. We bought some serious shirts, pants, and playboy shoes—we were "dressed down." We then jumped on the subway and went to a strip club on 42nd Street in Manhattan. The lust of New York City entered our spirits as we explored this new playground that would later destroy our lives. When we went back to school, we were slick, wearing our new duds and hearing everybody say, "Man, they got over big time."

THE HUSTLERS GET HUSTLED

Right after I got my driver's license, Billy and I drove to Daytona Beach, Florida. My mom came with us to catch a ride to visit my grandmother. Although my mom was an activist, she was naive at times. She sat in the back seat of the car making ham-and-cheese sandwiches from the cooler as Billy and I were in the front seat smoking fat joints all the way to Florida. We lit incense to cover the smell of pot. Mom ended up with a "contact buzz" from smoke so close to her. But, she had the best time as we joked, laughed, and munched. We dropped Mom off at my grandmother's house in Orlando, and

Billy and I shot over to Daytona Beach.

By the time we got to the beach, we were out of pot. We found two guys and asked them if we could buy an ounce of pot. One guy stayed in our car while the other went to get the pot. We had given him $25 for an ounce. When the guy did not return with our pot or money, we took the drugs from his partner who was still in our car. He had some little aluminum packets that were supposed to be powdered speed. After we kicked him out of the car, Billy and I snorted the stuff. We could not get the taste out of our mouths, so we ate some ice cream. Then it hit us: This was not speed. It was the "fake stuff" made with quinine powder normally used to cut and stretch the drugs. The two master hustlers had been ripped off by the new young guns. We shook our heads and laughed, realizing we had just been burned by our own scam.

OUR BASKETBALL DAYS

Billy and I played basketball all the time. We knew our game, challenged anybody, and then beat them on the court. Wherever we were, we would get a game going. We could rock 'em. Billy had moves like "Pistol" Pete Maravich or today's version of "And One" Basketball on ESPN. His moves were ahead of his time. We won street ball contests with those moves. We could put the basketball through our opponents' legs, around their backs, or "shake and bake" them to the hoop. Being brought up with the Smith family, we had an advantage over most kids our own age. We had such aspirations of playing ball in college and dreamed about the NBA.

Because of our craving to party with girls, get high on drugs, and hustle money to support our growing addictions, it was impossible to commit to our high school basketball teams. We satisfied our passion for basketball playing street ball and competing in the parks and summer league tournaments.

LIVING FOR THE CITY

Billy had many girlfriends but didn't fall in love until after we graduated from high school. He was head over heels in love with Annie Navarro, a pretty Puerto Rican girl from Freeport, New York. Of course, her beautiful sister, Miriam, became my girl. They loved to dance and hang out with us, especially when we introduced them to New York City life.

Our days in the city came straight from the Stevie Wonder song "Living for the City":

His hair is long, his feet are hard and gritty
He spends his life walking the streets of New York City
He's almost dead from breathing in air pollution

He tried to vote but to him there's no solution
Living just enough, just enough for the city... Yeah, yeah, yeah!

In the beginning years of our relationships with Annie and Miriam, the four of us were inseparable. Billy moved into his sister Jackie's apartment in New York City. When he landed a job on Wall Street, his apartment became one of our hangouts. We thought we were on top of the world. We had gone from our clubhouse E-14 to a high-rise apartment building on the 31st floor overlooking the Statue of Liberty and the Twin Towers.

SHOOTING UP HEROIN

In 1978, when I was 20, Miriam and I began living together. Billy started shooting heroin and lost his job on Wall Street. He still lived in the city but stayed with Miriam and me in Long Island on the weekends to spend time with Annie. Billy got hooked on heroin and ruined his relationship with Annie because he did not care about anything but getting high. One time I got so mad at him that I smacked him around for shooting heroin. Although I was high on cocaine, I still felt this righteous anger because I thought he crossed the line when he started shooting dope.

Jimmy, Miriam, and Billy at Bobby and Dianne's wedding reception.

Before too long, I was snorting heroin as well. Billy showed me how and where to buy heroin. The heroin dealers set up shop in dilapidated buildings on the Lower East Side of New York City. We scored at the Garage, the Spot, and 7-Ups. These locations had their own security system made up of gang members packing .44 Magnums to protect the dealers and the product. The little paper waxed bags of heroin they sold were about 1-inch in diameter with stamped names like "poison," "skull," and "death."

Billy and I were nearly shot many times. The most dangerous places were the "shooting galleries." A shooting gallery was a place to score heroin, buy needles or borrow someone else's "works" (needle), and get high on the premises. AIDS was not known at this time, so it was common to use other people's needles. It was a dog-eat-dog scene. Fights broke out, cops busted in, or other hard-core addicts would stick you up and rob you. Billy and I went there so he could buy or borrow a needle to inject heroin and get high. Located in broken-down, rat- and roach-infested apartments, each decrepit room was filled with strung-out drug addicts: young girls to 70-year-old junkies. Some of them were leaning back, feeling the heroin pumping through their vein with a belt or piece of string wrapped around their arm and a hypodermic needle still dangling from their vein, or even from the jugular vein in their neck. Others just nodded in the hallways, oblivious to the acrid stench of urine that filled the air.

I never shot dope (heroin) because of my fear of needles. I only snorted heroin. While I was in the shooting galleries, I was often accused of being an undercover cop. This resulted in suspicion and threats. Often, I would have to leave quickly because of the danger of getting stabbed or shot.

I came close to using a needle many times. I made Billy promise that if I ever asked him to shoot me up (inject the drugs in my arm), he had to refuse. A number of times, I did get to that point. I would hold my arm out, pleading, "Go ahead, Billy, do it." He never did. Billy's loyalty probably saved my life. I never got the HIV virus that destroyed his life and infected so many of our friends who are dead today from AIDS.

After Billy lost his job on Wall Street, he became a major player in the drug scene. He worked Washington Square Park, a tourist attraction downtown where street performers put on spontaneous shows. It became one of our meeting places. Billy and I hustled drugs, mostly fake, and sold them to rookie users. Sometimes, Billy sold fake dope to experienced drug users. When they found out, they came after him. In fact, one day he sold fake acid (LSD) to a man who attacked him with a hammer. Billy was badly injured, but it did not stop him. We considered it just another necessary hazard of the hustle game.

DETOX DAYS

On one occasion, after hanging out in the city for three days, I was so guilt-ridden for leaving Miriam by herself and desperate for a sympathy plan that I persuaded Billy to join me in checking into a detox program. When we signed in, we pretended we did not know each other. Later I said to the staff worker, "Hey, he seems like a good guy. Can you let him be my roommate?" They put us in the same room. Before long we were running the place.

In detox, everyone was given a sedative at bedtime. We convinced the other residents to save their pills by placing them under their tongues. Billy and I then hustled the other residents on the pool table for the pills. One night we collected 10 to 12 pills each and took them all at once. When the nurse tried to wake us in the morning, we were disoriented, hung-over, and unable to get up. We laughed hysterically, blind to the risks we were taking.

We were surprised to see Joni, a girl from the projects, in detox. She grew up with us and even lived with our family when she was homeless. She was there to kick heroin. They prescribed liquid methadone to wean her off of the heroin. One afternoon, she nodded off while eating some soup. She fell face first into the bowl of hot soup. At first, we laughed at the air bubbles coming up from her nose in the soup until we realized she was drowning. Only Billy and I, seeing her and lifting her head, saved her from drowning in her soup.

During a counseling meeting with the residents, I noticed Billy sitting next to Joni. When I saw the two of them nodding out, I realized Billy had hustled some methadone from her and had not shared it with me. I confronted him angrily as he innocently claimed that he did not want to tease me since there was not enough for the both of us. He smiled and I just laughed. He was such a hustler. It never dawned on us that we were in detox trying to get clean off drugs. We were just living for the moment, unaware we were wasting our lives.

In that same program, we met a heavy-set girl whose father was wealthy. She fancied herself to be a singer, so we told her how beautiful she was and what a great voice she had. It was just a hustle to get her father to smuggle in cartons of cigarettes. We now had another victim to joke on and pass the time away. Billy and I set up a show one night during our free time and asked her to be our featured singer. We made it out to sound like it was going to be a grand concert. She was excited—her dreams were coming true. She was going to be a star—maybe this was the beginning of *American Idol*.

We set up tables and chairs in the recreation room and invited all the residents. Then, we put her up on a table made into a stage and gave her a banana to use as a microphone. Her choice of songs was awful and her singing was off-key. She sang as though she was in a Broadway theater. She was having a great time. Billy and I were so high on the pot we smuggled in that we were under a table, laughing hysterically. We made her the international star of detox that night.

Finally, Billy and I checked out of detox. We promised ourselves we would stay sober, but Billy bought a beer as soon as we were out the front door.

ONE MORE CHANCE

After God resurrected Billy on the Lower East Side, it should have been the end. I asked God to show me He was real and He did. Even after the fear of God came upon me, it was not enough to stop me from doing drugs. I promised God that I would stop getting high with Billy in the streets. I was determined to keep my promise and honor the miracle of God bringing Billy back to life.

From that day forward, we never got high together again.

As I shared in chapter 7, I got a phone call a few weeks later telling me Billy had been stabbed in the chest up in Spanish Harlem and was near death. I got on my knees in my sister's house and cried out to God. Billy survived and when he checked himself out of the hospital I took him directly to Sheepgate Assembly of God to ask Pastor Joe to pray for us. This time I didn't care if he wanted to lay hands on me, throw me on the floor, or flip me. We just needed help, and I was ready to go down. To my surprise, there was no sideshow. Pastor Joe looked at us and prayed, "God, raise these boys up to know Jesus as their Lord and Savior." God was at work.

A MIRACULOUS TRANSFORMATION

After I went into Teen Challenge and gave my life to Christ at 26, Billy visited me with Miriam. He was usually high when he came.

"Billy, "I pleaded, "you've got to get into the program or you're going to die!"

Six months later Billy finally said, "I'm gonna do it. I am coming to Teen Challenge."

It seemed like whatever I did, Billy followed. When he entered the crisis center in Brooklyn, I had moved on to the second phase of the program in upstate New York. It seemed like he was just going through the motions in Brooklyn, looking to get to Camp Champion so we could start taking over like we always did.

Each time I asked the leadership how Billy was, they would answer, "Well, his hat is still crooked... he's still on the fence." I was disappointed because he had been in the program for a couple of months with no breakthrough. The boy was out of the street, but the street was not out of the boy.

The residents of Brooklyn Teen Challenge joined us at Camp Champion for a retreat and I was able to visit with Billy and mingle with the other students. It was exciting for Miriam, Billy, and me to share the weekend. In an evening service at Abundant Life Chapel, Brother Don Wilkerson preached and gave an altar call, inviting those who wanted to give their hearts to Jesus to come forward. Billy responded, knelt at the altar, and began to weep. I gently placed my hand on his shoulders as I continued to pray.

As he asked Christ into his heart, Billy cried and cried. He looked up at me with tears streaming down his cheeks and sobbed, "Jimmy, I don't know why I can't stop crying."

I said, "Billy, you're crying because God is touching you. God is giving you a new heart and melting away the old." This is a memory forged in the depths of my heart. I thank God for allowing me to be there. Having been with Billy through so many death experiences, it was such a blessing to see his ultimate life experience.

DAVID WILKERSON'S WORLD CHALLENGE MINISTRIES

After I graduated from Teen Challenge and went to Central Bible College, Billy joined David Wilkerson's staff of World Challenge in New York City. Brother Dave moved back to New York because God had called him to start Times Square Church. He bought a vacant mansion next to the Teen Challenge center in Brooklyn and renovated it to house the World Challenge staff and headquarters. Billy joined Gary and Greg Wilkerson, Brother Dave's sons, who headed that street outreach ministry and carried a passion for the lost just like their dad.

One of Gary's assistants was Jimmy Lilley, a street warrior who graduated Philadelphia Teen Challenge in the 1970's. Jimmy was a black brother called "Nums," because he was missing a thumb and a finger. He had an incredible testimony and loved evangelism. Gary, Jimmy, and Billy opened coffeehouses in Spanish Harlem, Brooklyn, and other places. They had tremendous zeal. I was in Bible College getting reports of what was happening. I went to New York during the summers to join Billy and help Gary with the World Challenge outreaches.

A DESTRUCTIVE COMPROMISE

For my birthday, Billy visited me in Missouri. No one told me he was coming. I was in my trailer, and when I looked out the window, I saw a guy wearing a black sombrero. I thought, Boy, that guy looks just like Billy. Billy burst in the front door. Miriam and I were so excited. Billy stayed with us for about a week.

While he was with us, I noticed some things that concerned me in his music and his walk, but I rationalized it away. I thought, Well, Billy was always a little wild, even in his walk with the Lord. Since he was accountable to some good people, I did not say anything.

During my summer breaks from Bible College, I worked in the crusades and coffeehouse outreaches for Brooklyn Teen Challenge and World Challenge. I noticed Billy was listening to secular music, walking with a big tip, and his hat was back on the slant. I confronted him and shared my love and concern. I told him I saw the compromise in his life, but he would not listen.

One day, I was so burdened for Billy that I told two pastors, "We've got to pray for Billy. I feel like he's going to fall." He was working for World Challenge, but I knew something was wrong. My brother, Hughie, was working with us at World Challenge, as well.

We had a street rally in Spanish Harlem and Brother Dave Wilkerson preached a powerful message. After he preached, we showed a movie, Cry for Freedom that featured Miriam and me. After the movie, Billy and I gave our testimonies and many people gave their hearts to the Lord. I left Billy to break down and close up the rally and went back to the World Challenge headquarters, going to bed about midnight. Around 2 a.m., I was awakened by Hughie pounding on my door. He gasped, "Jimmy, Jimmy, Billy's not breathing."

Hughie and I ran up the stairs to Billy's room on the third floor. We found him unconscious on the floor—blue and with no signs of life. Hughie and I picked Billy up, carried him all the way down to the first floor's foyer, and laid his lifeless body on the floor.

Gary and Greg woke up. We all laid hands on Billy and began to pray. I gave him mouth-to-mouth resuscitation and pumped his chest. We kept saying, "Billy, Billy, wake up!"

It was another overdose. Again paramedics came, took him to the hospital, and once again Billy recovered. I wondered if Billy was running out of chances. How long would God's grace keep giving him another chance and another and another?

I walked into the emergency room and saw Billy lying there. I said, "Billy, now do you understand what I'm talking about when I tell you about compromise?"

He looked up at me and said, "Jimmy, I'm tired and I'm lonely. Jimmy, I am so lonely."

I hugged him and cried, "It's all right, buddy. It's going to be all right."

The lyrics of Stevie Wonder's song, "Living Just Enough for the City," echoed in my mind over and over again in a tug-of-war between faith and despair:

I hope you hear inside my voice of sorrow,
And that it motivates you to make a better tomorrow,
This place is cruel, nowhere could be much colder,
If we don't change the world will soon be over,
Living just enough, stop giving just enough for the city!

IT'S GOING TO BE ALL RIGHT, BILLY

We sent Billy to a restoration program for 6 months. That was 1986. AIDS became a public threat in the mid-1980's and intravenous drug users were advised to be tested for the HIV virus. After the test, Billy asked me to come and visit him there.

When I met him, he held me, looked in my eyes, and said, "Jimmy, I have the AIDS virus." He began to cry.

I hugged him and said, "Bill, it's gonna be all right. We're gonna make it, buddy."

After that, he was restored and back on fire for God. Billy joined forces again with Gary Wilkerson and gave everything he had to serving at World Challenge. He was instrumental in helping Brother Dave pioneer Timothy House, a drug program for men, and the Upper Room coffeehouse next to the Port Authority on 41st Street and 9th Avenue in New York City.

Billy worked at the Upper Room outreach, a ministry that took homeless and transients off the streets of New York City and placed them in Teen Challenge programs across the country. Billy and I served coffee and sandwiches to the homeless. We shared our testimonies and God's Word. It was an awesome outreach in midtown Manhattan. Hundreds of hopeless people were saved and many are now in ministry. Billy was involved in the pioneer days of Times Square Church, but most of all he loved street ministry.

Billy met his wife, Debbie, at Times Square Church and started to date her with Brother Dave's permission. Debbie knew Billy had AIDS, but still they were married on December 2, 1989. I prayed that this would be the end of his loneliness and the final turning point in his life.

As my ministry grew on Long Island, Billy joined me. His condition worsened, and he was put on a medication that had to be taken intravenously. Many addicts are not just addicted to the drugs, they can become addicted to the needle. When Billy got high on the street, he loved "booting up." He would often inject the drug, draw his blood back up the needle, shoot it back in, then back it up, and shoot again just to get the sensation of the injection. With his history of heroin addiction and use of needles, I knew this was going to be a big temptation. So I advised him and Debbie to move out to Long Island where there were fewer temptations. Debbie refused to move, so Billy often made lonely trips out to Long Island by himself. Sometimes he stayed with us for weeks at a time.

In 1992, Billy was experiencing personal problems, but he continued to work. He often stayed at my house. He moved away from his wife at this time and lived with Miriam and me and Jackie.

Many nights he slept at our house on a little cot. Billy's disease caused profuse nosebleeds and he was often in agony. I spent many nights praying with him. He told me one night, "You know, Jimmy, I'm reminded all the time that I have AIDS. Every time I look in the mirror, I'm reminded I have AIDS. It's so difficult."

I would hug him and say, "Trust Jesus. Keep the faith, bro. We're gonna make it."

Billy loved to play with his sisters' children and it hurt him that he had to wear a surgical mask in order to hold her new baby. At that time no one knew how to handle the virus. Billy faced AIDS, loneliness, discouragement, and fear. I encouraged him to be faithful to Jesus. My son, David, was 4 at this time, and Billy was his best friend. They wrestled together. When Billy opened his roll-a-way bed to get ready for bed, David would run and jump in his bed and hide under his covers attempting to scare him. My daughter, Dionnza, was 2. Billy loved picking her up, throwing her in the air, and catching her. We treated Billy as though he did not have AIDS. Our home became his sanctuary.

Late one night, the ringing shattered the silence of our bedroom. "I'm so miserable, Jimmy. I'm ready to go. I'm ready to do it—I'm just ready to give in." Billy was at his sister's apartment in Manhattan. He said he had a gun and a pint of whiskey beside him and was going to end it.

"Billy, you can't! Don't do it, Billy!" I knew the medication was altering his judgment and he was getting sicker and weaker by the day.

"You listen to me, Billy." I told him, "Go down to the Hudson River and throw the whiskey bottle and the gun into the river and just come to my house." After much counsel and prayer over the phone, he finally listened to me and threw the gun and whiskey in the river.

WE'RE NEVER ALONE

Things seemed to improve for Billy. He moved back in with his wife and continued in ministry. One day when I was at the Teen Challenge Training Center in Pennsylvania ready to speak at a spiritual emphasis conference, an emergency phone call came for me. I was just about to begin to speak, but the messenger said, "It is urgent, you must respond now." All of my children and Miriam were with me, so I was unsure what the emergency was.

I picked up the phone and recognized the voice of Billy's sister, Marilyn, even though it was broken and weeping. She was yelling, "Jimmy, Jimmy, you've got to come home. Billy's dead. Billy's dead."

I asked, "Where is he?"

"He was found in the city and the police notified me," she told me. "You have to go to identify his body in the New York City morgue."

My heart was broken and I began to cry. Our love was genuine, out of the ordinary. Since we had become Christians, what we had was even deeper than what we shared on the streets. I thought Billy had a lot of time left. I knew he had AIDS and problems in his personal life, but he seemed fine when I spoke to him the day before.

It was impossible for me to continue in the service. I was a wreck. Tears were rushing down my face. I told them I had to go because of an emergency. My family and I started the 3-hour drive to the city morgue. I put in a cassette tape of The Brooklyn Tabernacle Choir and let one of my favorite songs, "Never Alone," minister to my heart. I must have listened to the same song over 30 times, crying and praying that it really was not Billy in the morgue.

I drove straight to the city morgue and told them that I was there to identify my brother, Billy Laan. Someone showed me two Polaroid pictures of Billy lying dead on a gurney with his face cut up, nose broken, cheeks bruised, head gashed, and numerous contusions.

I said, "I am Billy Laan's brother, friend, and pastor. I need to see him, and I am not leaving until I see him." After the staff worker spoke to her supervisor, she came back and escorted me to the basement of the morgue. Out of the icebox they took a lifeless form, transferred it to a gurney, and wheeled it over to me. They pulled down the sheet and I looked at Billy's lifeless, swollen face and broken, dead body. I sobbed. No bright eyes. No silly smile to make me laugh. Just a broken shell of the man of God who had gone from partying to laboring for the Kingdom by my side.

I silently cried, "Oh, my God. Billy, what did they do to you?" I had no idea what happened, although I suspected drugs were involved. His face looked like someone had hit him with a metal bar.

All of these things flooded my mind as I looked at him on that cold, cloudy Saturday in the city morgue. I combed my hands through his soft, black hair that he kept so neat. I leaned over and hugged him and cried, "Billy, I receive your mantle of ministry. By God's grace, I will do double what I was called to do for the kingdom of God. The devil will pay for this." I remember stumbling to my car, trembling and sobbing. I clutched the back of the car to hold myself up and reached out to God for some comfort, some solace, and some reason for this.

A MEMORIAL SERVICE FOR MY FRIEND

I had no idea how he had died, but I knew how his funeral was going to be conducted because he had already planned it with me. We thought he still had many years left when he planned it. How could we have known? So sudden. So unexpected.

I went with my brothers to the Sunday morning service at Times Square Church and spoke with Brother Dave Wilkerson after service. I gave him the outline of the funeral service that Billy and I had put together and asked if he would help us carry out Billy's last wishes. Billy wanted the choir from Times Square Church to sing the songs "God Is" and "I Want to See Jesus." He wanted Pastor Ben Torres from Church of the Revelation and Brother Don to pray and Brother Dave to preach. Billy wanted me to direct the service because he knew that my grief would not permit me to do anything else.

Brother Don agreed to pray and Pastor Ben promised to be there. As busy as Brother Dave's schedule was with demands all over the world, he made time for us and graciously agreed to speak. "Of course, I'll preach at Billy's funeral. I'll be there for Billy," he said tenderly.

WHAT REALLY HAPPENED TO BILLY

With the funeral arrangements completed, I went downtown to the apartment building where his body was found. My brothers and Billy's brother-in-law, Paul, found the stairwell of the apartment complex where he had fallen. We pieced together what must have happened.

We believe that on the night I left for Pennsylvania, Billy felt lonely and depressed. The medication he was on, his sickness, and his personal life were taking their toll. After an argument with his wife, he was depressed and hopeless. He went into the city to cop a bag of heroin. He bought a bag of dope on the street, found a building, and went up the third floor stairwell that led to the roof. We do not think he was alone because we found an assortment of drug paraphernalia and empty bags littering the scene.

Because of my past experience with Billy, I could read the scene: he apparently took the needle to shoot the dope into his arm. It must have been a "bad" cut. Let me explain: when street dealers get heroin, they cut it (i.e. mix it with other ingredients to stretch it and increase their profits). There is no way to know the actual purity of the bag bought on the street until it is used. Sometimes it is not blended thoroughly or evenly. Billy must have had a "bad" cut, which is almost pure heroin.

On the street, you learn that when you feel the rush from the drugs going through your body, you instantly stand up to prevent your heart from stopping and try to keep yourself from falling unconscious. Under normal circumstances, you can catch yourself. Apparently, Billy passed out and fell face-forward down two flights of steel stairs and onto the landing. It was a gory scene. There were remnants of blood everywhere. It was like I was outside of time looking in at this surreal scene where my best friend had so tragically died.

My brothers and I knocked on doors throughout the apartment house to ask if anyone knew anything about Billy's death. No one seemed to know anything. As we were preparing to leave the building, a young lady walked by and entered the building. As we walked away, the Holy Spirit whispered, "Ask her."

"Ma'am, do you happen to know anything about a young man who was found dead up here in the stairwell? "Oh, yes," she answered. "I'm the one who called the police. I'm the one who heard him."

My heart leapt as I asked her, "Please tell me what happened!"

The young woman said that she was awakened about 4 a.m. by the sound of a cry, followed by groaning. She said her apartment was on the third floor and her door opened near the stairwell where Billy landed. She listened to him for about an hour but was afraid to go outside her door.

"He groaned and groaned for a long time," she said. Her husband had to get up at 5 a.m. to get ready for work so she let him sleep until then. At 6 a.m. they continued to hear the groaning. When her husband was dressed and leaving for work, he saw Billy's body and called the police. When the police got there, Billy was dead.

"Oh, ma'am, thank you so much. We needed to know."

We began to leave and then she grabbed my arm, looking in my eyes almost like an angel, and gently said, "You know what, sir? Let me tell you something about your friend. He groaned, but the groans didn't sound like he was in pain. There was something different about the sound. I can't understand, but they weren't from a painful heart."

Those words so touched my heart and opened up my understanding of Billy's last moments on earth and God's loving mercy. I realized that the Holy Spirit had been interceding for Billy with groaning according to Romans 8:26 "Likewise the Spirit also helps in our weaknesses. For we do not know what we should pray for as we ought, but the Spirit Himself makes intercession for us with groaning which cannot be uttered."

God was so faithful to reveal this insight into His grace that I had never seen before. I knew that Billy was groaning and getting right with God in his last moments. God's intercession. What mercy. What grace. What love God has for us.

We could debate why the woman did not call 911 when she heard him. Some wonder why God might allow Billy to suffer alone. But, I have such assurance that even in those last moments, Christ was there with him, comforting him. He was not alone.

Billy's funeral was held at Brooklyn Teen Challenge where he began his faith journey and was later married. The place was filled with people who loved him. Billy was an ordained minister who served at Times Square Church. The choir sang the songs he had requested (they even mentioned his name in the songs), Ben Torres and Don Wilkerson prayed, and David Wilkerson preached a very deep message. He said Billy had missed his destiny because of his disobedience to God—it was heavy. He preached the truth and challenged the people. After the service everyone paid their respects—and it was over.

As I was standing by Billy's casket as his armor bearer, a nervous Spanish dude, full of drugs, approached the casket. He knelt down and prayed, and then he looked at me and said, "I'm one of Billy's friends. I know him."

As he finished his sentence, he ran out of the building. The Holy Spirit revealed to me that this was the man who was with Billy when he was getting high on the stairwell. I prayed, "Lord, save that man—that's what Billy would want."

EVEN THEN, THERE IS A FRIEND WHO STICKS CLOSER THAN A BROTHER

This chapter is about friendship. "There is a friend who sticks closer than a brother" (Proverbs 18:24). Christ was with Billy at his deathbed; at the threshold of death, Christ was interceding: "He always lives to make intercession for them" (Hebrews 7:25). What a friend we have in Jesus. Billy and I had a deep friendship, the kind of friendship that is rare. It comes around only once in a lifetime. I miss Billy. He is not here to experience the wonderful growth that has taken place in our ministry or watch my children grow up.

During Billy's funeral a new student from Long Island Teen Challenge approached me and said he would like to be my new best friend—to take Billy's place. He was sincere, but I realized he did not have a clue about real friendship. Billy and I had 24 years of fun, folly, pain, commitment, history, and love.

About 14 years after Billy was buried, my youngest daughter, Dominique, who was born just after Billy passed away, was going through one of my private files and pulled out a folder with Billy's name on it. She was reading through it, looking at the program. I hadn't looked at it since the funeral. It gave me a chance to talk with her about the whole situation. I found these two letters. Here are the letters from Billy's sisters, which they wrote a few weeks after the funeral.

Dear Jimmy,

Who would have ever thought that your initial encounter on the basketball courts with Billy would result in such a wonderful friendship. You two are so lucky you are able to share such a wonderful relationship. Even now you can continue your conversations and you will know what Billy would probably say.

How many people can you really say that you love unconditionally no matter what they do? Billy was certainly loved that way by you.

I know as difficult as it was for you, my family and I appreciate everything you've done for Billy in helping him and putting together the wonderful funeral services on his behalf. It was so comforting to us. I'm afraid my words do not express all my feelings. Call me any time.

Thank God for you, Jimmy.

Love, Jackie

Dear Jimmy,

I know when this is all over and things have quieted down, there will be a time when you will be overwhelmed with what has happened. My heart breaks for you. You were Billy's best friend. He loved you. You could do no wrong in his eyes. You have been a true friend.

You made all the arrangements. It was you who pulled it all together. My mother and sister were so proud at the memorial service. We were so touched by the love in the room. A complete stranger came up to me and said, "Billy brought the Lord into my life and it's changed my life." There was such happiness in her eyes. I will not forget that. She held my hand so tightly. I don't even know her name.

I want to consider you my little brother. And perhaps from time to time I can come over with my kids and visit you.

I know you and Miriam did the best you could to help Billy. I'm glad we all grew close in the last few months. It was meant to be.

I have never seen a truer, loving friendship than the one you and Billy had. He was blessed to have you.

Love, Marilyn

If you have a close friend or perhaps a spouse, keep the relationship pure and loyal, just as you do with Christ and Christ does with you. Do not assume there will be another tomorrow. There are so many things I wished I had said or could have said. Do not wait until tomorrow. You do not know where their struggle may lead them. But even then, there is a friend that sticks closer than a brother—Jesus.

CHAPTER 11
MY HOMEBOYS BECOME
MY ARMOR BEARERS

A prominent newspaper on Long Island (Newsday)
featured our lifelong friendship through our journey
from crime to the Cross. From top: Me, Barry Baugh,
Joe Spallino, and my brother-in-law, Bobby Lloyd.

One of the most amazing aspects of this story is how God has taken men whose only goal was to take, take, take, and now has brought them back to the city to give. I have watched as He has taken the hopeless and turned them into givers of hope. Never was that clearer than in September 2001. On September 11, 2001, we awoke to the most catastrophic scene of my lifetime. As Miriam and I witnessed terrorists crashing planes into the World Trade Center and watched it transform into a towering inferno, I could not believe my eyes.

As the towers began to crumble, my wife and I stood, grabbed each other's hands and began to weep and pray, realizing that thousands of people were dying before our eyes. At Teen Challenge and Freedom Chapel we gathered to pray and intercede.

While we understood that prayer was important, we knew we needed to take action. We had to go to Ground Zero to share God's love. Churches and Teen Challenge centers around the country began to call asking, "What can we do?" With their help we purchased hundreds of bottles of Gatorade, water, work gloves, hard hats, and headed into the city by faith.

Two Freedom Chapel assistant pastors, two deacons, and I drove to the crater that was once the Twin Towers of the World Trade Center. All five of us were graduates of Teen Challenge. We headed out to work alongside these giants and heroes at Ground Zero. At the entrance of the devastation of Westside Highway, Lower Manhattan, we first entered the Office of Emergency Management where we were granted full access. One of the supervisors who saw the sincerity of our hearts offered to escort us personally to the "front line." Before we left his office, we laid hands on him and prayed. Later, he told us that he was exhausted, carrying such a burden, yet he felt a thousand pounds were lifted after we prayed. He escorted us right through the barricades and told the soldiers who were guarding the fenced doorway to Ground Zero to allow us to go in and minister.

As we walked through that entrance, we witnessed destruction reminiscent of the Blitzkrieg of World War II or the devastation my father must have seen from the back of his plane. Two New York police officers standing on guard gazed at us with such bewilderment. I asked them if they would like prayer. They immediately said, "Yes." As we prayed, they turned their lives over to Jesus. Afterward, we began to embrace firemen, policemen, and rescue workers with prayer, words of encouragement, and supplies. In the midst of all the devastation, just our presence meant so much to them.

Serving workers at Ground Zero.

As a mist of rain began to fall, the smell of the smoldering ruins, burned vehicles, and death lingered in the air. Through the smoke rising from the ruins of the World Trade Center, we watched lines of brave workers combing for survivors or bodies through piles of wreckage and debris. Huge steel girders bent like pretzels balanced precariously over our heads. It looked like "the valley of despair." There was just emptiness where these huge buildings

*Viewing the devastation at Ground Zero with Dennis Griffith,
Executive Director of Teen Challenge Southern California.*

once majestically towered over the New York skyline. In the rubble was the wreckage of bent and twisted fire engines and other emergency vehicles. Realizing that brave policemen, firemen, and thousands of people were dead, crushed, or trapped in the debris was tragic and sobering.

At the same time, in the midst of the tragedy, was the heroism of hundreds of New York firefighters, policemen, transit authority, EMT workers, construction workers, welders, and officials who joined with hundreds of people from all over the country working in harmony. They modeled the spirit of unity from Psalm 133. Believers or not, they were fulfilling what God is calling the Church to do. They were of the same mind and in the same judgment (1 Corinthians 1:10), working with one accord in the same place (Acts 2:1), having all things in common (Acts 4:32).

We watched as they dragged bodies out of the rubble. We wept and prayed as we crawled over burned, crushed fire trucks that looked like toys. All around were windows blown out, buildings crushed and demolished. But in the midst of all this devastation, we ran into Vinny, a Teen Challenge graduate.

Deep in the heart of man there's recognition that we are nothing without God. I realized for myself, while watching the towers crumble, that some of my security was derived from America's power and prosperity, and I was deeply convicted and humbled by God. I pray that this same spirit of humility will continue to prevail in our hearts as we attempt to recover and restore our country, never forgetting our need for the Lord Jesus Christ in our lives. This sense of destiny is what makes the way God brought the homeboys to be the partners and armor bearers of this vision so amazing.

LOYALTY IS ESSENTIAL

Friend after friend came to the Lord and went through Teen Challenge. Many are now my partners in ministry (the Bible calls this an armor bearer). In my experience in ministry, I have discovered four character traits that define a faithful armor bearer:

1. Love God with all your heart, soul, mind, and strength.
2. Love people of all cultures and backgrounds.
3. Have a loyal heart to your leadership and the ministry God has placed you in.
4. Have a servant's heart and demonstrate a foot-washing mentality, a doorkeeper's mentality, and a second-mile mentality.

Loyalty is indispensable. Some fruits of loyalty manifested in a godly leader are honor, trust, integrity, faithfulness, dependability, and the ability to embrace constructive criticism for one's development in personal righteousness.

STAND IN THE GAP FOR YOUR LEADER

The armor bearer must have as much of a desire to serve a leader through the exciting, smooth workings of ministry as during the toughest storms of affliction. Jesus fully explained servanthood when He defined His office to the disciples: "For even the Son of Man did not come to be served, but to serve, and to give His life as a ransom for many" (Mark 10:45). Jesus demonstrated a servant's mentality and amazed the disciples as He washed their feet.

My staff trusts me to correct, instruct, develop, and guide them into truth, and they do the same for me. We have each other's back. We do not protect each other when we are in sin; we protect each other from sin. When it seems that compromise, sin, or a spirit of division tries to infiltrate our lives or ministry, we confront, pray for one another, and bear one another's burden. Galatians 6:1-2 instructs us, "Brethren, if a man is overtaken in any trespass, you who are spiritual restore such a one in a spirit of gentleness, considering yourself lest you also be tempted. Bear one another's burdens, and so fulfill the law of Christ."

In our ministry, as it was on the streets, we protect our friends and comrades. However, as Christians, this loyalty is different. On the street, we looked out for others by covering up for those who broke the law so they would not get caught and busted, or as the street saying goes, "Help them get over." In God's kingdom, if someone is sinning and breaking the commandments, we don't cover sin; we expose it. We help restore people in love, intimately and personally holding them up, and guiding them back to the road of righteousness. Having each other's back in the kingdom of God includes loyalty not only to one's brother, but also unto the Lord and His Word.

AN UNORTHODOX LOYALTY

Ricardo, a Hispanic brother from the school of hard knocks and a graduate of Long Island Teen Challenge, told me a story that defined his principle of loyalty.

After graduating our program, Ricardo became a staff member at the Teen Challenge Training Center. Situated on 500 acres, this beautiful facility is a place of healing for over 270 men through the power and love of Jesus. One day the staff was discussing potential speakers for their spiritual emphasis conference. My name was mentioned.

Jose, a staff member at the Training Center, retorted, "Ah, Jimmy Jack is full of pride—he's trying to build his own kingdom."

No one said anything (even after that reference) and I was chosen to be the speaker. Jose did not realize that Ricardo was one of my armor bearers. Ricardo did not respond to the comment during the meeting. After the meeting Ricardo asked Jose to give him a ride into town to the store.

As soon as they got off the campus, Ricardo said, "Jose, pull over. I need to talk with you about something."

As soon as Jose stopped the car, Ricardo grabbed him by the throat and said, "If you ever talk about my pastor like that again, I'll break your neck."

While it certainly was an unorthodox approach, Ricardo displayed his loyalty. It was the right message, but the wrong method.

NATURAL ABILITY

From the time I was a young boy and then throughout my young adulthood, I had the ability to unite friends. Because my friends had diverse temperaments, there was always conflict. God gave me the ability to disarm conflict, unite the gang, and develop a game plan, directing each of the personalities to accomplish our goal. Before I came to the Lord, the devil distorted these leadership qualities and our activities and goals were destructive in nature.

Before Christ I was a natural builder and led my friends to construct clubhouses, pigeon coops, go-carts, and electrical gadgets. After I became a Christian, God began to use these talents to build His kingdom. He allowed me to become a leader of diverse warriors for His kingdom.

DAVID AND HIS MIGHTY MEN

David is a biblical character I admire. I have learned from his leadership, especially when he chose his warriors in the cave of Adullam.

First Samuel 22:1-2 says, "David therefore departed from there and escaped to the cave of Adullam. And when his brothers and all his father's house heard it, they went down there to him. And everyone who was in distress, everyone who was in debt, and everyone who was discontented gathered to him. So he became captain over them. And there were about four hundred men with him."

Imagine a congregation in distress, in debt, and discontented. God chose and appointed five warriors out of the ranks of David's already outstanding army to have David's back at all times. I can relate to King David's boys: Adino, Eleazar, Shammah, Abishai, and Beneniah (cf. 2 Samuel 23), because God has raised up incredible men to help me fight in the frontlines of ministry.

Adino the Eznite's name means "skinny the spearhead." He was not much to look at, but he defeated 800 men in one battle.

Next was Eleazar, the son of Dodo (you know you have to learn to fight at a young age when your dad's name is Dodo). He fought so hard that after the victory his fingers had to be pried from his sword. Have you ever taken hold of God's Word until someone had to pry you from the promise of God?

Shammah, David's nephew, took a stand in a field of lentils. It was not a particularly strategic location, but he made up his mind not to give one inch to the enemy. He killed the Philistines and possessed the land. His courage brought about a great victory.

Abishai also stood by David's side. On one occasion Abishai was armed with only a spear, fought against 300 men, and killed each one. In the latter days of David's reign when he fought the fifth giant of Gath, Ishbi Benob, he grew tired. Abishai stepped in and basically said to David, "I've got your back, King David. Rest while I take him out."

Finally, Beneniah fought two Moabites, a lion in a snowy pit, and an Egyptian. These are types of victory over the flesh, the devil, and the world.

These valiant leaders remind me of my homeboys who turned into my armor bearers. Often, I receive credit for establishing the ministries of Long Island Teen Challenge and Freedom Chapel. These ministries have become internationally known; however, I know I do not deserve the credit. My armor bearers are fighting the enemy in prayer, interceding, loving me, strengthening me, and taking care of the ministry so we can fulfill the vision God has given us. There is nothing like having the homeboys you grew up with become your armor bearers.

Much of my miracle life revolves around my family and my boyhood friends. Members of my family have supported me in the ministry. Billy came from the shooting galleries of New York City to become my armor bearer from Times Square Church. He was not the only miracle; there are others with much happier endings.

BOBBY AND DIANNE LLOYD— MY FIRST ARMOR BEARERS

Dianne was a drug addict until she encountered Christ. She always was a tough cookie, wild, and a street fighter as a kid. When she started using heroin in her 20's, she almost died from hepatitis and the hustling lifestyle associated with being an addict. After she met Christ, she began to pray for us because she knew Christ was the only hope for our family. She went on a crusade to reach us with the gospel. At every family gathering, she was sharing the gospel. She even came into the discos after us.

Dianne was always praying, preaching, and believing for me. She has not stopped. From the coffeehouse outreach to the birth and growth of Freedom Chapel, she has prayed and walked with me through the storms we have faced. When the going gets tough, Dianne gets going. She is always there with a loyal heart, a word of encouragement from her heart and the Bible, and faith to overcome any obstacle.

Her husband, Bobby, has been my assistant pastor at Freedom Chapel from its inception. Bobby was one of the most notorious drug dealers and gangsters in the projects of Rockville Centre and on all of Long Island. He was a bright, cool, smooth black brother best defined by the Curtis Mayfield 70s tune:

Diamonds in the back, sunroof top,
diggin' the scene with the gangster lean.

This was Bobby—a gangster who drove a Cadillac and wore expensive clothes like Superfly in the early 1970's. He was like a big brother to me when I was growing up. We used to get high together; but after he accepted Jesus as his Savior and entered Teen Challenge, he paved the way for the rest of us.

As I shared, my father nicknamed him "The Black Knight" because he was always there whenever we needed help. Some of the kids we grew up with from the projects became heroin addicts and began to rob our house because they knew we never locked our doors. One night, as we were sleeping, an addict snuck into my mother's room to steal her pocketbook. She woke up to his face inches from hers and shrieked. She leapt from the bed and chased him out of the house, down the block, and all the way back into the projects.

Dianne called Bobby who came right over with several of his bodyguards.

Bobby told one of the bodyguards, "Go over there with Jimmy and look around in those bushes."

When we got down in the bushes, the bodyguard pulled out a .38 caliber gun. My mind flashed, "Oh no, this guy's gonna kill me because Bobby's the one who robbed our house and he wants to get rid of me."

My suspicions were wrong. He was just doing what Bobby had trained him to do. He tucked the gun back in the holster under his arm and said, "Ain't nobody here. Let's go."

That was just a typical day at the Jack home.

When I was 10, Bobby walked into the house carrying a bag. I thought it was sugar. When he dropped it on the floor, I grabbed it, holding it up innocently as I asked, "Is this yours?"

He looked around to see if anyone saw and quickly snatched the bag from my little hand and murmured, "Yeah, that's mine. Thanks." From his tone it was obvious that there was something wrong. Later I realized that the bag was filled with heroin.

When I got my first firearm, a BB gun, I was putting it together in my room. Mom saw me and immediately called Bobby. He came over, took it, and told me not to ever fool around with guns. Obviously, Bobby knew he had taken a wrong turn in life and wanted something better for me.

As much as Bobby influenced us in gang involvement and drug abuse, he became one of the greatest influences for good in my life. He was the first one to turn his life over to the Lord and come into Teen Challenge. I followed his footsteps, entering Teen Challenge 6 months later. God rescued him from the pit of hell, and today he is one of the greatest armor bearers a man could ask for.

In addition to his work with Teen Challenge and Freedom Chapel, Bobby is founder and Executive Director of Long Island Citizens for Community Values (LICCV). He saw the trail of destruction from the sex industry on Long Island and in New York City and took steps to combat it at the root. He has been at the front lines of this conflict, served on NYC Mayor Rudy Guiliani's task force to clean up 42nd Street in midtown Manhattan, converted adult bookstores into Christian bookstores, and ministered the message of sexual purity and freedom in Christ to thousands. God has given him a national pulpit and international influence in the war against pornography and sexual abuse crimes committed against women and children.

JOE SPALLINO—A CREATIVE GENIUS

Joe Spallino is another homeboy who graduated Teen Challenge. He became a licensed minister and choir director for our church, but no one could have seen that even in 1990. Joe was a close friend of my brother, Johnny, and grew up with us, but became a drug-crazed heroin addict and a lunatic.

Joe was a great athlete in high school and was blessed with great intellect. He is also a gifted guitarist and loved to play Hendrix. He often came over to our house to do drugs. I would be inside the house attempting to write a report on a book I had never read, and Joe would ask, "What book do you need a report on?"

"Anyone will do," I would answer.

Joe could think of a book and dictate a report to me. That was how I turned it into my teacher.

He attended the University of Massachusetts, played basketball, hooked up with some crazy friends, and started to spiral down. After his college days, Joe began to expand his criminal activities. He and one of his friends stole a 41-foot yacht from Staten Island and sailed it out to Long Island—they named it Debauchery. Joey ran around in the boat in his little tiger bikini partying with his friends until he got arrested and went to jail.

When I first entered Teen Challenge, I was supposed to be the best man at Johnny's wedding. Because I could not leave the program for the wedding, Joey took my place. He and I were the same tux size, so he wore my rented tuxedo and was Johnny's best man. As usual, Joey rocked the place. Always the life of the party, he was jumping and dancing on tables and running into the bathroom, shooting heroin and cocaine.

On the day of my brother's wedding, I sat looking out the window at Brooklyn Teen Challenge, praying that each friend and member of my family at the wedding would meet Christ.

Five years later, Joey visited Johnny at my mom's house. By this time, Bobby and I were crusading to rescue our family and friends. We cornered Joey by the pool and told him about the hope, love, and freedom we had found in Jesus Christ.

He said, "That is great for you, but I'm just not ready to surrender my life to Christ." We prayed for him, and he went on his way.

In 1990, I got a call from my brother, Johnny, asking if I would visit Joey in a hospital in New York City. Johnny had seen the transformation in my life and told Joey that his only hope was the power we found in Teen Challenge. Joey was hospitalized as a result of his cocaine and heroin abuse. His body was almost destroyed. He was lying in a hospital bed, shaking, and near death. Once again, I shared how God could touch his life and save him.

"Really, Jim?" He said with his eyes pleading for reassurance that it could be true.

"Yes, Joey," I said and asked if he was ready to surrender his life to the loving and healing power of Jesus Christ.

Joe looked at me intently, the left side of his mouth drooping from nerve damage caused by his drug abuse. He nodded his head and said, "Yes."

Not long afterward, he entered Teen Challenge, graduated from the program, and eventually became the supervisor of both of our men's homes. Joey started the choir at our coffeehouse. The Lord has since blessed him with a beautiful wife, Tami, who was raised in a Christian home. As our choir directors, they electrify our congregation in worship, write and direct our church holiday plays, and have produced a CD. Joe's original song "The Joy of the Lord Is My Strength" has been sung by Teen Challenge choirs on three continents.

BARRY HAZEL BAUGH—BAZEL

Barry Hazel was a cousin of the Smith's and like an older brother to me. He hung around our house for as long as I can remember. A 6-foot, 5-inch, 240-pound black man, he was a leader on the basketball court and always had an encouraging spirit. He would often say, "Let's go! Let's go!" Off the court his mantra was, "Let's party! Let's party!"

Barry wore a leather hat and leather vest over his matching jean shirt and pants and carried a boom box that blasted disco and soul music. He was always dancing and doing drugs. He played basketball against many NBA players over the years, but never fulfilled his potential because of his drug addiction and involvement with crime.

Barry turned me on to smoking cocaine. In fact, the last time I got high was with Barry. Shortly after that, I miraculously ended up at Teen Challenge.

After I finished Bible College, we started the coffeehouse in Amityville. Across the street was a gas station. In God's providence, one of my old friends who was at the coffeehouse walked across to the gas station to get some gum. He saw Barry and told him we were in the VFW Hall. Barry came bursting in with his charismatic self. Bobby, Joey, and I, along with Miriam and other family members, greeted Barry with hugs and kisses.

Barry was struggling with drugs and joined us frequently but never made a commitment to Christ. Then one day, he disappeared. At the same time that we were beginning our residential ministry, I heard that Barry was in jail and I went to visit him. He thought he was meeting his lawyer or a detective who was trying to stick him with another rap. When he walked in and saw me, his suspicion melted and he greeted me with one of the biggest smiles I had ever seen.

After a time of reflection, I said, "Barry, God has a calling on your life. You could do your time, get out, and most likely end up back in jail again. Or, you can turn your life over to Jesus, come into Teen Challenge, and become the man God ordained you to be."

He looked at me with such hope as he said "Jim, let's go. Let's go." We had no residential center for Barry at the time, so we made a place for him to live in our basement. That was our first residential home until we opened the center, and Barry was one of our first graduates.

After receiving Christ, Barry found his true love, Robin. Together they have five children; little Barry Jr. even sang the lead on "I Am a Friend of God" with our choir. For years he has overseen our evangelism ministries, and also founded and directs our Hoop Challenge basketball camps. In 2006, after serving as the Dean of Men at Teen Challenge, he moved on to new ministry challenges. Though Barry turned me on to the rock of cocaine, I got even with him. I turned him on to the Rock of Ages—Jesus Christ.

BOB RASCATI—A JOSHUA SPIRIT

While Billy was at the Teen Challenge Training Center, he traveled with the Teen Challenge choir. He toured nationally and became good friends with Bob Rascati, a graduate of Teen Challenge and then staff member. He and Bob became like brothers, and I met Bob later through Billy.

God knew I would need a brother to stand beside me when Billy died. He chose Bob. One morning in 1992, Bob called me and shared, "Jimmy, God spoke to my heart and told me I am to be your Joshua."

I was surprised. "Are you serious, Bob?"

"Yes, Jimmy, I'm serious," he replied. At that time Bob was working for the Teen Challenge Training Center and had a comfortable life in his own trailer with few expenses.

I explained, "Bob, the only place I can put you is in a little room in the basement. Your salary would only be about $50 a week."

Bob's response was, "Jimmy, I don't care where I live or what I make. God has called me to serve you and to serve Teen Challenge on Long Island."

Bob has incredible leadership abilities. With his help we expanded our residential capacity to provide for more hurting people. He became our Program Director and Assistant Pastor at Freedom Chapel. Bob served Teen Challenge faithfully, even though the small salary and humble living conditions.

Bob is now married to Terrie. She was our first outreach student—a fighter, crack-cocaine smoker, and drinker. She was a wild woman from the streets.

Because we did not have a home for ladies in crisis when we met Terrie, we worked with her for many years on an out-student basis. God beautifully restored her life, and she and Bob fell in love. Terrie became the Academic Dean for our ladies' program. When they married, Bob had two children from a former marriage and Terrie had three daughters of her own. God united their families and has also blessed them with a son, Rocco. Bob became an ordained minister and we have released him and Terrie to serve an emerging program in New Haven, Connecticut. Bob is another armor bearer for whom I thank God.

DENISE OLIVER—A WORSHIP WARRIOR

Denise was a church girl. She knew all there was to know about religion. She was also classically trained in voice and organ and carried her talents into the church. Denise was the organist in large Catholic and Baptist churches. Her desperate search for approval, though, was never satisfied by music. Dysfunctional relationships and a failed marriage only left her empty, desperate, and hooked on drugs.

Even while holding down a full-time position with the State of Virginia's Port Authority and two music positions, Denise continued her frantic search for hope. On Sundays, she would sit at the organ or piano and look at people's glowing faces, big hats, furs, and beautiful clothes. She stank of crack cocaine and wondered, "Can't anyone smell this? Doesn't anyone see how lost I am? Doesn't anyone care?"

One dark Thursday morning at 4 a.m. after Denise squandered hundreds of dollars on crack cocaine, the despair in her heart overwhelmed her. She looked in the mirror and did not recognize herself. Her money was all gone and she cried out, "Lord, I'm going to hell. I don't want to die. Please help me!"

When her pastor, Father Jim, called her in for a meeting a week later, she could tell by the look on his face that something was not right. "Denise," he said solemnly. "You have one of three choices. One, you can go into a 30-day detox. Two, you can meet with a young man who will tell you about a year-long program in New York. Or three, you are fired."

Her mind raced in confusion. All she could think was, Don't get fired!

Through her tears, she realized that she was not being rejected, but that God was answering her cry for help. Father Jim was doing the most loving thing for her. She knew a 30-day detox would not be enough. The next day Father Jim took her to meet with Barry Hazel Baugh.

"Jesus totally changed my life at Teen Challenge," he shared, as Barry testified of what God had done in his life.

All Denise had left in the world was an '86 Buick Electra 380 two-door coupe. She sold it to Barry to get money for the trip to New York. Unfortunately, when those hot hundreds hit her hands, the money never made it to the bus terminal. She was on the way to the dope man. She took one more run at the drugs till the money ran out. Finally, 30 days later with a ticket from her sister, she got on a bus to New York and her miracle began.

After graduating from Teen Challenge in 1995, Denise became the director of the women's program. She married the Men's Home program manager in 2006, directed our Teen Challenge choir, and recorded two CD's with them. She is also working on her first solo project. Denise no longer sings for approval, but because she has been forgiven and knows that it is God who approves of her.

KEVIN HENESY—DRUG DEALER TURNED PRISON CHAPLAIN

When I was 15, Kevin Henesy was our Quaalude supplier. He was a surfer dude and party animal. If he was not carrying his surfboard, he was running to Far Rockaway, Queens, to refill our drug supply.

After I had been in Brooklyn Teen Challenge for several days, I saw Kevin for the first time in at least 10 years. The last time I had seen him was the night we had been busted with about 30 people in a raid at a party at the Holiday Inn in Rockville Centre. I had sent my friends, Tony and Jackie, to break into a deli around the corner. They stole cases of beer and cartons of cigarettes. The cops followed them back to the hotel, and we all got busted.

So many people were arrested that the police ran out of handcuffs and had to use plastic zip ties around our wrists. Most of us were released. Kevin and I went back to the hotel with some girls to continue partying. Kevin left the next morning and went to Florida. I had not seen him since.

When I saw Kevin with some of the students and staff 10 years later, his countenance glowed. I thought, Look, I've got a homeboy in Teen Challenge.

I asked him, "Hey, Kev, what's happening? Are you a student?"

"No, I'm a counselor here," he said, "God has changed my life, and He put it on my heart to help people at Teen Challenge."

Kevin was a tremendous encouragement because he had "been there and done that." God placed him in my path at a strategic time not only as a student in the men's program, but also in the family ministry with Miriam. As Kevin shared God's Word in chapel, I was in awe as I listened to him preach with sincere faith and love for God and people.

When Kevin first became a Christian, he spent time with my dad just before he died. My dad gave him a cross as a testimony of his new faith. After I was in the program for several weeks, Kevin gave that cross to me in remembrance of my dad and my new faith. Encounters like that secured my walk.

Kevin was one of the first to put the seed to plant a Teen Challenge center for Long Island in my heart. He brought drug addicts to Brooklyn Teen Challenge from the streets of our hometown. Today, Kevin is a board member for Long Island Teen Challenge, a prison chaplain, and pastor of Calvary Chapel. He is married to a beautiful woman of God, Joanna, and continues to inspire my life.

CHARLES AND TERRI AGEE—
FROM THE PROJECTS TO THE PALACE

Charles Agee was one of the biggest pot and cocaine dealers in the projects. He supplied many of us with drugs. Since Charles is 10 years older than I am, as a kid I watched him hustle in the streets. When I was 16 and had the know-how to gamble, I was invited into his home to get high and play poker all night.

His wife, Terri, was his sidekick. Although Charles limited himself to alcohol, pot, and cocaine, Terri became addicted to heroin. In 1995, we started a coffeehouse in the Martin Luther King Center in front of the projects where we grew up. We served coffee and donuts, had a time of worship, praise, testimonies, and then the Word. We always ended with prayer.

Many kids would ask me to lay my hands on their heads and pray for them. As I prayed, they would giggle and laugh. One day Charles and Terri walked in. They came forward for prayer, but there was no giggling. They were touched by God.

Terri entered our ladies' program and Charles went to jail. When he was released, he entered our men's program. Both Charles and Terri are now deacons in our church and volunteers for Teen Challenge. Their niece, Cierra, was one of those little ones who used to giggle and laugh when I prayed for her. She has graduated from high school and is now in college.

Charles is presently on dialysis. The doctor said he would have to amputate Charles' legs because both of his kidneys had failed; but Scott, a young white man who graduated our program, offered to donate a kidney to Charles. Charles and Scott are 100 percent compatible, and Charles will soon be on his feet.

DENNIS VESIK—FAITHFUL FAMILY FRIEND

Dennis was a blond-haired, German boy with a muscular build and handsome chiseled features. His parents were immigrants from Germany, and his father was a hard-working carpenter. Dennis grew up with my family and was Hughie's best friend.

Dennis' father built him a clubhouse in his backyard. His workmanship was incredible with handcrafted bunk beds and furnishings. One night, he had a sleepover at his house with my brothers, and they invited me. When I saw the clubhouse, it was a dream come true.

My brothers were up all night laughing, joking, and drinking beer. In the early morning hours, the door suddenly burst open. There was Dennis' father, standing in his boxer shorts, shouting, "Vat are you doin' over dar? Keep da noise dahn." He slammed the door and went back to bed. We nicknamed Dennis' dad "Vesik Bloomers."

Dennis became an alcoholic. He drank away his marriage, family, and career. He heard about the change that had happened in our lives and about Teen Challenge. He entered Teen Challenge, but had a unique approach in his restoration: He entered Teen Challenge for 30 days. It seemed like he lived in 30-day increments, because every month I would have to encourage him to stay 30 more days. Even in his eleventh month, I had to encourage him to stay 30 more days to complete the full year in order to graduate. Four years later, Dennis is still by my side. He has served on our staff as the food coordinator and house manager for Timothy House—the graduate/reentry phase of our program. The Lord has restored his family and his future, even providing new employment for him. He is another faithful armor bearer.

GEORGE MOONEY—"MAD DOG" NO MORE

George Mooney was a schoolmate and black brother from the projects whom we called "Mad Dog." When I was helping in a coffeehouse in Hempstead in 1991, people came and we ministered to all of them. George came by the coffeehouse. Though I had not seen him in years, I instantly recognized him.

"Hey, George, what are you doing?" I asked.

"Nothing, man. Just doing drugs—and I'm homeless," he answered.

I invited George to come into the coffeehouse. He later graduated from Teen Challenge and now works full-time with Pure Life Ministries in Kentucky.

ROB BRYANT—FROM MESSED UP TO MISSIONS

Rob Bryant, a black brother, was a year younger than I was in high school. I was a cool, bad boy role model for Rob. He followed in my footsteps—played on the same basketball team, hung out in my clubhouse, and was heading in the same direction. With no concern for his schoolwork or future, he lived only for the moment. He was a perfect fit for our gang. After finishing high school, Rob and I bumped into each other on the basketball court or at parties in the projects. Both of us were hustling for our daily fix. We would hang out together and reminisce about our basketball days and times running with girls.

In 2000, Rob called me from detox. He had heard I was a minister and had started a Teen Challenge on Long Island. He told me he was messed up on drugs and needed to come into the program. After that call, Rob disappeared. Two years later, Rob called again, said he needed help, and was ready to give his life to God. This time Rob was for real.

Rob entered our crisis center and seriously surrendered his heart to the Lord. He has become a powerhouse for Jesus. Rob directed our Genesis men's crisis home, was a choir member at Freedom Chapel, and a Royal Rangers commander at our church. He has a heart for missions and traveled to the Dominican Republic with me where he sang with the crusade choir and helped us establish a Teen Challenge center in Santiago. Rob also has a vision to travel to Africa and minister there. I love to watch him as he pours his life into the men at our homes with the same love that he himself received from Jesus. What a miracle and what a mighty God we serve.

FAITHFUL LEADERS

People ask me, "How can you oversee the Teen Challenge programs; pioneer and build a church; direct Hoop Challenge basketball camps, Kids' Krusade bus ministry, Rock the Block hip-hop outreach to the urban culture of Long Island and New York City; and serve as the Northeast Regional Representative for Teen Challenge?" Others see my responsibilities as I travel across the United States and internationally—preaching, sharing our vision, and raising finances to support our growth and say, "How do you do it?" My answer is simple. I tell them, "I have faithful, godly leaders who serve with loyal hearts. My homeboys are my greatest armor bearers."

CHAPTER 12
THE TEEN CHALLENGE MIRACLE

Miriam and I with our son, David, receiving the Teen
Challenge Alumni Award for the Decade of 1980's,
with David and Gwen Wilkerson.

MIRACLE FAMILY

We named my dog TC, but his birth certificate records his real name—Teen Challenge. Some of you must be thinking: *You must really love this ministry to name your dog Teen Challenge. I guess it has had a miraculous impact on your life to name your dog after it.*

My reply is that Teen Challenge has been instrumental in reaching my entire family and friends. I love the ministry of Teen Challenge.

In 1986, just 2 years after I entered Teen Challenge, David Wilkerson said I had a messed-up family. My family now has a historic testimony: The Jack family is widely known in the Teen Challenge world as having the most family members go through the program. All eight of my siblings and my mother either went through a Teen Challenge residential program or through one of its outreaches.

Every year, and even as I write this book, my relatives and friends continue to receive healing, hope, and embrace their destiny in Christ through Teen Challenge. Since Brother Dave stated that I had a messed-up family, he revised his statement as I have told him of the scores of my family members who are now serving the Lord because of Teen Challenge. He smiled and said, "Jimmy, you have a miracle family."

THE BIRTH OF TEEN CHALLENGE

Teen Challenge was born in the heart of its founder in 1958, the year I was born. God knew I was going to need a powerful message and proven program to get me to the place where He could use me, so He birthed the ministry of Teen Challenge. I know, though, that God had tens of thousands of other addicts in mind, too.

In February 1958, David Wilkerson, an unknown preacher from the hills of Pennsylvania, was leafing through the pages of *Life* magazine. Then, the pen sketch of a trial taking place in New York City caught his eye. The drawing captured the look of confusion, hatred, and despair in the eyes of seven young boys. Suddenly, Brother Dave began to weep with compassion. Bewildered, he looked more closely at the picture and then read the caption under it. The boys, all teenagers, were members of a gang in New York City called the Egyptian Dragons. They were on trial for murdering Michael Farmer, a 15-year-old polio victim, who was stabbed to death in Highbridge Park, Manhattan by the Egyptian Dragons. They were reacting to a turf war with the Jesters over a community pool.

Suddenly, a thought entered David's heart. It was as though he heard the voice of God saying: *Go to New York City and help those boys!*

His natural response was "Me? Go to New York? I'd be a fool. I know nothing about kids like that. I don't want to know anything." But still, he knew these were the instructions from the Lord.

Brother Dave drove to the courthouse in Manhattan to try to speak to the gang members about the love of Jesus. Because the judge presiding over the case had received death threats from the Egyptian Dragons, security was tight. Everyone was searched before being admitted to the courtroom. Brother Dave knew he must make his move, or he might not have another chance to speak to these boys. He held up his Bible, hoping it would identify him as a minister, and ran to the front of the room.

"Your honor," Brother Dave called out as the judge angrily whirled around, jolting in fear because of the previous threats. Immediately, security guards picked Brother Dave up by his elbows and rushed him from the courtroom, handing him over to two policemen who escorted him into the vestibule.

Suspecting he was armed, the guards demanded to see the gun and searched him again while shouting more questions. Was he really a minister or was he with the Egyptian Dragons?

Out in the corridor newsmen waited with cameras ready. They taunted him to hold up his Bible, and flashbulbs popped. He was not prepared for the result: Front-page headlines accompanied by a picture of a wild-eyed, Bible-waving young preacher who had come to save the gangs of New York.

Brother Dave never did get to speak to the boys on trial. That episode opened other doors for him, however. He began meeting gang members who recognized him from the newspaper photograph—and they admired him. They thought he was like them because the cops threw him out of the courtroom. Since he had been rejected by the police just like they had, they listened. However, one particular gang member did not listen. His name was Nicky Cruz. He was vice president and sergeant-of-arms of a notorious gang called the Mau Maus.

Nicky was a violent man, full of hatred. He would cut people with his knife in a second. He was raised in a family involved in the occult who for years stuck him in closets and abused him. When Brother Dave shared God's love with him, Nicky got so upset he threatened Brother Dave, "You come near me, Preacher, and I'll kill you."

Brother Dave answered him, "You could cut me in a thousand pieces and lay them out in the street, and every piece would cry out 'I love you!'"

Nicky had never heard those words before—I love you. Those words haunted him.

Sixty-five churches in New York sponsored a 7-day youth rally in the St. Nicholas Arena, an old boxing center. Several major gangs had been invited to the rallies: The Mau Maus, the GGI's, the Chaplains, the Rebels, and the Egyptian Dragons. On the final night, a bus carrying the Mau Maus pulled up to the curb and about 50 teenagers spilled out, led by Nicky and Israel, the gang's president.

Brother Dave preached with the anointing of the Holy Spirit, explaining how Jesus was tortured on the cross and why: "'For God so loved the world that he gave his only begotten Son'(John 3:16). If you open up your heart tonight and receive Jesus, God will fill you with His love and give you a purpose and a destiny."

That night in July 1958, dozens of gang members received Jesus as Savior; Nicky Cruz was one of them. When Brother Dave opened up a house for drug addicts in Brooklyn, Nicky was the first director. Brother Dave and he became friends, and their friendship and association continues to this day.

WORLDWIDE IMPACT

This story is told in detail in the best-selling book, *The Cross and the Switchblade*. Thirty million copies in 40 languages have been sold. Pat Boone approached Brother Dave about making a movie. While Hollywood had said that no one would see it, Pat ignored the critics and personally took on the challenge to make this film. The movie has been translated into over 30 languages, shown in 150 countries, and viewed by 50 million people.

The success of the movie is only one part of the miracle: Pat Boone (who played David Wilkerson) and Erik Estrada (who played Nicky Cruz) were impacted eternally by Jesus Christ. David Wilkerson insisted that Pat Boone have a personal experience with Jesus and the infilling of the Holy Spirit before he would allow Pat to play him in the movie. During the filming of the movie, Erik Estrada refused to rehearse the scene in St. Nicks Arena when Nicky Cruz responds to the gospel. He wanted it to be real. The altar call became more than acting. The presence of God was so strong after the preaching of the word that Erik Estrada actually made a personal commitment to Christ at the altar as they filmed.

Teen Challenge has grown to become the largest and most successful drug and alcohol treatment program of its kind in the world. It has grown from that single house in Brooklyn to 191 centers with almost 6,000 beds in the United States. Under Don Wilkerson's leadership, Global Teen Challenge was launched in 1993. In 2007, they recognized over 652 centers and evangelistic outreaches in 87 countries, with dozens of centers in the implementation phase. There are invitations from 27 other countries.

Including coalitions formed in Russia and the Ukraine, there are over 20,000 residential care beds worldwide. It is difficult to evaluate the Global impact of Teen Challenge, Recently over 150 Teen Challenge centers (not included above) were discovered in Brazil which were launched through the spread of *The Cross and the Switchblade.*

Teen Challenge's success rate of 70 percent has been recognized and substantiated by studies done by the U.S. National Institute on Drug Abuse. Since the first residential center was opened, thousands of young men and women throughout the world have come into Teen Challenge and found hope in Jesus. They go back to their communities as faithful mothers, fathers, and family members. They return to their places of employment as successful teachers, pastors, missionaries, businesspeople, politicians, and military officers.

Teen Challenge is always there for people, no matter what time it is. When I crawled through the doors of Brooklyn Teen Challenge, it was 1 a.m. I was drunk and drug-crazed. I left the house but came back at 4 a.m. They took me back in; they did not tell me to come back another day or come back when I had my blood test and physical results. If they had, I might not be here today.

Teen Challenge is a place of compassion where the weary find rest and the brokenhearted are healed. At Teen Challenge a drug addict can be set free; the homeless find a home; the naked receive clothes; the hungry are fed. It is a place where broken people are trained to become the people that God created them to be. People become warriors for the kingdom of God, find their dreams, and fulfill their destinies. Not only are there residential homes for hurting people, but through the ministry we also reach out to the streets, highways, and byways, rescuing people from the grip of hell and teaching them to dream again.

TAKING IT TO THE STREETS

Miriam and I were ministering in Red Hook, Brooklyn, at a Teen Challenge street rally during one of our summer breaks from Bible College. During a rally we met a 12-year-old deaf and mute girl. Miriam and I fell in love with her. We had learned to sign a few words from classes in Bible College and communicated with her through sign language and hugs. Since her vocal cords did not allow speech, she used her stomach and intestines. However, when they were strained to make noise, a strong, putrid smell also came out with her speech.

Later, we introduced her to Mike Zello, a pioneer for Teen Challenge and the Executive Director of Brooklyn Teen Challenge at that time. He gave her a big hug, Miriam and I joked with her, and she responded with her funny little noises.

After graduating from Bible College, we were hired by Brooklyn Teen Challenge to pioneer Long Island Teen Challenge. A few years later, Mike Zello asked if I knew why they hired Miriam and me.

When I said, "No," he asked me if I remembered the street rally in Red Hook and the deaf and mute girl. He recalled the putrid and repulsive odor he had smelled from her mouth when Miriam and I introduced her to him. What he saw, despite the odor, was us loving and hugging this little girl. He said, "When I watched you embrace that girl with the compassionate love of God, I knew you were ready for the ministry."

God is not so much concerned with our abilities. He is looking for people who know how to love. When you know how to love, other abilities follow. One of the greatest Gospel witnesses is not to tell people you love them, but to show them. When you have a compassionate heart, you are able to love those who cannot love you in return.

LA PELLA—A MODERN-DAY LEPER COLONY

In 1987, Miriam and I visited La Pella, a village in Puerto Rico internationally known for its drug infestation. Entering the village under a rickety bridge, we saw villagers hustling around, scratching, sniffing, shaking, and just trying to get their next hit of heroin. Entering alleyways we observed little make-shift homes turned into shooting galleries, with dope fiends sitting around broken tables and on milk boxes. People everywhere were injecting heroin-filled needles into their arms, hands, legs, and necks. It was horrible to see these ladies and men of all ages shaking, straining, and trying to find a vein to "get off."

The addicts had so many abscesses and open ulcers they resembled lepers. But the Teen Challenge team reached out with love, compassion, and hugs. Some outreach workers were washing open wounds, while others wrapped loving arms around bent, broken, and bound people, praying and interceding for God to resurrect them with the overwhelming love of Jesus Christ.

We were searching for Martha, a woman who had asked a worker for help the previous day. Before locating Martha, we met Lulu, a striking beauty, sitting in a dingy stairwell. At first glance, I was struck by her face. From a distance she was so beautiful that she could have been a model. As we got closer, I could see the blood-stained, grimy sweat that covered the infected abscesses on her arms. She was trying to inject heroin into one of her knuckles. All of her veins had collapsed so the only place left to shoot heroin was into the capillaries in her hands. She was only 21, but even the dim light of that stairwell revealed lines of age on her face far beyond her years.

Miriam and I embraced her and encouraged her to come to Teen Challenge with us. I asked, "Lulu, what happened?"

She shared that she was originally from a happy, quiet village. When she was 18, however, she wandered into a house in La Pella where they offered her some drugs. When she injected the heroin, she was instantly hooked. She never left La Pella.

Lulu turned her attention back to her knuckles, growing more and more frantic as she desperately searched for a vein. As we pleaded with her, Miriam began to cry. Lulu put her head down, facing away from us, relentlessly seeking a way to pump in the poison into her hand. Miriam and I learned that not every story has a happy ending. Lulu was convinced she was hopeless. Heroin had control of her. The monster was winning and there was nothing we could do but pray for her and continue search for Martha.

As we scoured the village, we finally found Martha hunched over in a steamy, dilapidated apartment. As we prayed for her and brought her outside to take her to Teen Challenge, suddenly angry men with rifles and guns barged onto the street and shouted, "Drop the drugs and put your hands up."

Miriam and I had our hands up in the air with our Bibles. We did not know if these raging, gun-slinging men were the police or guerillas. We were exercising God's command to love people and trusted His faithfulness. As they shouted in Spanish and menacingly pointed their rifles at us, Miriam and I looked at each other with confidence.

We both thought, *What a way to go to heaven together, after loving on a bunch of lepers!* We believed that Jesus would personally receive us with a high five and say, "You got it" (or as the kids say nowadays, "You da bomb!").

Then, as suddenly as the men came, they released us. We left and placed Martha in Teen Challenge. From the pits of hell to the gates of heaven, Martha was given an open door to a new chance at life. Teen Challenge is a place where people learn to dream again.

LOVE BROKE THROUGH

Billy and I worked at a David Wilkerson street crusade in Spanish Harlem many years ago. On my way up from the subway system, I saw Billy ministering to a big Spanish dude named Ramon. He had a bandana around his head, rosary beads around his neck, a goatee, and bottle of Colt 45 beer in one hand.

His finger was in Billy's face as he screamed, "Don't you tell me that I don't know Jesus, you no-good, blankety-blank-blank."

Since Billy was filled with the Holy Ghost, I thought, *He can handle himself.*

I didn't want to interfere with this "evangelism explosion," so I just passed by as I shared, "Billy. I'll be down the block."

Unfortunately I was not fast enough. Billy grabbed me by the arm and said, "Jimmy, this is Ramon. Ramon, this is my brother Jimmy. I gotta go." And, he left me with Ramon.

Ramon hated me even though I had only just met him. He took one look at me and blasted off, "Look at you, coming up here with your Bible. I got God..." He grabbed his rosary beads and continued, "Don't you tell me about God, you no-good, blankety-blank-blank."

I said, "Ramon, Ramon, listen to me. Please, Ramon." He stopped and said, "What?"

I said, "Ramon, I love you, that's why I'm here. And, now I gotta go."

I turned and left. I met up with Billy, and we began to prepare for the street rally. Ten minutes later, I got a tap on my shoulder. It was Ramon. He was respectful. His beer was gone and he asked, "Can I hang with you for a while?"

"Yeah, of course you can, Ramon," I said.

I found out later that everybody hated Ramon. He was kicked out of his house at 10 and rejected by his family. Everyone from his neighborhood hated him—the street cop, the man in the Spanish bodega store, even his dog. When I shared that I loved him, it was the first time that Ramon heard those words in many years. I prayed for him and led him to the Lord.

Love breaks down walls, prejudice, pain, anger, and bitterness. I did not pull out my Bible college manual from Personal Evangelism 101 class to convince Ramon he was depraved and going to hell. Instead, I gave him the greatest witness mankind can ever hear:

I told Ramon, "I love you and God loves you."

That is what Jesus said to you and me, isn't it? When He died on the cross, He spread out His arms and said, "Jimmy, I love you." That is what the Gospel is about—the love of Jesus breaking through even the hardest heart. When we operated the coffeehouse in Hempstead, we served coffee and donuts in a storefront on Main Street. We ministered to drug addicts, prostitutes, and homeless people. Some are in ministry today because they were changed and transformed by God's love.

One day an 18-year-old blond peeked in the coffeehouse. I met her at the door and asked her, "What is your name?"

She said, "Beth."

I said, "Beth, come on in."

She looked around in a panic as she frantically replied, "I can't."

Just then a big, ugly pimp walked behind her, grabbed her arm, and said, "Come on."

I realized she was a prostitute and said, "Wait a minute. Beth, listen to me and don't ever forget this: No matter what you are doing and no matter what you have ever done, God loves you and you are very special in His sight."

As I spoke, her pimp dragged her out.

Three months later, I went into the church behind the coffeehouse to get some supplies. As I walked in the door, there was a little blond girl working at a desk. She was neatly dressed with a pencil behind her ear, speaking on the telephone. I thought, Can this be Beth? Could this be that same prostitute?

She looked at me, somehow knowing what I was thinking. With blue eyes sparkling she said, "Jimmy, I'm Beth." She told me she could not get my words out of her head. She came back to the church and gave her heart to Jesus. It was that message of love that transformed Beth's life. It is the only message that can convince a world of hurting, suffering, and dying people to dream again.

TEEN CHALLENGE GOES THE EXTRA MILE

Jesus defined outreach when He gave His seminar on evangelism during The Sermon on the Mount. He said, "And whoever compels you to go one mile, go with him two" (Matthew 5:41). The following stories about Wayne define this teaching to a T.

Wayne was the light-skinned, African-American brother I met when I first entered Brooklyn Teen Challenge. He entered the program one week before me. Raised on the streets of New York City, he became a homeless drug addict, living in and out of shelters and on rooftops. Wayne was dropped off on the stoop of Brooklyn Teen Challenge in a last-ditch effort by his brother to save his life. He had an earring in his nose with a chain attached that led to his ear, a joint in his mouth, a pint of Wild Irish Rose wine in one hand, and a handgun in his pocket. Wayne was accepted into Teen Challenge as he was, but the paraphernalia had to go.

When I met Wayne, we hit it off. We were both crazy, and crazy people either attack or attract. He had a great sense of humor, and we bonded instantly. At Camp Champion we were placed in the same room.

As students, Wayne and I cooked breakfast for all the residents. We coined a phrase, "It's time to put the feed bag on." Wayne knew how to "throw down" and proved it. One morning our group leader Mr. Fitch came into the kitchen just before we were about to cook the Saturday morning brunch. He handed us two squirrels he had just shot.

He said, "Here, cook these for breakfast." Wayne grabbed them and said, "No problem."

I was the assistant chef so I was ready to learn from Wayne how to cook squirrel. He filleted the squirrels like Davy Crockett. He began my first seminar on cooking squirrels with the instruction: "You cut the heads off, grab the skin, and pull their drawers down." Then, he threw them into the frying pan with some oil, and bingo, fried squirrel.

When we rang the chow bell, the rest of the brothers came in excited to eat. When we sat down to pray, it was quiet. The breakfast table was the final resting place for scrambled eggs and toast, as well as two fried squirrels lying on their backs with arms and legs pointing toward the heavens. Everyone passed on the squirrels. I had a "no thank you" portion.

Wayne said, "Well, if y'all ain't gonna eat 'em, I will." And he did.

Another morning Wayne got up on the wrong side of the bed and was in quite a mood. He and I were in charge of cleaning the breakfast dishes, and our group leader was rushing us.

I said, "Wayne, I'll clean the dishes and you dry them." Then we heard our group leader yell, "Hurry Up!" again.

When I handed Wayne the dishes to dry, he opened the back door that led into the woods and began to fling the plates like Frisbees out the door, saying with a rebellious tone, "He wants us to hurry up. OK, this is the quickest way to dry these stupid dishes."

At times we all need an attitude adjustment, but Wayne needed more of God's grace and love to break through his rebellion.

Within a month, the men's program was phased out and Wayne was transferred to another Teen Challenge center. I married Miriam and we joined the family ministry. I heard Wayne left the program he was in. For the next 6 years, I often found Wayne in the streets and brought him home with me. After cleaning him up, we would get him into another Teen Challenge program. Wayne became a part of my family, and my mother took him in like he was her son.

Some people told me to leave Wayne alone and let him help himself, saying, "When he's ready, he will get it right." But, I could not give up on him because I remembered what those brothers at Teen Challenge did for me the night that I entered the program so rebellious and full of pain. I knew that if I let Wayne go, he would die. Finally, after either being dismissed or prematurely leaving 12 Teen Challenge programs, Wayne graduated Teen Challenge in 1993. Wayne met and married Stacey, a beautiful Christian woman who was one of our first Teen Challenge volunteers and people to attend Freedom Chapel.

Wayne and Stacey moved to Missouri and went to Central Bible College. While there, the Lord blessed them with a beautiful child, Nicole. I will never forget the day I visited Wayne in Springfield. When I entered his home, he welcomed me with a bear hug and gave me a tour of his new "crib." The first attraction he pointed out was the new leather couch and large TV. Then, he guided me into his kitchen, opening the refrigerator packed with food. He opened a freezer full of steaks and ice cream. He opened his wallet and showed me a credit card that had his name on it and said, "They're all mine."

Then, he opened his bedroom door and showed me his king-size bed. We were giving each other high fives by this time. Finally, we opened the door that led into his daughter's room. There I saw his biggest miracle—a beautiful, healthy baby lying in her crib. The colorful room was filled with toys, a sweet fragrance, and the peace of God.

I rejoice more than anyone when I tell this story because I know how Wayne lived in the drug world. Tragedy followed him. He was living on a roof with his girlfriend when she went into labor. The baby was born on a cold rooftop and died. Today, he is an ordained minister with a singing ministry who owns a beautiful home on Long Island. His daughter attends a Christian school, and the entire family is committed to their church. Wayne frequently stops by Teen Challenge to say hello and volunteer. Teen Challenge reaches out to the outcasts of society and goes the second mile.

FAMILIES CAN DREAM AGAIN

In 1995, several concerned family members escorted a drunk into my office for an interview, hoping he would enter our program. Jim was the walking embodiment of a wet noodle or wet brain. On the surface he was a successful lawyer and father, but no amount of good intentions and promises could stop the flow of booze that was gradually stealing his life.

Vodka was his drink, and for 10 years he nearly drank himself to death. Jim destroyed his marriage, devastated his two children, and lost his practice. As I prayed for Jim, he was in another world and had no clue that we were even praying for him.

We took him into our crisis center; but halfway through the program, Jim left against our counsel, believing he was ready to be restored to his family. Jim's wife, Angela, divorced him, and he came back into the program with a heart finally prepared to do the will of God. After graduating from the program, he stayed on as an intern.

I had the honor of officiating his wedding when he remarried his wife. He now has a thriving practice, provides legal counsel for Teen Challenge and Freedom Chapel, and volunteers his services to help others.

Prior to Jim coming into Teen Challenge, his children had no hope and little faith in God. Years later, the words on his son James' college admission application tell the story through the eyes of a son who witnessed the miracle firsthand:

Dear Sir,

Throughout our lives people touch us. Some significantly while others brush by leaving only a trace. As I sit here trying to write this essay, it strikes me as ironic that the person who has most influenced my life, also almost shattered it. This person is my father.

I was in the sixth grade when the floodgates opened. I was swept away in a current of changes and could not stop them. I saw my father slip away until he was no longer recognizable as himself. Within a year my father had to leave the house because he was tearing it apart. I tried to pretend normalcy but the anchor was gone and no matter what I tried, I was drifting. Even on the happiest of days, there was that dull pain that overshadowed everything. I held onto hope that he would come back.

My father was gone from us three years when he finally entered Teen Challenge. Since other attempts in other places had failed, I was, to say the least, skeptical. In March 1999, in my sophomore year at St. Anthony's, my father was ready to leave the program. He got an apartment and began rebuilding. Incredible chains of events began falling into place for him. They were hard to shrug off as coincidences or luck. He truly believed they were blessings. Slowly my skepticism began to fade.

He won us all back with his perseverance and moved back with us. He is still rebuilding his professional life and has made major progress. I am again at peace with him. He has my trust, my respect and is a daily inspiration to me. He has taught me to never lose faith and solidified my

faith in God. The unfortunate invasion into our lives, although taking away precious years, has forever strengthened my character. I am, as my dad would say, "Blessed."
        James

CALLED TO A PURE LIFE

Lying under the shadows of the massive 59th Street bridge in Queens is a derelict housing project called Long Island City. Forty to 50 brick buildings are crammed together, separated only by the muddy remnants of what was once a beautiful lawn. Each 5-story apartment building houses 10 families, intensifying the misery and frustration of the congested living quarters. Jeff Colon (pronounced cologne) found himself on another crack-cocaine binge in the rundown apartment of a prostitute he had picked up that night.

After 3 days of constant drug use and 2 nights without sleep, he was slipping out of reality. Jeff locked himself into the seedy bathroom as a stocky black man in his 40's, carrying a butcher knife, beat on the door. He waved it in Jeff's face, telling him to get out of the girl's apartment. Jeff was so burned out that he just wanted to die so he refused to leave. A stranger managed to talk the burly man out of stabbing Jeff and then convinced him to leave.

When Jeff woke up the next day, the reality of how hard-hearted he had become frightened him. He knew how far he was from God. His mind wandered back to his childhood on Long Island: How did all this happen?

Jeff had grown up in Long Island's Suffolk County in a middle-class home. He got into a life of drugs and promiscuity at an early age. What began as recreation soon developed into a habit. With that came a lifestyle of crime and violence. He began to develop a sexual addiction as well. At times he would spend entire nights in hotel rooms smoking crack and watching pornography. This led to increasing involvement with prostitutes. His father, an honorable man, could barely tolerate seeing his son throw his life away.

God intervened in Jeff's life when he was 19. One morning, after spending a night in jail for drunk driving and assaulting two police officers, his oldest sister bailed him out of jail. She shared the Lord with him. He made a commitment to Christ, but the next several years were marked by an up-and-down double life of drugs, sex, and Christianity. He married a Christian girl named Rose, had a good job as an elevator mechanic, and they attended church together. Then, Jeff began disappearing for days at a time to binge on drugs and prostitutes. Finally, with pressure from his family and friends, Jeff admitted himself into Long Island Teen Challenge. After graduating from the program, he became a leader in our choir.

Jeff moved back home but after battling the constant temptations of New

York City for eight months, his strength and determination gave out. He vanished on another two-day binge, leaving his wife, Rose, sick with worry.

When he came back home, we confronted him. Rose was at the end of her rope, "You can't come home, Jeff. I've had it!" Some were suggesting he come back into Teen Challenge.

As his pastor, I told him, "Jeff, you can't come back to the church this time. You are hurting too many people here. You need to go to Pure Life Ministries in Kentucky. They deal with sexual sin—this is the root of your problem. They can help you."

He was angry with this ultimatum. He had become so hardened he was ready to forget his experience with Christ. Before the evening was over, though, he was on a bus to Kentucky.

Today, Jeff is reunited with his family and serves as the Executive Director of Pure Life Ministries. When one of the men struggles, Jeff is able to empathize with their struggle. He can share, "I remember what a struggle I had," as he encourages them with his own victories. Now Jeff helps others to dream again.

MENDING BROKEN PEOPLE

Teen Challenge climbs over racial and denominational barriers to minister to people who are in desperate need. When Jesus came to earth, He broke through the walls of tradition. He took the church out to the highways and byways. He took the church to the people.

Teen Challenge is the Bride of Christ getting outside herself to pick up what society has labeled as lost, hopeless, and dead. Teen Challenge is touching men, women, and families who were once prostitutes, heroin and crack addicts, thieves, scoundrels, and outcasts of society. They are transformed into students, educators, businessmen, evangelists, pastors, and missionaries. They not only become citizens of the kingdom of God, but also soldiers of the Cross.

Teen Challenge is the arm of the church that invests monies, talents, strengths, gifts, and efforts not into buildings, cathedrals, or comfortable cushions, but into helping hurting people and mending broken lives.

Teen Challenge is a ministry loving the unloved. It holds up the hopeless until they find hope. Teen Challenge is a ministry of outstretched arms with hands unashamedly committed to getting dirty in the grubby work of restoring lost people. It is a ministry with backbone, willing to stand up and lift the outcast. This ministry delivers the derelict from depravity as it houses, feeds, and schools them in godly disciplines. This is a ministry that sees what many want to ignore or pretend is not there. Teen Challenge is dedicated to the

Great Commission and maximizing its ability to see young men, women, and families saved, sanctified, and secured in Jesus Christ, our only hope.

WILLIE, FROM GANGS TO GOD'S GRACE

Willie was a tough gang member from the mean streets of Bridgeport, Connecticut. After being shot several times, he entered Teen Challenge, where he met God. Today, as a licensed minister, godly father, and loving husband, Willie is not only one of our aspiring graduates of Long Island Teen Challenge, he is now the director of the program.

Willie shares his testimony:

I have heard it said, "It is not how you start, it is how you finish." That quote has been proven in my life. I could have been written off as a statistic, were it not for the grace of God. My father was a drug and alcohol abuser. He owned his own liquor store and often used it as a means to deal drugs. Often my dad would come home in a drunken- high rage and physically assault my mother, many times in front of my brother and me. Since I was the oldest, I had more freedom and so turned to the streets as a source of comfort and direction.

By 15, I began to use drugs, first as a casual user and then as a dealer. As the amount of drugs I pushed increased, so did my ambition to hit the big time. Because of my drug-infested lifestyle, I found myself in and out of gangs.

One evening when I was walking home from a club, two houses away from where I lived, I was robbed and gunned down by two rival gang members. I was stripped of my clothes, jewelry, and money. Then they told me to turn around and start running. "Bam, bam, bam!" The sound of shots ringing behind me was deafening. Suddenly, I felt a piercing pain burning through my leg. I fell to the ground. In the distance I saw my assailants darting up to me to finish the me off, but just as they were about to shoot, my neighbor pulled up in his car. They fled in fear because they thought it was the police. My neighbor had unknowingly saved my life.

I had been shot with a 9 millimeter. My neighbor immediately called an ambulance. When I arrived at the hospital, they had to perform emergency surgery because one of the bullets pierced a major artery in my leg. As I lay in a hospital bed recovering from my injuries, I knew that something had to change or else I would die.

My mother brought me to a Teen Challenge in Brooklyn, New York. I had no idea that the decision to enter the program would radically change my life. It was at Brooklyn Teen Challenge that I began to learn about Jesus Christ, how to make godly decisions, and that Jesus had a purpose for my life.

But the trials were not over. Eleven months into the program I was preparing for full-time ministry and ready to enroll into Bible College. With one month to graduation, the FBI came to pick me up on an attempted murder charge from a knife fight in a barroom brawl.

In one instant, my plans, my future, and my life seemed gone. All that I had worked for in the last couple of years seemed wasted. I even questioned my faith in God. But Scripture states that even when we are faithless, He is still faithful! It seemed like the only words that were ringing in my ears and beating in my heart were, "It's not how you start, it is how you finish."

The charges were dropped to a lesser charge. I had to serve a sentence in a Texas prison. Upon release, I decided to go back to Teen Challenge, this time in Long Island, New York. Upon entering the program I met Pastor Jimmy, executive director of Long Island Teen Challenge. Through our relationship, he imparted into my life leadership skills, practical ministry insights, and a love for hurting people. In no time I graduated the program, but I decided to remain on staff for another two years. Once I traveled with Pastor Jimmy to Springfield, Missouri, to learn about Central Bible College. God continued to remind me of my call into ministry, so I applied to CBC for the fall semester of 1999.

God had another blessing in store for me. The summer before I left for school, I met a beautiful, godly woman named Anna at the Ladies' Home of Long Island Teen Challenge. She had just graduated Central Bible College and was completing her internship at the Women's Home when we met and became good friends. Instantly I knew that she was going to be my wife. Sure enough, the next summer Anna and I were married on August 19, 2000.

Both of us graduated in the spring of 2003, me with a B.A. in Pastoral Ministry from Central Bible College and Anna with an M.A. in Counseling from Assemblies of God Theological Seminary. We both became licensed ministers and headed into full-time ministry at Long Island Teen Challenge, where I am presently the program director and assistant pastor at Freedom Chapel Assembly of God. Within a year, we added a blessed and precious member of our household: our son, Caleb.

Despite all the experiences that I have encountered, whether it was trials or triumphs, sorrow or splendor, burdens or blessings, pain or peace, I learned that no matter who you are or where you have been, when Jesus Christ enters your heart, "It's not how you start; it's how you finish!"

CHAPTER 13
THE BEST IS YET TO COME

Jimmy Jack ministering God's Word in Santiago, Dominican Republic. Evangelism is his passion and his one desire is to maximize the gifts that God has provided to win the lost.

FULFILLING YOUR DESTINY

While I was in Poland, speaking at the European Teen Challenge conference in 2002, Joao Martins, National Director of Portugal Teen Challenge, spoke from Ecclesiastes: "The end of a thing is better than its beginning; the patient in spirit is better than the proud in spirit" (Ecclesiastes 7:8). He passionately shared the reality that as our love for Christ matures, our faith will mature and the vision God has for our lives will become more vivid. God accomplishes greater works as we exercise and maximize our gifts for the kingdom of God.

Through life's journey, we all experience mistakes, afflictions, and trials. When we learn from these experiences, we mature in what we are called to do. When it seems our efforts are futile, insignificant, or just a collection of blunders, we can approach these situations with a humble attitude and a heart of faith. Our spirits can declare what Solomon said—essentially, "The best is yet to come." Today, tomorrow, and for years to come, this will be our legacy through obedience, faith, and love.

My mission statement is Philippians 3:12-14: "Not that I have already attained, or am already perfected; but I press on, that I may lay hold of that for which Christ Jesus has also laid hold of me. Brethren, I do not count myself to have apprehended; but one thing I do, forgetting those things which are behind and reaching forward to those things which are ahead, I press toward the goal for the prize of the upward call of God in Christ Jesus."

Paul says God has a calling for each of us. We are not perfect: "Not that I have already attained or am already perfected." But, we have to keep pressing on and realize the reason God has laid hold of us is to fulfill the purpose He has for us: "That I may lay hold of that for which Christ Jesus has also laid hold of me." Often I pray, "God, I want to pursue and fulfill Your purpose for my life." Through this Scripture I understand that God had chosen something special for me. I want to fulfill my "that"—whatever it is.

Paul also says he has not mastered anything except one thing: "One thing I do, forgetting those things which are behind and reaching forward to those things which are ahead, I press toward the goal for the prize of the upward call of God in Christ Jesus." By not allowing our past failures to detour our present or future purpose, we can realize our God-ordained calling and, in turn, strive to fulfill our destiny.

ELEVATING FAITH

Paul wrote of the persevering faith that elevates us into a supernatural realm in Ephesians 3:20: "Now to Him who is able to do exceedingly abundantly above all that we ask or think, according to the power that works in us, to Him be glory in the church by Christ Jesus to all generations, forever and ever. Amen." I have witnessed this truth in my mentors. And now I see this in my ministry and life, as well as those who have stepped out in faith with me.

People limit themselves when they do not realize the purpose and potential in their God-given calling. Because they subconsciously put reins on their belief system, their faith is stunted and their destiny is limited. However, Jesus said: "I have come that they may have life, and that they may have it more abundantly" (John 10:10). The word "life" in the Greek is zoe. This means more than just surviving or being alive. There is life, hope, health, joy, and divine intervention wrapped up in Zoe, the abundant life Christ spoke of. It is God adding His "super" to our "natural."

For centuries it was believed no one could run a mile in less than four minutes. Then on May 6, 1954, a British college student, Roger Bannister, ran the mile in 3 minutes, 59.4 seconds, at the Iffley Road track in Oxford. In the next year hundreds broke the 4-minute mile. This accomplishment caused other runners to believe they too could achieve a new level. Their belief system was challenged and expanded by Bannister's accomplishment. In the same way, our faith grows as we shake off the limits and reins of our past failures in order to trust and embrace the reality of our calling—not because of what we can accomplish, but because of what He can accomplish through us.

The elevation of our faith is a process. When people were healed, Jesus reminded them it was by their faith that they received His healing power. Jesus said if we had faith the size of a mustard seed we could speak to mountains and they would move (Matthew 17:20). After 20 years of ministry I am beginning to understand this truth.

In the process of being faithful, faith reproduces and matures. Elisha's ministry is an example of maturing faith. When Elijah called Elisha to join him, Elisha was a farmer, plowing his field. In obedience, Elisha burned his plows and barbecued his bulls to follow Elijah. Elisha clung to his mentor and started on the journey that developed his faith.

In 2 Kings 2, Elijah took Elisha from Jericho to Gilgal to Bethel and finally to the Jordan River. "When they had crossed over, Elijah said to Elisha, 'Ask! What may I do for you, before I am taken from you'" (v.9).

Elijah asked the question and Elisha said, "Please let a double portion of your spirit be upon me" (v.9).

Elijah responded, "You have asked a hard thing" (v.10). In other words, "To whom much is given, much is required."

Elijah asked Elisha if he was ready for everything that would come with the double portion. Often the double portion includes burdens, battles, bruises, added trials, and intense responsibilities. Elisha did receive Elijah's mantle. The results of his elevated faith are clear. Second Kings reports that Elijah performed 21 miracles and Elisha performed 42. But, what was in Elisha's heart that God could trust him with such power and elevate his faith? It was his obedience to his calling and his desire to maximize his God-given potential.

As I think back to when I entered Brooklyn Teen Challenge so hopelessly lost, I am amazed at what God has done since then. How could God allow me to pioneer Long Island Teen Challenge, Freedom Chapel, and become Executive Director for Brooklyn Teen Challenge, the place where He changed my life? God has opened the doors for me to serve on the Teen Challenge USA board. I was also appointed the first president of the Teen Challenge USA Alumni Association in 2003. I have preached in streets, parks, churches, and stadiums around the world and founded Teen Challenge centers in Albany, New York, and Santiago, Dominican Republic. These accomplishments were not achieved by sheer determination or a planned goal, but by a desire to maximize my God- given purpose. My destiny is then naturally realized. All glory goes to God. As 2 Corinthians 10:17-18 says, "But 'he who glories, let him glory in the Lord.' For not he who commends himself is approved, but whom the Lord commends." It is only God at work in my life who has inspired and anointed me to embrace my purpose and fulfill my destiny for His kingdom.

As I walk obediently with Jesus and follow the leading of the Holy Spirit, my faith continues to be elevated. The dreams, visions, and desires in my heart for the kingdom of God and my family are not a fantasy; they are attainable realities no matter how impossible they may seem. My desire is to press on and fulfill the vision God has given me. I boast only in the Lord, and challenge you to go after your dreams. As you do, your faith will be elevated, and you will accomplish the destiny God planned for you before the world was created.

THE VISION

My introduction to ministry was not the product of one single event, but rather the result of an intense process. After graduating from Teen Challenge, Miriam and I dedicated ourselves to a year of working in Brooklyn Teen Challenge. We became group leaders for Brooklyn Teen Challenge's family ministry. During that year we were able to solidify the Biblical truths we had learned from loving people at Teen Challenge. At the end of that year, we went to Central Bible College and learned more about each other and our faith and relationship with Jesus. At CBC, in a Pastoral Ministries class I was challenged to write the vision of where I thought I would be in 10 years.

Following is an excerpt from that report written in 1988 (by the way, I received an A+):

The Vision

- Church: New Testament Assembly of God, Long Island, New York
- Teen Challenge program: Men's program including phases 1, 2, 3, for ages 17 and up
- Teen Challenge program: Ladies' program including phases 1, 2, 3, for ages 17 and up
- Teen Challenge program: Family program including phases 2, 3, for ages 17 and up, and capacity for four children under age 15.

It's Monday morning, 8 a.m., and the day is full. First thing to do is have a special time with Miriam. After a time of prayer and Bible reading, we discuss the day's activities together and share some thoughts and give opinions on the important items for the day. We then will communicate thoroughly about each other's plans, and I will make sure Miriam's needs are met for the day.

Off we go to the church for the daily Monday morning staff meeting. The members who will be joining us are as follows: two group leaders from the men's program, two group leaders from the women's program, two group leaders from the family program, the program's academic dean, pastors, and the secretary.

We join together and lift up the needs of the church and the programs. If there are special needs we take time out for them. The meeting begins with an overall outlook on the church and the congregation. After our focus on the church and congregation we then review the Teen Challenge programs and the evangelism ministries. Next we receive an update on the programs. Each group leader is asked to give an account of students pertaining to their progress in the phases of the program.

This report was fully realized in 2003 when we pioneered our Teen Challenge family ministry, a home where married couples could be restored from their drug addictions. I have seen the basis for that assignment in Habakkuk 2:2-3: "Write the vision and make it plain on tablets, that he may run who reads it. For the vision is yet for an appointed time; but at the end it will speak, and it will not lie. Though it tarries, wait for it; because it will surely come, it will not tarry."

For the past 20 years, God has fulfilled His call on my life, enlarged my vision, and given me a glimpse of what Jabez prayed for: "And Jabez called on the God of Israel saying, 'Oh, that You would bless me indeed, and enlarge my territory, that Your hand would be with me, and that You would keep me from evil, that I may not cause pain!' So God granted him what he requested" (1 Chronicles 4:10).

FILLING THE VESSELS

One of my philosophies is to maximize people's purposes and potentials for the kingdom of God. Our staff at Long Island Teen Challenge and Freedom Chapel has embraced this mentality. With time designated for fasting, prayer, physical exercise, and the inspiration of the Holy Spirit, we maximize our potential in discipleship, evangelism, physical development, and personal maturity.

We do everything we can to reach lost and hurting people. We go to the highways and byways to rescue people from the streets of Long Island and New York City. We reach out to the homeless, hungry, sick, and drug addicted, and bring them into our residential homes. We provide for their needs and spiritually nurture them for their ministries, occupations, educations, and families. These precious souls often join our church and begin to cultivate their gifts.

Our resources are plentiful only because of our faith and God's provisions. We seek, knock, and ask, and are never without. Elisha stayed with a widow who was about to lose her two sons to pay off her debts because she had no other finances. Elisha's instructions concerning God's provision spoke profoundly to me.

"So Elisha said to her, 'What shall I do for you? Tell me, what do you have in the house?' And she said, 'Your maidservant has nothing in the house but a jar of oil.' Then he said, 'Go, borrow vessels from everywhere, from all your neighbors—empty vessels; do not gather just a few. And when you have come in, you shall shut the door behind you and your sons; then pour it into all those vessels, and set aside the full ones.' So she went from him and shut the door behind her and her sons, who brought the vessels to her; and she poured it out. Now it came to pass, when the vessels were full, that she said to her son, 'Bring me another vessel.' And he said to her, 'There is not another vessel.' So the oil ceased" (2 Kings 4:1-6).

Elisha instructed the widow to find as many vessels as possible—"not just a few." Every vessel she gathered she filled with oil. When the vessels ran out, so did the oil. The proceeds from the widow's oil sale paid her debts and her sons were safe.

The Lord spoke to me when we were experiencing a financial drought: "As long as you keep bringing empty hurting vessels into your ministry, I will always provide the resources to fill every one of those vessels."

God has done that. Every year we bring in more and more hurting young ladies, men, and families. We fill them not only with food, clothing, and a home; but more importantly, we fill them with love, faith, hope, and a bright future in Jesus Christ.

GOD'S HEART AND OUR PASSION

One addiction of the new millennium is pornography. My brother-in-law and associate pastor, Bobby Lloyd, established Long Island Citizens for Community Values 10 years ago, a coalition that fights pornography and sexual abuse toward women and children. As I have united with Bobby, we have been able to close adult bookstores and help New York state legislators pass laws to protect our communities from the sex industry. One adult bookstore on Long Island was shut down by laws that LICCV helped to establish. Through our efforts and prayers that place is now a Christian bookstore.

We have also united with Pure Life Ministries. Steve Gallagher, a former Los Angeles police officer turned pastor and evangelist, pioneered this residential ministry in Kentucky with the mission to restore sexually addicted adults through biblical principles and the healing of Jesus Christ. When pornography-addicted people need intense care, we refer them to Pure Life. Pure Life houses 75 men and also has an outreach program for ladies. Graduates of our Teen Challenge program, Jeff Colon and George Mooney, are directors and network with us.

With these outreaches we meet many needs and fulfill the heart of God proclaimed by the prophet Isaiah and fulfilled by Christ: "The Spirit of the Lord is upon Me, because He has anointed Me to preach the Gospel to the poor; he has sent Me to heal the brokenhearted, to proclaim liberty to the captives and recovery of sight to the blind, to set at liberty those who are oppressed; To proclaim the acceptable year of the Lord" (Luke 4:18-19). That is our heart, our passion, and our mission.

EXPANDING THE VISION

I have a goal to expand our Teen Challenge residential ministry. We want to secure a facility that will provide a 100-bed program for young men and turn our present men's campus into a 50-bed ladies home. We also want to expand our family ministry from a five-bedroom home to a complex that will accommodate 20 families.

The original Freedom Chapel facility held a maximum of 350 people, but only like sardines in a can—wall-to-wall people. We were packed every Sunday morning as our choir rocked the house. We have a powerful prayer meeting on Tuesday night with people crying out to God. It is a birthing chamber where people are saved, healed, restored, and refreshed. Friday night is our Teen Challenge coffeehouse outreach. Before service we invite people from the streets and shelters to come. We serve coffee, juice, bagels, and pastries. The Teen Challenge choir leads worship, and our students testify of their new lives in Christ. The last Friday of every month is a graduation service—a celebration when ladies, men, and married couples who are graduating the program

receive certificates of completion. The atmosphere is filled with tears of joy as graduates testify and often ask forgiveness from those whom they have hurt. These testimonies inspire our staff to sacrifice to restore people.

Freedom Chapel International Worship Center

When they hear the students testify, they applaud and lift their hands toward heaven as they realize it is worth it all.

Another ministry of our Friday outreach is Royal Rangers and Missionettes, programs for boys and girls, ages 4-17. Precious warriors who come from single-parent or foster homes meet in children's church trailers. On any given

Friday evening, you can open a door in the church that would normally lead to a storage room or bookkeeping room and find Missionettes or Royal Rangers meeting.

Our facility was originally a warehouse, 50-feet wide by 100-feet long. There was barely enough space to accommodate the needs we have. We turned the upstairs storage areas into a makeshift nursery and offices. In the parking lot adjacent to our church we secured two construction office trailers and refurbished them for children's church. When we dismiss the Royal Rangers and Missionettes for class on Friday evening, 50 young boys and girls march from the back to the front of the sanctuary with the American and Christian flags with our congregation cheering them. Every time I witness this I am inspired and realize that children from our neighborhood are receiving God's love and instruction for their destiny.

We were grateful for our facility but also saw the need to expand. God gave us an incredible vision for our church. We developed architectural plans that maximized our two-acre property in order to build the largest building possible. Since we had little parking available, we wrestled and worked with the town board to receive a special variance to build. Because of the testimony of our ministries over the years, our plans were approved.

Although such plans required funds and resources, we were hoping and praying for a Nehemiah Miracle. Upon completion, the church would hold 1,000 people and provide classroom space for our children, youth, and outreach ministries and Bible Institute. The new building was not about numbers; it was about meeting the needs of people. Mothers, fathers, young people, and children of all ages, cultures, and economic status from Long Island and New York City would soon fill our sanctuary with great expectation and adoration to the Lord. And the Lord did provide—as you'll see in the coming chapter.

We also approved plans and permits to renovate our present building into a youth center. The Freedom Outreach Center will house youth activities, as well as after-school programs, Hoop Challenge basketball camps, youth rallies, Missionettes and Royal Rangers programs, a children's evangelism ministry called Super Saturday Kids' Krusade, and food distribution ministry.

Another dynamic of our ministry is our International Evangelism Bible Institute, the beginning of a vision that will include a 2-year training program for Teen Challenge graduates and others who have a burning desire to pioneer churches and outreach ministries in the United States and throughout the world. Students enrolled in the Evangelism Bible Institute will be committed to Bible, evangelism, and leadership classes during the fall and winter. During the spring and summer, they will commit to practical, personal evangelism through our Super Saturday Kids' Krusade, Rock the Block youth explosions, and street rallies and crusades in the New York metro area, throughout the United States, and overseas. Once the new building is finished, we are trusting God to expand our Evangelism Bible Institute with dormitories for ladies and men. The student body will be fired up and trained to rock the world for the glory of God!

A NEW THING

The Lord spoke to the prophet Isaiah in Isaiah 43:18: "Do not remember the former things of old, nor even consider them, behold I desire to do a new thing." For over 20 years our ministry has set up street rallies throughout New York City and Long Island. I have preached to thousands of people and witnessed their hearts open to receive the gospel of Jesus Christ. However, I realized that the urban dynamics of our generation have changed. Youth were no longer identifying with our evangelism methodology. They saw our invitational flyers and thought of a children's event. We attracted children and their parents, but were losing people ages 15-30. As I watched young people walk by without even glancing at what we were doing, God opened my eyes to a new thing. We have transformed our Freedom Outreach theme and mission and pioneered Rock the Block Ministries. The mission of Rock the Block is to evangelize the urban culture of America through contemporary gospel music, praise, hip hop, dance, and dynamic preaching.

Rock the Block is a new form of evangelism to the inner city that integrates contemporary methods to reach those living in the concrete jungles of New York City and other major cities in the United States. Youth groups, mission teams, and other radical warriors for Christ are joining us to bring the gospel to the streets of New York City. This cutting-edge ministry is impacting their lives and igniting them to return home and light a fire for evangelism in their own community. Our website, www.rocktheblock.org, gets hundreds of hits every day from compassionate people of all denominations who want to reach youth and direct them to their God-given destiny.

THE LAW OF THE HARVEST

When you dedicate your life to helping hurting people, you will experience the principle of multiplication through the law of the harvest in three ways:
1. What you sow you reap.
2. You reap later than you sow.
3. You always reap more than you sow.

We have experienced this truth from the inception of our ministry and in a greater way through a mission trip to the Dominican Republic. I spoke at conferences and crusades overseas for several years. However, there were no opportunities for 2004. When Ramon, one of our on-fire, Teen Challenge graduates and our Blessingdales thrift store manager, shared an encounter while attending his grandfather's funeral in the Dominican Republic, I got a burden for Santiago. While in Santiago, Ramon's hometown, a boy came to him begging for money. Ramon became a little irritated and questioned him why he needed money. The boy said, "I'm trying to raise money for my Royal Rangers uniform." This touched Ramon's heart. When he returned home and told me, I told Ramon to contact the pastors in Santiago and ask if we could bring a missions team to Santiago to come alongside the churches there and do street witnessing.

Our simple plan turned into one of the most inspiring gospel events in Santiago's history. The association of pastors from Santiago secured the 20,000 seat baseball stadium for a crusade. Our mission teams passed out flyers and tracts throughout the city. We raised enough money to rent 80 buses to bring people from outside the city to the stadium. International gospel singers Ron Kenoly and Jocelyn Arias Quezada heard about our mission and joined our combined choir from Freedom Chapel and Teen Challenge. From Thursday through Saturday the choir ministered in worship and I preached to 15,000 people. As I gave the invitation for people to receive Jesus, thousands flooded the stadium's in-field to give their hearts to Jesus.

Ephesians 3:20 says, "Now to Him who is able to do exceedingly abundantly above all that we ask or think, according to the power that works in us." During the Friday evening service, we collected an offering to pioneer a Teen Challenge men's crisis home. By the following Monday, we secured a large home to accommodate 20 men and began the necessary renovations.

One year later we were invited back, and I led a team of 35 short term missionaries to host a four-day crusade in the city's basketball arena. On Friday and Saturday afternoon, our children's team, led by Juanita Florez, held a Kids' Crusade where over 5,000 children experienced the love of Jesus. The arena was filled each evening with worship, and I preached. People were saved and healed. On Friday evening we officially opened the Teen Challenge center and installed the first supervisor. The home is filled with men once bound by the demons of substance abuse who are now receiving salvation and healing.

MIRACLES IN CUBA

When our team arrived back in New York, I received an e-mail two weeks later from Daniel Torres, the National Youth Director of the Cuban Assemblies of God. He heard of our crusade in the Dominican Republic and asked us to come with a team to participate in their upcoming national youth convention. He asked me to be the guest speaker and to pray for God's favor to pioneer a Teen Challenge center in Cuba.

Though we had returned from the Dominican Republic in June and the youth convention was scheduled for September, we immediately recognized this as a miraculous open door. This missions trip was not without resistance. We prayerfully selected our team as only 15 tourist visas were available. Ramon and I applied for religious visas. Although the government did grant the tourist visas, the religious visas were denied. Without a religious visa I would not be able to preach; I could give a welcome without my Bible or any notes and spontaneously share a message each evening. We submitted this matter to prayer and continued to prepare.

As we landed in Miami, in preparation for our flight into Cuba, we were warned that Tropical Storm Rita was heading our way. Residents began boarding up windows, and evacuation orders were in place for the Florida Keys. The Hurricane Center observed that conditions were ideal for the storm to quickly gather strength and grow into a Category 4 hurricane. Twelve hours later Tropical Storm Rita had not intensified. Our flight to Cuba was delayed only one day.

In Cuba, we were greeted by Daniel and his family. Everyone passed through customs without problems. As we exited the terminal to the parking lot, it was like visiting an antique car show. President Fidel Castro came into power in the late 1950's, and shortly after the United States established an embargo. All industrial exports from the United States into Cuba were stopped by the end of the 1950's. The last vehicles to be exported to Cuba were manufactured in the late 1950's; therefore, common vehicles owned by Cubans are 1948-1957 Chevy's and Dodges. These vehicles were a variety of bright blue, green, red, black, and grey. They were all modified with truck engines and wheels and plexiglass replacement windows. Because the climate is warm and no rock salt is used, the cars' bodies are in mint condition. I love the 1957 Chevy. In Cuba I had a chance to see a restored classic on every corner.

Now that we had landed in Camaguey, there was still the matter of the denied religious visas. This city is carefully monitored for a number of reasons. Camaguey, situated on a savannah midway between Havana and Santiago de Cuba, is an important cultural center and Cuba's third largest city. Over 2,000 young people were expected to attend the convention. It was clear that without approved papers and visas, our ministry would be limited.

Rev. Torres prayerfully appealed the refusal of our religious visas despite the fact that he had never had one of these denials overturned for him before. On the opening day of the convention, we visited the Regional Presbyter's home for prayer. During our visit, his wife burst into the room beaming with excitement.

"Rejoice! The news! The news!" She exclaimed and a deluge of Spanish poured out of her.

The presbyter wept at hearing the news.

Every eye was on Ramon. "What, Ramon? What did she say?" I asked.

Ramon translated, "She said, 'I have never heard of this happening—not in all of my life!'"

"What? Heard what?!" Everyone asked, almost shouting in anticipation.

"The government officials have been trying to decide what to do with you. Well, word from Havana has just come through today. The message is simple: 'Let the foreigners minister.'"

The presbyter wept and out poured another torrent of Spanish. "What, Ramon? What did he say?" I asked.

He said, "I too have never heard of this happening—not in all my life."

The Cuban people were tender and inviting, despite extremely hot weather and frequent electrical blackouts. One power shortage delayed the start of the service for one hour, but the young people waited patiently in the dark, singing and praying until the lights came on. Our team prayed with literally hundreds at the altar each evening. At the end of the convention, I had each team member share a word. The young people reached out and personally saw God answer their prayers and honor their faith. I was impressed by the intelligence, level of commitment, and quality of relationship demonstrated by these young people.

As thrilling as it was to pray for masses, the times ministering one-on-one on the streets were even more special. Prostitutes, drug addicts, and bicycle taxi drivers came to faith in Christ. We were welcomed into the Cuban culture and invited into homes. One family even wanted to roast a pig in our honor. We played basketball with a local team. Later, many of the players came to the services and prayed with our team. By the end of the trip, many of our team had given away most of their clothes and shoes.

I was challenged by one Pentecostal leader who had spent time in prison rather than obey the government's order to close nearly 80 churches. He told the government leaders, "God saved me to open churches, not close them." He held out his arms to be shackled and taken to prison.

Even after the convention God was not finished with us. While we were there, we befriended many street people and the bicycle taxi drivers. These drivers were powerful men who pedaled these "rickshaws" on the bumpy cobbled streets of Camaguey with tourists in 100-degree heat. As we were packing to leave, one of the local drivers, an atheist, issued a challenge, "It is not just New York City people who can rap and sing," he told us. "We challenge you right now to Rock the Block—Cuban Style."

It was amazing to see dozens of bicycle taxis line up to take us across town to Plaza del Cristo (Plaza of Christ). This name had not been changed by the Communists because of its cultural and historical significance. As they danced and rapped for us, we had a wonderful time of laughter and music.

As the Rock the Block team took center stage to share, Plaza del Cristo was transformed, because in 2006 it once again resounded with God's love. The Plaza of Christ reverberated with rejoicing once again. As the crowd grew to several hundred, we seized the opportunity to share the gospel. The hunger for the Word was obvious. As the power of the Holy Spirit descended upon the plaza, an invitation to pray and receive Christ as Savior was given and over 100 responded. Among those that responded was the bicycle taxi driver who wept as he met God. Spontaneous opportunities for the gospel like that are so special and unique.

As we left Cuba, a torrential rainstorm shut down the airport and grounded our flight for several hours. As we stood in line hoping for the airport to reopen, we prayed and thanked God for all of the miracles.

While we were in Cuba, we examined two possible properties for Teen Challenge. The planning for Cuba Teen Challenge continues with formal meetings between government officials, community leaders, an Assemblies of God missionary, and representatives from Teen Challenge USA and Global Teen Challenge. The local pastors are committed to opening a crisis center, and even have encouragement from the government to do so.

NEW INVITATIONS, AFRICAN DREAM

Word of the miracles that God did in Camaguey and Santiago began to spread. The center we had launched grew and opened another men's home, a ladies' home, and a ministry to families.

Within 6 months, Reverend Hector Hunter, General Superintendent of the Assemblies of God in Cuba, asked me to come to minister at a national Youth Convention for several thousand young people and to lay the groundwork for Teen Challenge in Cuba. I took a team, and we saw God move powerfully.

From there, invitations began to stream in from around the world—even from Africa. An evangelist from Tanzania appeared on our doorstep to plead with us to come to his country to do a crusade and launch a new Teen Challenge center in the capital, Dar Es Salaam. As we began to plan, we realized we could strategically combine this project with a mission to a center in Nairobi, Kenya, which David Wilkerson had launched the year before and would also welcome our ministry efforts. We trusted that this was the Lord, leading us to expand the reach of Jimmy Jack Ministries.

FREEDOM CHAPEL

We had a vision for Africa, but we still had to trust God for the finances it would take to stage two huge crusades—one in Nairobi and one in Dar Es Salaam. God miraculously provided $80,000 through a special events evangelism grant from the Four Square Foundation. This was good news, but the challenge would be raising an additional $80,000 in matching funds to cover expenses and qualify for the funding.

Although we only had 6 months to raise that money, the new Freedom Chapel International Worship Center was nearing completion and also faced serious financial challenges. The need was so great that we knew we could not do it on our own. We needed over $100,000 for materials and thousands of hours of labor to complete the sanctuary and first floor. The task seemed impossible.

A year earlier, we had slated our opening for Easter Sunday. Rational advisors began to suggest that we postpone the date. But as I went to the Lord in prayer, He led me to Nehemiah 6:15, which says, "the wall was completed in 52 days."

God confirmed in my heart, "That is your promise." I rallied the pastors, elders, and deacons and challenged the church to believe. We displayed a banner in large letters, "Nehemiah Miracle," and under that, "The wall was completed in 52 days. Nehemiah 6:15." It was a challenge to all of us to pray earnestly for our Nehemiah Miracle. For 52 days the miracle continued in a flurry of financial gifts and volunteer activity "for the people had a heart to build." It culminated with a Victory Celebration in our beautiful new sanctuary April 12, Easter Sunday, with over 1,000 rejoicing at what the Lord had done.

While common sense called for a vacation, there was still an $80,000 mountain to climb for the upcoming mission to Africa. So we went to prayer: for finances, for souls, for addicts, for all of East Africa. I prayed, "God, please speak to someone to send us a large check to meet the need." That was my plan, but God showed Himself in a different way. In small increments we inched toward our

goal, as checks, offerings, and twenty-dollar bills came in. By August 15, God had met this need through His people.

We sent an advance team to both sites—Nairobi, Kenya, and Dar Es Salaam, Tanzania—to "scout out the land" and determine the best location for our upcoming crusades. The team was headed by Ramon Rosa, my crusade coordinator, and Bernie Gillott, Africa Evangelism Coordinator of Global Teen Challenge.

KENYA—ADVANCE TEAM

The advance team first headed to Nairobi, Kenya. They identified a potential crusade site on the Kamukunji grounds, along the border of one of Africa's cruelest slums. Through the sauntering hustle and bustle of the clogged city avenues, our team heard a cry from the street—a cry from the hearts of addicts bound in sin. Crippled by addiction to changaa (a devastating mix of moonshine and formaldehyde brewed in back alleys), over 1 million were desperately in need of a way out of poverty and despair.

The Kamukunji grounds were also the site of bloody political riots two decades earlier. On July 7, 1990, protestors defied the Moi-Kanu dictatorship and were mercilessly gunned down. This dictatorship was eventually overthrown, but by 2009, there was a new dictator on the scene: addiction. Changaa, weed, and heroin had enslaved countless Kenyans.

Because of this history, Christians often saw the Kamukunji grounds as too dangerous or frightening for ministry—and non-Christians often believed the area was cursed. But Jimmy Jack Hope and Destiny ministries believed that this was the community God was calling us to.

TANZANIA-ADVANCE TEAM

Our advance team continued on to Dar Es Salaam, Tanzania, a Muslim stronghold. The obvious opportunity for a crusade was in one of the capital city's large stadiums; but our team felt led to the Jangwani grounds, an open space of dirt soccer fields in the very heart of the city. The grounds were surrounded by both poverty-stricken and working-class communities, and were easily accessible by car or bus. We knew that this site would allow our crusade to be a beacon to the city and help us to take the message to those who needed it most.

KENYA-CRUSADE

In August of 2009, our team of 24 vibrant evangelistic warriors set foot on East African soil with a zeal to preach the Gospel of Jesus Christ. The Nairobi crusade commenced on the Kamukunji grounds, and tens of thousands came—not to battle for political freedom, but for spiritual freedom, and to break the tyranny of addiction. Despite the devastating poverty and pain in this slum, the people were hungry for hope.

Just behind the large, beautiful stage—set up and decorated by local church volunteers, a testimony in itself to their dedication—was a devastating urban backdrop: a slum of tin huts housing a population of 300,000. These slums continued in both directions of the stage, and around the sides of the Kamukunji grounds, exhibiting the great needs of the city. And thousands of individuals from those slums poured into our crusade each night.

Our ministry team included internationally renowned Gospel singer Ron Kenoly; our own Rock the Block East Africa Team, featuring my daughters Dionnza and Dominique Jack who ministered in song and dance; and Jaz,

a vibrant young man from the streets of Harlem whose rap with a positive message engaged not only the young people, but everyone there. Many of the church leaders had never seen culturally relevant, Christ-centered hip- hop music, dance and rap—and even the most traditional of them were amazed at the

Dominique and Dionnza Jack minister in dance and music.

impact of Rock the Block as thousands and thousands of young people streamed to the altars to meet Jesus Christ.

The Kenyan church also came out in force to see what God was doing

Tens of Thousands gather for ministry in Dar Es Salaam, Tanzania.

and take back this territory for the gospel. A mass choir composed of worship leaders and choir members of local Nairobi churches ministered in song, and the Kenya Teen Challenge choir also shared songs and testimonies.

I closed the crusade by preaching from Isaiah 61:1: "The Spirit of the Lord God is on me, because the Lord has anointed me to bring good news to the poor. He has sent me to heal the brokenhearted, to proclaim liberty to the captives, and freedom to the prisoners." The altars were flooded with Kenyans responding to the Gospel—but what touched me most was when I saw a 5-year-old boy come up to the altar.

His eyes were bloodshot and full of tears. He was intoxicated by the changaa drink. I realized that his own parents had given him this drink—not to get him high, but to take away his hunger pains. I looked into his eyes, and was overwhelmed. But I praise God his parents heard the message of Christ, and we pray that one day they will thirst for righteousness and drink of the true living water.

5 year old boy intoxicated at the Kenya Crusade Grounds.

This was the first major Christian outreach on the Kamukunji grounds in over two decades. During the opening days of Hope and Destiny, some believers were afraid to set foot on this dangerous plot of ground. But by the third and final night, leaders shared that these grounds had now been staked out for the kingdom and they were occupying it for the King. One of the pastors shared, "This is not the last time we will be here. We are coming back." The chains of fear were broken and the Gospel released to go forth.

TANZANIA-CRUSADE

Our Hope and Destiny Crusade in Dar Es Salaam, Tanzania began at the launch of Ramadan, the greatest religious observance in Islam. As darkness fell each night, Muslim prayers blaring from the speakers surrounding Jangwani Grounds. Amidst threats of violence and machete-bearing guards with armed police patrolling the site, we nevertheless heard the voice of God saying, "Trust Me. I will exalt the name of My Son, Jesus, during this Ramadan."

Ron Kenoly and the Rock the Block team went with us to Tanzania and again ministered powerfully; a coalition of Tanzanian churches came together a joint choir. I concluded the crusade by sharing a message based on Hannah, titled "The Miracle of the Misunderstood Woman." Hannah was mocked, miserable, misunderstood, but through it all she poured out her soul to the Lord. Even in her brokenness, she believed her vision would come to pass and she became a woman of miracles.

As we opened up the altars for people to respond, God's Spirit flowed out, and people ran to the altars, calling for God. Bishops and pastors from Tanzania had joined us in ministry and went into the crowds to anoint and lay hands on the sick and demon-possessed. Some were even carried to prayer tents for further deliverance and healing. Over 25,000 Books of Hope were distributed to people at altars, who cried out to Jesus during the Hope and Destiny Crusades.

Pastor Jimmy ministers the word on the Eve of a major Muslim holiday, Ramadan's Lailatul-Qadr (Night of Power).

Another goal of the Tanzania outreach was to establish the first Teen Challenge center in that country. By the end of our crusade, scores were begging us to do just that. Over 35 Tanzanian pastors and businessmen met with Africa Global Teen Challenge Director Mike Zello to show their support. Before we left, a steering committee had formed and they were moving forward to launch their first Teen Challenge.

FUTURE PLANS

As Jimmy Jack Ministries expands its outreach, we see the value of partnering with Global Teen Challenge to use the crusade format to plant new Teen Challenge centers around the world, impact families through the ministry of Jimmy Jack Crusades, and engage the culture through the cutting-edge Rock the Block Ministry.

DREAM AGAIN

My life is just one testimony of what God can do through His love and power. Although the enemy wants to destroy our dreams and detour our destiny, God redeems even the most broken dreams. When I stumbled into Brooklyn Teen Challenge in 1984, who could have dreamed that one day God would be using me to pioneer Teen Challenge centers throughout the world? No one saw it or even thought it possible. But our God is a miracle- working God.

My prayer is that you would embrace your purpose and that revival will overflow from your relationship with Christ to your family and then out to your community. I am believing for an encounter with the living God that you might dream again.

Forget about the past. Forget everything that people have told you that you cannot do. Leave the failures of yesterday behind. Please, join with us together as we believe God that He will energize your heart and super-charge your life to Dream Again. Please send us a letter so we can rejoice with you as God fulfills His promise as you are able to say from first-hand experience, "I Can Dream Again."

Haiti Crusade in Port-au-Prince, one year after the devastating earthquake. Our mission team experienced life-threatening encounters with angry gang members, but God took over and transformed rage into miracles of souls saved.

LONG ISLAND TEEN CHALLENGE
OUTREACH PROFILE: OUR MISSION

As Long Island Teen Challenge celebrates nearly 2 decades of ministry, we thank God for years of needs met, miracles performed, and lives changed. From humble beginnings in the coffeehouse outreach in 1990, Long Island Teen Challenge has grown to a thriving complex of homes across Long Island. God has established a haven for the hurting where lives are changed. The center includes three homes for men, a women's home, a married couple's home, a reentry home, a thrift store, as well as an auto repair and donation center.

At the core of our ministry is Christ-centered residential treatment. In 2002 we admitted 143 new students. By 2007, admissions had increased to over 300 new students per year. Last year we provided over 20,000 days of residential care. Our men's and ladies' residences, family residential center, and newly established home in Albany, New York were filled with hurting people who came through our doors seeking refuge and healing through the power of the Lord Jesus Christ.

These students collectively have suffered over 4,400 years of drug

addiction, alcoholism, or crime. Various students under our care served 187 years in prison for drug-related crimes. Over $6.5 million in tax monies were squandered to incarcerate them without getting them off drugs. Other court-mandated students faced 57 years in prison. At an average cost of $35,000 per year for incarceration, sending them to Teen Challenge will save the taxpayers $1,785,000. The truth is that though crime doesn't pay, the community does. God is blessing us to turn these ladies and men from a burden on the taxpayers to contributing members of the community.

GENESIS HOUSE MEN'S HOME PHASE I

Genesis is our crisis home, houses 40 men. In Phase I, students move from at-risk surroundings, to a drug-free, structured environment, and learn to make positive life decisions. This provides them not only with a change and the chance to detox, but also an encounter with the love of Jesus Christ. They get practical life skills to cope with the roots of their addiction. Students complete 14 Group Studies for New Christians, 8 character studies and 8 personal studies in the academic division, job skills training in the vocational division, and social interaction within 4 months. After completing these studies they are awarded a graduation certificate and advance to Phase II.

SHEKINAH MEN'S HOME PHASE II

Shekinah houses 24 men, all students who have completed Phase I and have moved on to the second phase. Phase II is completed either in Long Island, or at the Teen Challenge Training Center, the 500-acre farm in Rehrersburg, Pennsylvania. This has been an exciting year as we have completed the new wing, adding a classroom, chapel, dining room, and 25 new beds.

During Phase II we provide "power tools" for success. In addition to life skills that address the roots of their addiction, students need additional academic and work skills to be prepared educationally and vocationally after graduation. They continue their studies with an interactive curriculum, additional job skills preparation, counseling sessions and GED training.

GRACE LADIES' HOME

The program for our ladies is structured similar to the men's, combining God's love, discipline, academics and vocational training. Our beautiful ladies' home was filled to capacity throughout the year, housing 15 students and 6 staff members. We provided over 5,000 days of free residential care.

Building a Ladies Home Extension to provide more beds for hurting ladies who come to us desperately seeking healing.

TIMOTHY HOUSE PHASE III
EXTENDED TRAINING

The Timothy House, pictured below, provides an ongoing Christ-centered environment to advance the growth process for Teen Challenge graduates. It provides continuing stabilization as they navigate the challenge of re-entry and prepare to become staff. Our graduates in Timothy House serve at Teen Challenge while they continue their education or pursue other opportunities for advancement following graduation.

Men's Extended Training House for our graduates.

EXTEND TRAINING HOUSE

The previous Extended Training house, shown below, contributed to the growth of our staff since 2003, in Brentwood, New York. In June 2009, we underwent a transition to move the Extended Training Center to Amityville, just around the corner from Freedom Chapel. This house is under heavy construction as the Lord also reconstructs the lives of those who will be living there.

This previously abandoned house, is soon going to be filled to overflowing with the love of God ushered in by the men of women serving the Lord in the ministry. Their hands that once did so much harm in the world, now are being used to restore places broken and abandoned for the glory of God!

TEEN CHALLENGE VOCATIONAL TRAINING PROGRAM

Blessingdales is an outreach of Long Island Teen Challenge and has been providing families in the community with affordable clothing, children's toys, and assorted household items since it first opened its doors in 1999. We successfully expanded the store, adding a dry cleaning, computer, and furniture sections. The thrift store remains a tremendous opportunity for vocational training for our students and provides income for the ministry. It also provides jobs for Long Island Teen Challenge graduates. We open up our store to local shelters and foster care homes for clothing and personal needs.

TEEN CHALLENGE AUTO REPAIR
AND REDEMPTION CENTER

In 2004, we expanded our vocational training program with the addition of an auto repair center located adjacent to our thrift store. "TC Auto" provides valuable training for staff and students, while also providing much needed repair services for our fleet of ministry vehicles. The shop includes two bays with car lifts, an office for the manager, a waiting area, and a parking lot on site. Donated vehicles are redeemed and restored for ministry use or resale.

HOOP CHALLENGE

We saw a need within the surrounding area to reach out to these at-risk children since many of their family members were coming to us for help with substance abuse. For young people raised in an environment of drugs and drug-related violence, there were no visible means of prevention and intervention. We incorporated the popular sport of basketball, combining fundamental skills learned on the courts with the skills needed to succeed in a drug- and crime-free life on the streets.

Hoop Challenge Basketball Camp is a valuable tool in our multifaceted outreach strategy. In up to three separate camps with 170 at risk youth, we teach basketball and life skills. At Hoop Challenge, "campers" are challenged to resist the lure of drugs, alcohol and lawlessness and encouraged to pursue their future, education, purpose and dreams. More importantly, we do not offer empty hope; we offer Jesus Christ as the power to win that battle.

We provide an atmosphere for character building through mentoring and positive role model relationships with "coaches." These coaches and other staff are all volunteers with Teen Challenge or visiting out of state coaches who offer more than basketball skills. They offer a hand up by encouraging them to find a dream, apply themselves and succeed. Each participant receives a daily lunch, beverages, an All Star T-shirt, trophies and prizes. Most importantly, they have an opportunity to encounter Jesus.

Sharing the Gospel of Jesus Christ to at-risk boys and girls through the discipline of basketball.

OUTREACH AND ROCK THE BLOCK MINISTRIES

Rock the Block is a cutting-edge, culturally relevant urban evangelistic street ministry featuring contemporary gospel music, praise, dance, drama and preaching. Evangelism teams from Teen Challenge programs across the country have partnered with us, including groups from Brooklyn, Philadelphia, Rehrersburg, PA; Garrison, NY; Florida; North Carolina; New England; and Oklahoma. We Rocked the Block in New York City, Long Island, Florida, Connecticut, Virginia, and Santiago, the Dominican Republic. We held 16 Rock

the Block outreaches with over 20,000 in attendance and 8,106 first-time commitments to Christ. We held over 144 outreaches through our street rallies in drug-infested communities, local school assemblies, Super Saturday Kids' Outreaches, basketball camps, church services, and our Friday night coffeehouse outreach. A total of 40,775 were in attendance.

SUPER SATURDAY KIDS' KRUSADE

Our emphasis on mentoring continues with Super Saturday Kids' Krusade. We bus over 150 children to our church from drug-infested communities on Long Island from October through December for fun, free giveaways, lunch, and the Gospel. Using puppets, games, and interactive activities, we share life skills training and God's love. We also host a special Christmas event. Each year we give away over 125 bikes and Christmas stockings with toys, treats and candy to over 350 precious children. We have seen the critical need to develop a comprehensive strategy to reach these children *before* they are lost and need Teen Challenge.

Freedom Kids Christmas Outreach -
Sharing the gift of Jesus Christ.

ALBANY NEW YORK TEEN CHALLENGE

In 2005, a campus in Albany County was donated to Long Island Teen Challenge. In our continuing effort to strategically address the needs of addicts in crisis throughout the state of New York, we took possession of the property and have renovated the parsonage into a men's crisis home. The church is now used for our dining hall, classroom and chapel. The gym is used for our multipurpose functions and youth outreach.

Albany New York Teen Challenge Men's Victory Home
Restoring Broken Lives, Fulfilling Destinies

SANTIAGO TEEN CHALLENGE

In 2004, following a crusade in the city's largest baseball stadium, we established a Teen Challenge men's home in Santiago, Dominican Republic. The 30-bed facility now meets the needs of addicts through the love of Jesus. Jose Martinez is the men's program director. They have also established a "Blessingdales" thrift store. We send our surplus from Long Island Teen Challenge Blessingdales to help support their work. Santiago is self sufficient and restoring many broken lives. The center has experienced continued growth. With 24 men in treatment and a long waiting list, we are preparing to open a new women's home.

Desafio Juvenil, Teen Challenge Santiago

THE NEW FREEDOM CHAPEL
INTERNATIONAL WORSHIP CENTER

Easter 2009 marked a day of big dreams coming to reality. This is the day the new *Freedom Chapel International Worship Center* opened it's doors for the first time to over 1,500 congregants. Packed to capacity, Pastor Jimmy Jack preached a fiery Easter word that raised the dead community to their feet to worship the God of their salvation. Seated in the front row was his aunt (his mother's sister), a reminder of days long past and the fulfillment of a sputtering mouth that declared, "my cup overflows."

This new house of worship holds accredited Bible classes, a full scale children's church, men's and women's ministries, and most importantly, the precious lives of families looking for hope and destiny. Brimming with excitement and life, this is truly a church with no limits! Freedom Chapel has already hosted events such as an island-wide Greg Laurie pre-crusade concert, an opera/praise concert, an engagement featuring CBC President Denbow, and many more.

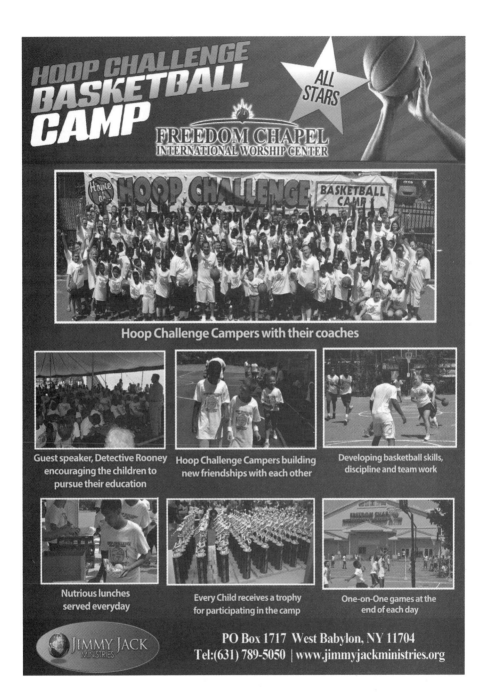

Hoop Challenge Campers with their coaches

Guest speaker, Detective Rooney encouraging the children to pursue their education

Hoop Challenge Campers building new friendships with each other

Developing basketball skills, discipline and team work

Nutrious lunches served everyday

Every Child receives a trophy for participating in the camp

One-on-One games at the end of each day

PO Box 1717 West Babylon, NY 11704
Tel:(631) 789-5050 | www.jimmyjackministries.org

New Book Releases...

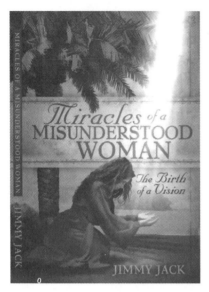 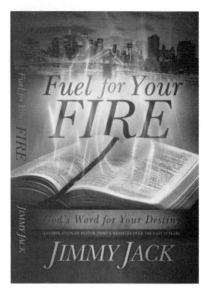

Miracles of a Misunderstood Woman defines the journey of Hannah's life, a woman barren yet filled with a vision. Seven chapters capture this woman of faith's mission and marriage, while bearing the burden of being marked, miserable, marred and misunderstood. From a woman defeated to a woman of miracles, God turned Hannah's bitterness into beauty, her misery into a miracle, her pain into praise, her sorrow into song and her tragedy into triumph!

Fuel for Your Fire is a power-packed book of dynamic messages written by Jimmy Jack. These teachings were birthed out of his heart and preached in the streets of New York City, International Crusades, and Conferences and at his Church, Freedom Chapel International Worship Center. From "Gethsemane Experience" to "Maturing through Hard Times," "Passion for Your Purpose," "Desiring a Double Portion" and your "Supernatural Burning Destiny," these messages will inspire, ignite and influence you to walk deeper with God, while developing your leadership and servanthood skills!

If you would like to receive the new release of *Miracles of a Misunderstood Woman* or other resources, please call us at (631) 789-5050.

We pray that this book has been a blessing to you. If it has, please let us know. If you would like a copy to send to a friend or need additional resources, please contact us at:

Jimmy Jack Ministries
641 Broadway
Amityville, NY 11701
Phone: (631) 789-5050

E-mail: Info@jimmyjackministries.org
Websites: http://www.litcny.org
http://www.rocktheblock.org
http://www.freedomchapelny.org
http://www.jimmyjackstory.com

Twitter: @jimmyjackny
Facebook: Jimmyjackministries

Copies are available above or online
through Amazon, eBay and
www.jimmyjackny.org

If you, or someone you love are in need of help,
please call Long Island Teen Challenge at
631-321-7070 or e-mail info@litcny.org

There is a miracle waiting for you!
You can dream again!